Jenni Calder was born in Chicago in 1941 and came to England when she was nine. She read for her B.A. at New Hall, Cambridge, and for her M.Phil. at Birkbeck College, London, where she made a special study of George Orwell. Her previous books include *Chronicles of Conscience: a study of George Orwell and Arthur Koestler,* and a study of Sir Walter Scott.

Jenni Calder

THERE MUST BE
A LONE RANGER

The Myth and Reality
of the American Wild West

ABACUS edition published in 1976
by Sphere Books Ltd
30/32 Gray's Inn Road, London WC1X 8JL

First published in Great Britain
by Hamish Hamilton Ltd 1974
Copyright © 1974 by Jenni Calder

Set in Plantin

Printed in the Channel Islands by
The Guernsey Press Co., Ltd

O, God . . . I must have a belt that glows green
in the dark. Where is my Captain Midnight decoder??
I can't understand what Superman is saying!

THERE *MUST* BE A LONE RANGER!!!

Le Roi Jones

Since undertaking to write this book I have met and talked with many people who have an enthusiasm for Westerns. I am in debt to all of them for their interest and encouragement. For more specific help I am especially grateful to Jim Stewart, Harvey Ginsberg and Liz Austin who provided me with elusive material, to Lady Ritchie-Calder for her help at a hectic time, and to David Dorsey for his sympathetic criticism. Above all, my thanks to Dave McCormick for his patience and enthusiasm in reading the typescript more than once, and his conversation, advice and support.

This book is dedicated to Angus Calder, a token of our shared experience of countless Westerns, the pleasure we have found in them, and the many hours of discussion that helped to bring this book to birth.

Contents

Introduction

The American West is loaded with myth. It has been interpreted endlessly. It has been the subject of almost every type of entertainment from circus acts to weighty novels. Its brief thirty years of heyday have been studied, exploded, loved and enjoyed. And all this activity has not destroyed its magnetic appeal. For more than a century there has flourished an industry devoted to the propagation of all there is to know, imagine and invent about America's last frontier, and in spite of some lean years it continues.

I have attempted a book about the spell the Western has cast over our imaginations for so long. The myths of these last ruthless years of America's expansion on her own territory almost preceded the reality. While the West was yet untamed, the stories of how men had brought justice and order to the wild became a national legend. They provided meat for a country that was hungry for heroes as well as for beef. While anarchy and sometimes terror were endemic in the Western territories, civilisation devoured the frontier's men of action, and fed back its own idea of what the hero should be. Battered real life Westerners were seized by the East and inflated into colourful symbols of American prowess. Kit Carson, Wild Bill Hickok, Buffalo Bill and many others—outlaws, sheriffs and adventurers—were sublimated into a superb fiction while they still lived. Indians in showy costumes performed in New York and London while others fought their last battles in the deserts and mountains, or starved on the reservations.

From the beginning the American West contained such paradoxes. These were bequeathed to the celebratory fiction that began to gallop alongside events in the West only a few years after the end of the Civil War. Much of this fiction has tried to tame its material and temper the harshness. Some of the most memorable has deliberately made use of the contradictions that were produced by an adulation of the wild that did not impinge on a profound respect for civilising institutions. Neither approach has dulled the astringency of these contradictions; both have helped to feed the world's fascination with the heroes, the hardships and the triumphs of the West.

From the first dime novels to the latest sophisticated movies, the relationship between the fact and fiction of the West has been incestuous. Mutations are frequent. Real men become immortal heroes of fiction and movie stars become, for their public, genuine Westerners. Authenticity is a hub around which reality and legend spin in colourful confusion. The Western produced on inception a license to claim almost anything as authentic. It has always respected historical fact not for what it is but for what it can become. In the Western, as in many other myths of other countries and other times, historical fact can take on a life of its own.

Historically I have begun with the end of the Civil War and finished with the century, for it is those years that have yielded most of what has characterised the Western. Where appropriate I have gone back to the 1840s and '50s, the years of transcontinent travel, and forward into the twentieth century with the Westerns that have done the same. The historical limits are dictated by the myth itself, for my purpose has been primarily to write about the West of the imagination. I have tried also to illuminate those things that have fed this legendary West and helped it to grow into a national monument that can exist quite independently of the past—and of the present.

The Western's absorption of this material has been as anarchic and varied as the material itself; its reproduction of it has only too often been tedious, repetitive and inept. I have ignored much, but not all, of what is bad. The quantity of material is dense, ranging as it does from ghost written memoirs to slick hack fiction, from orthodox histories to comics, from shoddy television horse opera to ambitious wide screen epics. It has all contributed to our idea of the West, and is therefore pertinent to this book, but there is a limit to a sustained interest in the third rate.

Many books have compared the fact and fiction of the West, but I have been much more concerned with examining the particular potency of a myth that continually outwits history. In the case of the West the relationship between history and imagination is far too sinuous and suggestive for the exercise of comparison to be more than interesting. We may know that it was virtually impossible for a man to fire with accuracy a Colt revolver from a moving horse, but do we think of this when our hero kills from the saddle? We may know that the typical Western cow pony was an ill-looking beast, but does this make our enjoyment of our hero's handsome steed any less? No amount of elucidation of the facts will destroy the myth.

Why should this be so? This is one of the questions I have had in mind throughout this book. In some respects the Western seems to have survived in spite of rather than because of the West. The

Western defies the limitations of history, just as all myths tend to defy their origins, and just as so much popular expression tends to defy the imagination's more serious and studied efforts. The Western myth continues to live after a hundred years and more repetition than any other basic myth in the world's history. And, forgetting for a moment the pleasure it has given, its significance is much greater than its relationship to fact and the process of its growth. It is a national and local myth that has reached out to countries that are relishing their own nationalism, as well as nourishing the aggressive patriotism of America herself. It appeals to adults and children, intellectuals and illiterates, Americans, Europeans, Asians and Africans. Limited as it is historically and in locality (and, because the history is recent and locality in many respects unchanged, this restriction is much greater than in the case of many older myths) the Western contains profoundly basic elements. They are elements that degrees of sophistication do not necessarily render impotent.

My intention has been to describe and explain the essential ingredients of the Western in terms of the contribution to the myth and their appeal. It is this that has suggested the shape of the book rather than chronology—it is not a history, or a catalogue. I have allowed myself a measure of freedom in the use of immensely varied material that is sometimes difficult to categorise, and I hope that readers will not find this lack of compartition confusing. With screened material I have concentrated on films of the last twenty-five years, for reasons of availability and personal preference, and also because it is these films that are most likely to have been seen and remembered by those who take pleasure in Westerns.

Alongside questions concerning the nature of the myth, its appeal, its progress and its relationship with history are questions of the Western's implications and influence. The cultural and political implications of the Western are perhaps more insistent than is at first apparent. In the last chapters of the book particularly I have looked at some of these implications both in terms of the myth's origins and its present relevance. The Western has had pale moments, but there are still many people who believe in the legendary West not as historical fact but as historical force. There were just men on the last frontier. There were heroes of skill and courage. There were situations in which action had meaning. These simple elements constitute a lost world as attractive to the imagination as El Dorado. Like El Dorado the legendary world of the Old West has never quite been found in fact, and while most Westerns are concerned with preserving the myth, reality still tugs. It has been a highly productive situation, and a challenging one for those who feel that the Western has more to say.

ONE

The Frontier

... in spite of environment, and in spite of custom, each frontier did indeed furnish a new field of opportunity, a gate of escape from the bondage of the past; and freshness, and confidence, and scorn of older society, impatience of its restraints and its ideas, and in-difference to its lessons, have accompanied the frontier.

> Frederick Jackson Turner 'The Frontier in American History'

Thrice armed is he that hath his quarrel just,
But six times armed that gets his punch in fust.

> Anon.

[1]

A lonely and rugged hero has captured the imaginations of the millions exposed to American culture. He is central to the myth of America's last frontier. He carries the myth repeatedly to its triumphant conclu-sions, and his constant rebirth keeps the frontier myth as satisfyingly alive as it ever was. The myth's vast territory and intense action, its subversive tug and its readiness to submit obediently under the great American harness, its realism and its romanticism, never stray from the dominant hero at the centre.

The country itself furbishes the hero. The sheer splendour of the Western terrain could have inspired writers and movie makers to invent a history to match it. The plains, the mountains, the deserts and the forests each have an individual brand of beauty. In each case there is also a cruel power: the beauty is ominous. The vastness of the empty spaces and the height of the Rocky Mountains engender awe, and our response is enriched when we realise that for frontier people the beauty was part of the challenge. The threat of this splendid emptiness was manifest in their daily existence.

The territory and the lonely hero fuse into a myth that has tempted generation after generation into seeing the thirty climactic years of the West as containing a crucial statement about American history and the American people. They are a reminder of past glory, of a period when the wild summoned the best out of men and women, and gave them a license to act with fierce independence. There is nostalgia in the pleasure that the West and Western engender, as well as excitement. The Western hero, from the trappers, traders and guides of the 1830s and '40s to the town tamers of the '70s and '80s suggests what ought to be a unique best in the American character. It is not difficult to believe that to imitate the action of the independent Westerner, to uphold the surging values of the frontier, is to be true to American history.

It is the 1850s and a young man leaves the security of the wagon train and the love of his girl to travel south-west towards the Mexican border in search of good cattle country. This is Howard Hawks' film *Red River* (1948) and the young man is John Wayne in the role that he has in essence been repeating for the past twenty years. Wayne chooses his land, reinforces his claim with his gun, and with the help of an old timer and a young boy builds up a vast herd of prime cattle. In 1865, the year that Chisolm cut his famed trail to Kansas, there is no market for cattle except in the East. Wayne, determined, tough, sure he is doing the right thing and sure that the right thing must be done, prepares to drive his cattle a thousand miles.

It is a movie of epic dimensions that says something of intrinsic importance about the individual's role in the Western myth. The historical background is convincing. The Kansas Pacific railroad, moving westward, provided a vital link with Eastern markets which enabled cattle ranchers from the south-west to avoid the more risky proposition of driving to Missouri. Someone like Wayne's Tom Dunson could well have been the first to make that historic drive to Abilene. Wayne's hero is a man of pride, courage and personal ambition—but his ambitions happen to coincide with the good of the country. While he makes money from his cows he is providing beef to feed the nation and every step on his way to profit helps to open up the frontier.

To protect his cattle and bring them to market Wayne needs all the qualities the frontier has celebrated: courage, skill, an understanding of the country and its hazards, authority, cussedness. With these comes, inevitably, two traits that nourish each other, loneliness and intolerance. In rejecting the advice of his friends, in doing things his own way, the right way, he reinforces both. If a challenge is there it has to be met, regardless of sacrifice, whether it be women, lives, friendship or security that have to go. When at the film's end the young boy whom Wayne has reared and trained (and nearly killed) gets his girl Wayne can satisfy himself that his struggles and sacrifices have cleared the way for the younger generation. The young people can afford to love, but the task of the old ones is not done. They remain as watch dogs.

Wayne renounces women and community for cows. The fight to conquer new territory, as glorified by one hundred years of cultural expression, lies not in the charge of the U.S. cavalry so much as in the lone combat of an individual. Loneliness is a persistent theme in the saga of the old frontier. Fenimore Cooper captured it first in Hawkeye, who is both proud and melancholy in his solitariness. It is not essentially different in the Lone Ranger or any other of Hollywood's mighty heroes ex machina. Like his independence and his freedom the loneliness of the frontier hero is irresistible.

Loneliness heightens the signal importance of comradeship. Cooper's Hawkeye and Chingachgook, white man and Indian, have a silent and instinctive appreciation of each other's qualities and feelings. They are extensions of each other. In *Red River* Wayne needs his companions, if only because they, in spite of criticism and rebellion, acknowledge his skills and achievement. The boy has lost his family but gained a heroic father-figure. For a lonely boy comradeship is sustenance, and he owes to the more experienced frontiersman not only survival but his training in the essential Western skills and qualities. He represents the countless raw youths, from the fictional Huck Finn to the real Jack London, who lit out from established communities and were taught some salutary lessons from their experience of the wild.

Shared danger brings an intimacy akin to that of shared love. Under threat men are vulnerable. At the end of *Red River* Wayne and the young man, played by Montgomery Clift, have shared an elemental and territory-building experience which strengthens them as heroes and enhances their achievement as myth-makers. They have glimpsed each other's vulnerability, acknowledged it, and acknowledged each other's ability to conquer it. To us, the audience, the brief exposure can only add to the appeal.

In A. B. Guthrie's *The Big Sky* (1947), a novel that takes us back to the mountain men of the 1830s and '40s, the splicing of loneliness, comradeship and self-reliance carries the main theme, and ultimately renders the hero unfit for life east of the Missouri. The mountain men conquered their vulnerability by making a virtue of solitude. It was because they were alone that they became so cannily skilful in the art of survival. An annual orgy of squaws, cards and raw whisky equipped them for the loneliness of the year to follow.

The Big Sky shows how the demands of frontier country—and the mountain men operated in territory beyond the frontier—built up qualities and talents which find no outlet in civilisation. Once the art of survival in the wild is mastered—though of course it can never be totally mastered—the East becomes irrelevant, and the Western hero rarely returns to the civilised world from which he has probably sprung. (The degree of civilisation may only be relative.) The attraction of a savage country where his survival proves him a conqueror outweighs the pull of home and family, though he may have fond memories of ma on the old homestead. The Western archetype, whether William Sublette the trapper or Clyde Barrow the gangster, proves that he can exist without the bolstering of community and all that that implies. He shakes off the entrenched social order, the established hierarchy. If he survives he is a superior being, wielding a measure of power over an untamed world.

We admire him and envy him. In the Western hero we do not see the struggle for upward mobility or for acceptance, but a victory over hardship and the unknown, fear and evil. It is an elemental struggle, influenced, sometimes totally characterised, by the nature of the country. It involves killing, but an important feature of the Western myth is its implicit attack on the sordid and the corrupt, on hypocrisy and backstage power struggles. On the frontier, the myth suggests, the fighting is straight and open; clean violence rather than tainted corruption. It is a false antithesis, but lingers, although history and many recent Westerns challenge it.

Behind the aggressive heroism of the individual hero lies the sheer capacity for endurance which characterised the settlement of the West. The endurance and survival of hardship does not itself amount to individual heroism in the Western myth, but it is an essential part of the collective experience that nourishes the hero. Of this the covered wagon is a potent symbol. The legend of the prairie schooners does not generally celebrate the individual, but it does provide opportunities for the hero, guide, Indian fighter, to show his paces. He leads the families, the plain pioneering people, to safety and success. It is of interest that this particular aspect of the pioneering spirit has become less popular in the last ten or fifteen years. And the men who knew the mountain passes and the water holes and the Indians, who advised and succoured the greenhorns have not been granted much space in the Western. The first men to cross the Great Divide after the trappers and fur traders were missionaries. They were the heroes of this early stage in the opening up of the far West.

The wagon trains themselves were often ill-equipped, their captains ignorant. Enthusiasm was far greater than experience. Frequently the men with vital knowledge of the country hesitated to assist in what they felt instinctively as a threat to their own free existence. Settlement would mean the crowding out of the men without whom settlement was impossible. But even with experienced help there was suffering, sometimes disaster. Bad advice and an eagerness for short cuts wherever possible tempted weary immigrants. Even if the desert, Indians and sickness were survived winter weather often overtook the wagon trains on the mountains. This happened in the famous Donner Party incident, where quarrelling, madness, murder and cannibalism reduced the band of immigrants to nearly half. Through ignorance and stupidity and petty rivalry many others had appalling experiences of drought, starvation and disease—and did not survive.

Yet in the Western the wagon trains provide a ritual framework for glorifying individual action and the action is related easily and at once to a body of humanity. The group is brave but bewildered, the individual hero cool and skilled: that is the general pattern. There is nothing else in the Western that works quite like this, and it is much more difficult to dramatise a collective experience than individual heroism. It takes an understanding of history and people, and an ability to generalise without loss of detail. Among film makers—and it is easier on film—John Ford has an unrivalled ability to make us see the individual within the collective, and the collective beyond the individual. Many of his Westerns use a group of people as a dramatic pivot, wagon trains frequently, a company of cavalry, a tribe of Indians.

This relationship, between the individual and community experience, has always bothered American writers, and is strongly linked with the lack of cultural tradition and over-anxiety for cohesion. Alongside these lie the persistence of 'old world' ways and the ghetto cities that still exist. The frontier was an invitation to escape the ghetto, but a community self-consciousness very soon caught up with the pioneers if it did not travel in the covered wagons with them. Opening up the frontier meant bringing established civilised ways to a wild land. Immigrants could only use the tools of civilisation that they knew, and they were likely to cling to them more fervently the more distant they were from the bastions of order and authority. The contradictions that this situation produces tug at two hundred years of American writing, and the Western does not escape.

But pre-eminently the wagon trains were the movement westward. The flow is continuous from the 1840s on. 1846, the year of the Donner disaster, was the great trail breaking year to Oregon and California, although it was ten years earlier that Marcus and Narcissa Whitman had established their mission on the Walla Walla River. The Civil War did not halt the movement. Wagons, mule trains, the stagecoach, the pony express, the railroad: excitedly eastern America reached out across the Continent. The drifting cowboy has been incorporated into this movement, although he just as often travelled on a north-south axis, and the great cattle drives were south to north. The Western hero, though usually moving, is not necessarily moving West. The potency of the trail from east to west in nineteenth century American history has influenced everything connected with it.

Escape beckoned, the opportunity for heroic action beckoned. Horace Greeley's dramatic appeal in the *New York Tribune* to go West suggested limitless horizons of challenge and opportunity. Although the real motives may have been to do better and make more money the awareness of nation building could dazzle materialism. It was not only a vision of the Garden of Eden that lured men westward, it was the particular attraction of virgin land. Here was a true wilderness, untouched, unspoilt, waiting to be shaped by human hands, for individual profit and the nation's good.

The pioneer beyond the Mississippi almost had to be a hero, especially by the standards by which America had begun to judge her heroes. He blazed trails, broke prairie sod, subdued the Indians and built homes, then towns. For the homesteader five or six years on one quarter section, then another move West to start all over again. Restlessness itself became an heroic quality, to stay still anti-heroic. The belief in moving on contained its own drama. Only by movement could the vast territory be conquered. The plains were empty but for Indians and buffalo. The mountain ranges were endless. There would surely always be somewhere, and somewhere better, further into that emptiness. Yet land hunger, gold hunger and cattle hunger decimated the buffalo and the Indians (the only difference between them in the eyes of many frontier people being that you could make more money out of buffalo) and built towns, railroads and highways in almost every quarter of the West. By the Oklahoma landrush of 1889 the West was believed to be crowded. And it was perhaps at this point that it became vitally important psychologically to preserve the myth.

By 1889 the covered wagon had long gone. Oklahoma, the last territory to be opened to land settlement, had until then been partly owned by Indians. It seethed with outcasts and refugees from the law which tried to wield an iron hand from across the border in Arkansas. It was the scene of some of the most gruesome and irrational crime in the West. In 1889 North and South Dakota, Montana and Washington achieved statehood. Geronimo, legendary Apache chief, had surrendered three years before and Sitting Bull, returned from exile in Canada, would be killed two years later at Wounded Knee Creek, where soldiers, nervous at the revivalist Sioux Ghost Dance, perpetrated a last massacre. It was not quite the end of the Old West. In 1892, in Wyoming, Johnson County was gripped by one of the bitterest of the large scale range wars. By this time the Western hero was safely down on paper.

[2]

In a highly pleasurable film *Sam Whiskey* (1969), directed by Robert Aldrich, a brief and beautiful sequence takes us through shimmering grass lands. The sunlight filtered through leaves sparkles on the tall grass. The cattle browse undisturbed. It is only a glimpse, but the effect is rich and peaceful. Men move over the surface of a beautiful land, untroubled by it, almost in the shimmering light glowingly absorbed by it.

The landscape is there, and every Western maker who uses landscape consciously owes much of his effect to an independent existence. He does not create the beauty or its influence. The most memorable use of landscape emphasises that the country itself is more endurable than the action we are witnessing, than the celluloid on which it is reproduced, than ourselves. John Ford has a certain humility in his use of landscape which acknowledges its power and enables us to forgive much of his lack of humility in his portrait of the American people. To treat the Western terrain as a visual toy, which Sam Peckinpah tends to do when portraying the desert in his *Ballad of Cable Hogue* (1970), is bound to be unsatisfactory. The sense of discovery is lost, the uneasy awareness of manipulation very much present.

The source of the power of Western terrain is its simultaneous beauty and cruelty. It can encourage the romantic and dismay the realist. It can inspire ordinary people to conquer immense hazards—and it can defeat them totally. It can inspire the average Western writer to pause lyrically and coax a tough romanticism out of his hard living hero.

The day has died making a dark, vast expanse of the plain above which, in the west, stood now only a faint red glow, deepening lower into greens and blue against the utter black, knife-sharp and faintly jagged line of the horizon. Far away to the north and west the foothills, gradually raising their slope eastward, had turned purple.

Why they turned purple no one knew. It was a peculiarity of the rocks, the vegetation and the air, refracting the dying sun's rays, perhaps. In the daytime they were just hills and mountains, barren, forbidding. But now, at this hour, they held a man's glance and made him think of things he had not attained; things indefinable as dreams, as lofty purposes, as regrets ... a yearning for something ultimate ... [1]

In the midst of a life that was rough, demanding and usually short the big country could nourish dreams as well as act as a continual reminder of life's hazards. The response of a killer to a beautiful sunset can affect our attitude to him. Traditionally writers have felt that a response to nature enhances man's sensibilities. The hoariest old mountain man, because he has lived close to nature has something which, Western writers often suggest, the most refined intellect without these experiences has not.

But the most vivid sunset could not disguise the country's ruggedness. The Westerner had to triumph over the country in order to survive, but he did not necessarily want to tame it. He did not want to subdue its wild character entirely. The appeal of the cattleman was partly due to the fact that in the days of open range he was using the country, profitably certainly, but also naturally. The cattle simply did what the buffalo and antelope had always done. On the screen cattle spread out across a grassy valley look right, part of the country, in a way that man-constructed dwellings never can. In the early days it was possible to raise cattle with a minimum of construction. A rider on a horse is one with the landscape. Not only does the animal itself link the man with the terrain: our grasp of a lone man's dependence on the country he rides is emphasised.

The relationship is elemental. In better Westerns, with sympathetic actors, there is the feeling that the country has shaped the man, but does not dominate him. It is not only through the individual that this is communicated. In the case of the Indians their relationship with the terrain is felt as a people. When Thomas Ince spreads his war-bonneted, bare-back riding Indians over rolling, scrubby country in *The Battle of the Redmen* (1912) they look as natural as cattle, or antelope. When we see a dust-covered immigrant train straggled out along the trail, plodding oxen, plodding women and children, that too is a portrait of people as a group in relationship with the surface of the earth. Cavalry too, horsemen again, reflect in their movements the necessity of adapting to the demands of the land. If they do not, they perish.

Alongside this necessary sense of intimacy comes a kind of romantic awe. When Mrs. George Armstrong Custer described the departure of her husband's troops on their last march in the campaign against the Sioux in 1876 she was illustrating just how natural is the transition from hard reality to a thrilling impressionism.

From the hour of breaking camp, before the sun was up, a mist had enveloped everything. Soon the bright sun began to penetrate this veil and dispel the haze, and a scene of wonder and beauty appeared. The cavalry and infantry in the order named, the scouts, pack mules, and artillery, all behind the long line of white-covered wagons, made a column altogether some two miles in length. As the sun broke through the mist a mirage appeared, which took up about half the line of cavalry, and thenceforth for a little distance it marched, equally plain to the sight on the earth and in the sky.[2]

Mrs. Custer is describing a phenomenon of the elements, but the effect is to bind the general's troops irrevocably, and in the context of the subsequent massacre at the Little Big Horn ominously, to the country in which they are going to fight. The scene has poignancy and a striking beauty.

Throughout the West beauty is associated with riches. Rolling grass lands mean cattle. The majesty of mountains mean gold initially, then later silver, copper and lead. The pioneer considered the quality of the soil, the amount of cattle per acre, rich lodes in the rock, pebbles of gold glistening in the stream bed. For many Westerners, and aspiring Westerners, the country was beautiful because it fed dreams of riches. William Bell, member of an early survey party in the West, remarked, 'Money-making is, of course, the great desideratum which attracts the white man to so out-of-the-way country, far from home, and often also from all that is dear to him. Once here, he cares little what he does provided it pays.' [3]

For a man like John Clay, an emigrant Scot, a highly successful cattleman, an astute business man and a gentleman always able blandly to reconcile opposites, the blended appeal of beauty and riches was not difficult to grasp.

The year 1882 saw cowpunching in all its glory with a colour of carmine around it. It was fashionable. The hunter for big game from European shores had told the wondrous tale of free grass and fat beef, of buffalo, elk, and antelope, of a wild, free life with little restraint, of invigorating days under the shadows of mountains that almost matched the Alps, of champagne air that was a tonic to body and soul; and dangling before them, as a result of these charming surroundings, was wealth and the ease and dignity that comes with it.[4]

John Clay himself had the opportunity to sample some of this ease and dignity. But most frontier people were not so lucky. The magic ring of 'free grass' grew hollow in the face of barbed wire fences and range wars. The charming surroundings remained, but they did not guarantee good land to the settler or good pay to the miner. In fact what Clay is writing about is not the reality but the dream that brought so many thousands West. For a very few the dream did come true and Clay, one of the lucky ones, can write with a certain smugness.

John Clay was able to relish the clear air and tall mountains, making the West sound like a playground for the rich. But the mountains and successful men like Clay were responsible, directly and indirectly, for the deaths of many pioneers. Some writers and many Westerns emphasise the emptiness and the loneliness. For the men who did the vital work on the cattle ranges, and especially for their wives, the wide open spaces meant a solitary life, hard work and not much money. The mountains were a barrier in travel, treacherous, and even where they yielded rich metal that metal did not come to light without backbreaking toil and heartbreaking disappointment. Yet the promise was always there, both on the prairies and the mountains. 'We must be crazy people to live in a leaky mud hut, at the utter end of desolation, and put our money down a hole,' [5] a character in one of Alan Le May's stories says. In another of Le May's books a man remarks 'This is a rough country.... It's a country knows how to scour a human man right off the face of itself.' [6] Westerners could hardly be unaware of the hostility of the country. Yet the splendour is there all the time, in space and height, and much of the splendour lies in the country's power to dwarf humanity, to make men and women seem pitiful in the face of the giant natural hazards.

Frederick Jackson Turner commented on this in his famous essay on the American frontier. He felt that the demands of the frontier influenced the development of the American character and made him crucially different from the European, more like the Indian he was displacing.

The wilderness masters the colonist. It finds him a European in dress, industries, tools, modes of travel and thought. It takes him from the railroad car and puts him in a birch canoe.... Before long he has gone to planting Indian corn and plowing with a sharp stick; he shouts the war cry and takes the scalp in orthodox Indian fashion. In short at the frontier the environment is at first too strong for the man. He must accept the conditions which it furnishes, or perish, and so he fits himself into the Indian clearings and follows the Indian trails.[7]

If the birch canoe was not applicable on the plains and mountains the West was still making just these demands on the pioneers. The environment was indeed too strong for the Eastern civilised man. He had to change. The first generation of frontier dwellers had to be different from those back East who inherited the tame civilisation their forefathers had pioneered for. Whether from Liverpool or New York the change demanded was similar. In this, as much as in the rivers and mountains, lay the long-lasting barrier between East and West.

It was in the influence of the Western terrain as much as in its nature that the barriers were rooted. Railroads and cities could be built, but there was always going to be territory inaccessible to wheels and concrete. Mountains could be tunnelled and bridges constructed, but without razing the mountains to the ground and damming the rivers the environment was going to continue to dominate. Even the earliest settlers, whatever their anticipations of progress, recognised this. It must at times have been profoundly depressing. The fact that death could come so rapidly, whether by violence or by the wearing effect of endless toil and rough living, that a whole town could appear overnight and disappear almost as rapidly (to which the hundreds of ghost towns all over the West bear witness), underlay what was for many a constant awareness of mortality and insignificance. Only the struggle itself, and survival, could outweigh the insignificance.

Isabella Bird, a British visitor to the West in the 1870s, was much distressed by her observation of the effects of the hard life endured by most men and women on the frontier.

One of the most painful things in the Western States and Territories is the extinction of childhood. I have never seen any children, only debased imitations of men and women, cankered by greed and selfishness, and asserting and gaining complete independence of their parents at ten years old.[8]

Isabella Bird, an extraordinary woman who travelled alone through the roughest country, saw the worst. Westerners were ready to convert the worst into advantages. Independence at the age of ten did not cause them dismay. The child who had learnt to fend for himself at an early age, who could ride, and shoot, and hunt, and cook, illustrated the best of the frontier. Independence was a quality to be cherished. Children were expected to work hard. They were encouraged to carry out demanding tasks and undertake missions of responsibility. A fifteen-year-old boy was a man, and was expected to work and act like one. Children were a very serious investment in survival. The frontier was proud of this, and Westerns have nourished this pride. What Isabella Bird saw as greed and selfishness the frontier recognised as commendable aspiration. The motives that had brought the parents out West were encouraged in the children.

In the Western at its best the hardness of life and the nature of the country are interrelated. This was lost in the 'forties era of glossy singing cowboys, and frequently appears dressed up and improved, with success as the dominant note. In Westerns that emphasise the intrinsic goodness of simple settler life, as countless do, hard work is its own reward, and the landscape is something to be admired as the sun sets and the peace of evening descends. The women remain beautiful, the children childish, and the simple dwelling place a home worth fighting for. In these Westerns it is family and community that we are intended to value. In others, the family appears in significant contrast to the violent life of the gunman. *The Pistolero of Red River* (1967), a Glenn Ford Western directed by Richard

Thorpe, is an example of this, and it also illustrates how crude such a contrast can be. In it the hardened gunman pays a visit to a recently married couple and their new baby and eyes them reflectively. The young wife (a reformed prostitute, incidentally) is suitably homely and solicitous, a glow of contentment surrounds them: this is what the gunman denies himself when he pursues what the picture tries to present as the commitment of his trade.

The big country is explored by the lone frontiersman, redeemed and brought to fruition by the family first, then by the community with its responsible citizens, its church and school, and so on. In the case of the individual, the violent man shaped by the country is very often redeemed by a woman, a home, or sometimes by the mere ownership of land which suggests a commitment to solid values. One of Lewis Patten's heroes, Walt Rand in *Valley of Violent Men* (1957), is very much the product of environment, but it is not only the influence of the land that has shaped him. He works on it and for it and has a wife and home on it. The big country means something specific and solid to him.

Horse and rider moved like a speck across the empty immensity of land, across the sagebrush flat, through shaded quakie pocket, and at last, through the fringe of dark spruce which guarded the precipitous rim.

Here Rand halted, his eyes noting the sorrel hide of his horse with its thin coating of mud caused by mingling sweat and dust. In his nostrils was the sour-hot smell of the horse, the strong, pitchy smell of spruce and the tangy, wild smell of scrub sage crushed under his horse's hoofs.

He looked out across the shimmering heat haze in the valley and beyond, towards the purple shrouded, high slopes of Rampart Mesa, twenty miles southwards and across the Roaring Fork River.[9]

The interrelation of horse, rider and features of the terrain is strong here, with its suggestion of toughness, wildness and loneliness. The country is relentless and moulds the kind of life that can be lived there. Life is lived at a very basic level. But if the country is relentless it does produce determined men, and it is just this that provides the drama of Patten's story, as it does in so many Westerns. The drama springs from the country itself. Its harshness—and this is true of many Westerns, especially in the 'fifties—is softened because the theme involves the protection of property and the promise of a bright future for the hero with his beautiful young wife. If the hero himself escapes the softening of the harsh outline of elemental conflict then very often a passage or a sequence will remind us of what he is really fighting for. In spite of the savage influences of the big country the Western has been able to preserve its highly moral code because the value of the small town or the smaller family prevail. It is only recently that Westerns have deliberately attempted to break down this code. The town in the West was in reality more often an accident than a formed community—'The town was simply an eddy in the troubled stream of Western immigration, and it caught the odd bits of drift wood and wreck—the flotsam and jetsam of a chaotic flood.' [10] But in the Western it has become as valuable a focus as any amount of uninhabited wilderness.

[3]

Often what we see on the screen is a familiar square mile appearing repeatedly, supplied with a stage road, a hill, a rocky outcrop or two, perhaps a dried up river bed and a glimpse of distant mountains. The fact that often just when the action takes us out into the country the same footage is repeated in a number of films does grave injustice to the broad sweep of Western terrain. But a few directors are much concerned with giving us a sense of the country's scope and moods: John Ford, obviously, although even he is reluctant to leave his favourite Monument Valley and Ford fans have had numerous opportunities to relish its particular starkness and grandeur. This is not a complaint, for Ford uses his terrain, and there are many directors for whom rocks, mountains and river beds are no more or less useful than false fronted saloons or wooden sidewalks. There are others who are so concerned with epoch-making angles that a total effect, a total feeling for the landscape, is obscured.

The self-conscious approach can be as damaging as the perfunctory. Western scenery has produced a multitude of its very own clichés, and without striving for highly artificial effects it is indeed difficult to avoid them. In two movies, separated by twenty years and representative of countless others of the same time span, there are identical cliché openings. Fritz Lang's *Western Union* (1941) and Robert Aldrich's *The Last Sunset* (1961) both open with a lone horse and rider moving fast across the landscape. In both cases the country is spare, stony and glaring. In both cases there is something clearly distinctive about the rider; he is, of course, the hero. Fritz Lang's is a nicely handled Randolph Scott Western, a good story and attractive hero, while Aldrich's is a ponderous and bad attempt at a psychological study. They each employ a standard opening and in each case the first few minutes with their hint of dramatic action and mystery tempt our interest.

Duel at Diablo (1967), a memorable Western in many respects, directed by Ralph Nelson, is more impressive in relating the mood of its opening sequence. The drama of the landscape is used to convey a disturbing sense of doom. It is grey desert country, with tall rocks casting long shadows across the treacherous sand. The sheer heartlessness of the country is emphasised. A horse and rider collapse from thirst, dwarfed by the surrounding terrain, and Apaches emerge silently from the rocks as if they were the evil spirits of an evil land. Although the movie does not altogether live up to the promise of its beginning the ominous tone is sustained throughout, with the country collaborating with the enemy to sustain the threat.

It is the scenic variety the West can provide that delights us as much as anything. As a dramatic contrast with the stark, dry desert Anthony Mann in *Bend of the River* (1952) takes us to the high forests of Oregon where steep slopes and torrential rivers are the natural hazards. Mann's confrontations between individuals, which are a trademark of his highly distinguished Westerns, are set in a strongly coloured, strongly characterised background. The hero's final struggle takes place in a mountain river, and it is the river that kills and sweeps away the dead. Mann continually uses the Western terrain in this precise and specific way. It becomes a part of the action. The final fight in *Winchester '73* (1950) owes its harsh integrality to its location on barren rock, which is a crucial influence on the fight's outcome. The two bitterly intense rivals, brothers whose mutual hatred has been unequivocally established in the opening sequences, face each other at last in a battle that is devoid of all extraneous features. This really is naked conflict, the naked rock contributes to our sense of it. The entire action of the movie has been moving towards it.

In *The Scalphunters* (1967), essentially a comedy Western directed by Sidney Pollack, the landscape reinforces the effect of action in a rather different way. In the early part of the movie a band of Indians are massacred while they are watering their horses: the incident is all the more shocking for its location by a quiet river in peaceful woods. The relaxed, natural activities of the Indians and the gentleness of water and foliage are abruptly shattered. It is a tribute to Pollack's direction that the film regains its comic equilibrium fairly convincingly after this sequence.

Attempts to establish visually the relationship between the Westerner and his terrain do have a tendency to cliché, although they may in their own right have some impact. Horses and riders skylined on a diagonal slope have appeared frequently in recent years. In Robert Mulligan's *The Stalking Moon* (1969) and in Don Siegel's *Two Mules for Sister Sara* (1970) this particular shot does successfully suggest a blending of the terrain and living creatures while making them at the same time sharply distinct. The animals appear to grow out of the land yet are seen in striking outline. When in *The Stalking Moon* we see the horse's hoofs sinking into the sand and the effort that every step takes we see the conflict between beast and country.

In both these Westerns the land is hostile and the hostility durable. An armistice may perhaps be achieved, but never conquest. Sometimes, however, the countryside has a placidity which counters any suggestion of ruthlessness. The beauty is tame, and indicates solid prosperity rather than harsh challenge. We find this in a novel by William Cox, *Black Silver*, which uses the same characters and situation as the television series *Bonanza*. 'Ponderosa was his home. The spreading loveliness of it, reaching to the edge of Lake Washoe, was part and parcel of him, as much as his bones, his marrow. This was something the Cartwrights had built, great and profitable and beautiful.'[11] Space, beauty, profit. It should surely come as no surprise to learn that the owner of this magnificence is a man of gentlemanly manners, noble mien, paternalistic instincts—and fast on the draw.

The land here is tamed and exploited. It has not lost its beauty, but its beauty is intimately bound up with its profitability. We see the threats in the story not as the menace of a wild country but as the menace of disorder against established business. What we want to see in the Western terrain is the rich potential without a softening of the wildness. We find this in Anthony Mann and other directors of his stature. It is not so much that there is room for everyone that gives the country its appeal, but the fact that it contains a challenge. Dispersing this challenge acts counter to the best the Western has to offer.

The challenge is initially to the individual. The community comes later, and the challenge it has to face is partly concerned with the problems inherited from the individual's free fight with the frontier. The particular relationship between the lonely man and limitless, unpopulated space is still the most impressive fact of the big country. We are continually shown Western enterprises such as the raising of telegraph poles and the laying of steel rails in terms of individual challenge. In Western drama a corporate effort is very often whittled down to a battle between one man and thousands of miles of space, with all the hazards it contains. Randolph Scott pulls Western Union through. It is one man versus big country. The families and communities were very often slowly losing, but the Western hero makes it easy to overlook their failure.

Frontier country is perhaps the Western maker's greatest challenge also. It is too easy to regard it simply as a striking background, a gift to the camera, a delight to the eye, a license for purple passages. It has a role to play in every Western drama and to manipulate its influences without undermining its power is not always easy. It is essential to maintain the relationship between man and the surface of the earth, and many Western directors owe their achievement to their ability to do this. John Ford treats the country with respect and admiration. Peckinpah fidgets with symbols wrenched from the terrain. Mann rivets men and action to it. Aldrich succumbs happily to its influences. Burt Kennedy, one of the most interesting contemporary directors, but restless and unreliable, comes to grips with a bleak, splendid, tyrannical landscape.

The visual temptation is there continually, yet the earliest Westerns were made in New Jersey, the most recent often in Spain, and many, some highly successful, are town Westerns with the camera hardly venturing beyond main street. The word does not have to describe, the camera portray, the landscape, but in this case it is essential for the hero himself to convey the rigours of the country—as he does in that most renowned of all town Westerns, *High Noon*.

Behind the Western hero lies, almost as a part of the landscape, all our impressions of the violence of the old West. The natural savagery in difficult terrain, drought, floods, sand and snow storms seems to breed violence. The hardships the emigrant pioneer had to endure were not the stuff of romance, but they became the ingredients of a solidly wrought legend in which aggression played a vital part. Winning through meant aggression. The journey itself, the breaking of virgin soil, the pacification of Indians, implied assault. In the Western myth suffering, endurance and aggression are inseparable.

The vision of the Pacific shore, the vision of rich, fertile valleys, the Mormon's vision of Zion, were not tame attractions. The sacrifices demanded in seeking them were hardly likely to encourage passivity. The lone trail breakers set an example of survival: weapons, skill in their use, identification of the enemy, these were all essential. The brighter the vision of promise, the more likely were the pioneers to fight for it, as the Mormons did, ruthlessly. There were legitimate targets, legitimate enemies. The earliest heroes of civilisation had weapons in their hands and the heroes of the West were no exception.

The mountain man, the guide, the breaker of trails and the breaker of virgin soil, are soon superseded by the most renowned of Westerners, the cowboy. He came into his own after the Civil War. In 1887 the first fictional cowboy hero made his debut, and it is now preeminently the saddle tramp who is, has been or will be a cow puncher, who is the Western hero. Essentially he is a man on horseback, with six shooter and Winchester, and no fixed abode. In his preface to *The Virginian* (1902), hailed by Eastern critics as the first, real, serious piece of cowboy fiction, Owen Wister wrote:

What has become of the horseman, the cow-puncher, the last romantic figure upon our soil? For he was romantic. Whatever he did, he did with his might. The bread that he earned was earned hard, the wages that he squandered were squandered hard .... Well, he will be among us always, invisible, waiting his chance to live and play as he would like. His wild kind has been among us always, since the beginning, a young man with his temptations, a hero without wings.[12]

The Virginian himself, the gentleman cowboy, is a far cry from the cheerful brutality of contemporaneous dime novels which first introduced the cowboy to the reading public. His moral agonies when he feels it necessary to lynch a group of cattle rustlers cannot be compared with the perfunctory despatch of outlaws that takes place in less lofty literature. But Wister was right. By 1890 the West was changing its character, its heyday over. Wister was concerned that its heroism should last in some form or other. His romantic horseman is essentially the same man who rode roughshod through the dime novels and who has murdered and lynched in film and fiction ever since. Whether he notches his gun or agonises over every 'necessary' killing he is one of 'the wild kind', 'a young man with his temptations'—and the conscious thrill in that phrase, 'the last romantic figure upon our soil', is still present.

Was this the frontier's finest product? It is interesting that in his diary Wister's entry for June 20, 1891, read:

I begin to conclude from five seasons of observation that life in this negligent irresponsible wilderness tends to turn people shiftless, cruel, and incompetent. I noticed in Wolcott in 1885, and I notice today, a sloth in doing anything and everything, that is born of the deceitful ease with which the makeshift answers here.[13]

There is no hint of romance or heroism here and this is not the picture of life that Wister purveys in his fiction. Yet the irresponsibility, the cruelty, the deceit and the shiftlessness are not so far from the ingredients of the Western heroic personality. Wister is describing here a town that does make its appearance in the Western, a town ripe for redemption, in a state of moral degradation that can only enhance the upright hero. It is the town of Firecreek in Victor McEveety's film of the same name (1967). Firecreek is morally soft centred. Mr. Whittier the store keeper, a failed lawyer back East, reproves the hero for trying to defend the town against a band of hired guns. Why die for a town full of failures, he asks. Mr. Whittier says Firecreek has no guts. Its citizens came West not with a pioneer vision, but to escape failure. The hero, James Stewart as an honest sod buster and stalwart family man, goes ahead and wins out. The town is saved and redeemed. But the man he kills, Henry Fonda as the gang leader, is the romantic figure. He is the man who has Wister's qualities, the hard riding, hard living horseman. He has come from across the mountains, powerful and mysterious. His men steal, attempt rape, lynch a halfwit, but Henry Fonda dying slowly on main street is our romantic Westerner.

The 'negligent irresponsible wilderness' is bound to enlarge the tough man on whichever side of the law he is. The man of quick decisions and positive action wields a solid power in a town full of people who are shiftless and incompetent. Wister's recognition and depressed expression of the true character of a Western town do not necessarily undermine this aspect of the Western myth. Frequently the Western pivots on a town rotten at the core rescued, redeemed or liberated by the frontier hero.

Wister refused to acknowledge the attraction of the cowboy on the wrong side of the law who kills without conscience. He makes his villains evil, and insidiously relates the Virginian's shy wooing of a pure schoolteacher from the East with his moral killing. Wister's chivalrous version of the West, or at least his version of the West's influential characters, is often crude. It is a different kind of crudity from the dime novels' blood and thunder, but sometimes just as blatant. It is the outlaw, sometimes the outcast rather than the criminal, who contains much of the myth's potency. Whether sadistic killer, repulsive thug or orphan with a grudge he can have a compulsive attraction. Certainly, many of the West's famous outlaws were brutal and perhaps psychopathic killers, and legend has elevated many of them to the status of Robin Hoods. But this itself suggests the power of their appeal, so great that legend has had to legitimise them.

The outcast need not be criminal, and the mysterious stranger, no questions asked, who radiates an aura of self-imposed exile from the community, is a standard figure in the myth. Shane, in Jack Schaefer's story and George Stevens' movie (1953) is the best of all possible examples of the mysterious stranger. It is darkly hinted that Shane has killed in dubious circumstances, but we never associate him with the rat-faced hired gun whom he ultimately despatches. It is Shane in his ambiguity, not the Virginian in his moral certainty, who convinces us that killing is necessary, and also that the man carrying a gun on the right side of the law shoulders a heavy responsibility which isolates him from the community he defends. Shane is outside the law in the sense that he has to shape the law. A frontiersman with his skill, experience and moral sense does not need the law to protect him, and the hint of an unacceptable past confirms our impression of him as essentially independent of the law.

This independence is a vital part of the outlaw's attraction. He shares it with the mysterious stranger. They are both symbols of the anarchy of the West, which along with the wide open spaces gives the frontier such scope for myth. A man has to learn to fend for himself. Once he has learnt this it is not easy for him to succumb to the values of the community that moves after him. And because his experience and understanding of the country give the frontiersman his crucial superiority very often the community has to adapt to the individual, not vice versa. There is anarchy in the towns, its ramifications in the saloons and brothels and local government, as well as on the prairies. An anarchic situation tempts the independent man to find his own way, and it can result, as it did in the West, in every degree of conflict and aggression.

Shane contains a standard type of Western conflict: cattleman versus sod buster, big range versus small claim, anarchic cowboy versus man of the community trying to put down roots. The theme is of especial interest because it is always in danger of reversing and destroying a vital element in the myth. In *Shane* and in *Firecreek* the sod buster, representing the worth of the community, wins, but if the decent American qualities this victory confirms are really what we are being encouraged to support we must condemn the cowboy and all that he represents. Shane has a melancholy about him which suggests an awareness that ultimately he is wrong. Nevertheless, he is the hero, not Joe the homesteader.

While we watch the dying outlaw in *Firecreek*, and suspect that perhaps Mr. Whittier was right, we are being asked to celebrate qualities that are often thought of as being particularly American, qualities which imply the centrality of the home, the family, the community, the vestments of democracy. They concern beliefs which specifically negate the loner. And yet it is just these that the loner so often fights for. Shane rides on; he cannot share in the victory. There is a tantalising contradiction here, yet the two halves are inseparable. The West is extolled because it can sustain simultaneously but not quite reconcile the anarchic qualities of the frontier hero and decent 'American' qualities. Not only is the loner allowed his freedom; the community, sometimes, is dependent on him.

The frontier always constituted a potential threat to the seat of government and established society, wherever the frontier was and wherever the government. Frederick Jackson Turner in his seminal essay suggests that the frontier experience confirmed the Americanism of Americans, and the frontier has been frequently discussed as melting pot and safety valve. But even when the frontier is seen as drawing off the pressure from the East the threat was always there, whether the frontier was Cooper's upper New York State or Bret Harte's California. The qualities that the frontier demanded were the qualities that society discouraged. Independence. Individualism. Ruthlessness. Conforming to established social values would not help much in the deserts and the mountains. But when a town caught up with you and the frontier moved on to community building you might be destroyed if you did not destroy first. It has been argued that civilisation created the criminal. America has spectacularly preserved a myth of pre-civilisation which encapsulates a hero free from the pressures of conformist society.

The relationship between collective experience and the individual has bothered many American writers and there is a parallel ambivalence in their treatment of the community. The dualism in the Western myth is not unique. Thomas Wolfe's *Look Homeward, Angel!* (1929) and Sinclair Lewis's *Main Street* (1920), two respected novels about town and community, both, although their object is to condemn, succeed in *confirming* community values while portraying the destruction of individuals by institutions Americans appear to value highly: the family and the community. Where a town symbolises victory in a battle against a hostile territory (and a hostile people) this is even more likely to happen.

The conflict between community and the individual, which occurs all the time in the Western, became also a conflict between history and the individual. Although the Western myth is virtually frozen in time the period within which it generally ranges, the 1860s to the 1890s, saw enormous changes, and the processes of history and the effects of change are incorporated into the myth. The myth absorbs the inevitable contradictions without reconciling them. The near tragic conflict in David Miller's memorable *Lonely Are the Brave* (1962), a contemporary Western, would have been appropriate sixty years earlier. The film tells us that there is no longer room for the cowboy, who must negotiate tarmac and barbed wire on his horse. It is not just that there are man-made hazards, but that there is no place for the man who wants to be independent of the community, who prefers his horse to a limousine, who prefers the open hills to the concrete town. The cowboy hero, played by Kirk Douglas, and his horse are mown down by a truck when they are crossing a wet highway at night. The horse is shot and the cowboy carried away on a stretcher. Yet it is accident that brings them down. Up to this point they have outwitted jeep and helicopter, survived rifle fire, crossed mountains. The myth survives. The machine is as fallible as the man, and fallibility emphasises the hero's significance, even in defeat.

Lonely Are the Brave is an unpretentious movie that makes its point simply and memorably. Unsatisfactorily clever, but allied in theme, is *Coogan's Bluff* (1968) directed by Don Siegel. Coogan (Clint Eastwood) is a deputy sheriff from Arizona sent to extradite a criminal from New York, not only a contemporary cowboy, but a contemporary cowboy in New York. We see him first tracking an Indian in a jeep. He is a nasty man who despises his prisoners and sleeps with other men's wives. He stalks cussedly through joints thick with LSD and turgid pop, a clean limbed Arizonian, a self-reliant loner, but vicious.

We are, it seems, intended to admire the strong, silent, sexy cowboy. His is the clean violence of wide open spaces. But as it is in the classic Western the antithesis is false, its crudeness a great deal more apparent at a distance from the frontier, for the implications are no longer cushioned by myth. It is difficult to transplant the Western, for as soon as it moves East it raises, in spite of itself, essentially moral issues, concerning violence, and in this case sexual behaviour, which cannot be glossed over. This film moves out of the Western form and out of the Western environment while trying to retain something of the myth. It doesn't work. The elaborate parallels, a motor bike chase instead of horses for example, emphasise the failure. Coogan is completely convincing as an illustration of the breakdown of the Western myth, but that does not seem to be what was intended.

The only threat the West still contains is the threat of sheer violence, unmodified by the romance of independent struggle and the demands of the frontier. The frontier has gone leaving oil fields and long range rocket stations in its wake. There are no outlets for the old pioneer spirit: the step from cowboy to Goldwater, John Wayne's alter ego, is a short one. If the qualities of heroic independence do not endure someone must be elected to ensure, or artificially promote, their survival. It is not as paradoxical as it may seem that this confirms the status and importance of the Western as a vehicle for celebrating many of the qualities that democratic Americans traditionally value.

Coogan shows us the decadence of the last frontier, the puzzled hero of Miller's film the nobility. Just as the hero of *The Big Sky* is rendered unfit for civilisation by his frontier experience, the westward movement, East moving West, has made the frontier experience irrelevant to the West also. It is an historical inevitability which the Western can transcend. While the Western myth absorbs historical change, eventually the myth defies history and lives its own independent existence.

Other modern Westerns, Martin Ritt's *Hud* and Sturges' *Bad Day at Black Rock*, illustrate frontier decadence. In Ritt's film the hero needs to do something, no matter what, with his frustrated power. He is amoral because the Western hero no longer has a context. He is wasted, as the infected cattle driven into the lime pit are wasted. Sturges' film is concerned with community guilt, a recurring theme in the Western, but bleaker in a contemporary setting. Racialism, hysteria and a terrible inbred demoralisation are the striking features. The frontier has passed by and forgotten its creations. The classic cold-eyed killer has become a slab fisted moron, and it is conscience rather than skill that moulds the hero.

These twentieth-century Westerns implicitly draw attention to the cultural and psychological necessity of preserving the frontier in all its glory. This is not a plea for romanticism or the falsification of history but a recognition of the legend's force. The rest of this book is very much concerned with all that has contributed to this legend, and the nature of its magnetism.

TWO

Post Bellum

A union depending not upon the constraint of force, but upon the loving devotion of a free people; 'and that all things may be so ordered and settled upon the best and surest foundations, that peace and happiness, truth and justice,· religion and piety, may be established among us for generations'.

President Hayes, Inaugural Address

[1]

Victory for the Union at Appomattox signalled the shifting of a battle-ground from the ravaged South to the still relatively empty West. After the Civil War thousands went West, fleeing a disorganised Union and any attempt to adjust to a settled life. Soldiers, guerrillas in the border States, freed negroes and the merely restless joined the Westward flow, and their vibratory presence in the opening territories shaped the character of the thirty years to follow. Post bellum chaos existed everywhere, but in the West there was nothing to hold it, no established institutions on which to fall back. Immediately after the War the West was not only in the throes of building a society almost from scratch. It was importing chaos to add to the legacy the War had left. It is with this legacy, and the more disruptive elements of this importation, that this chapter is concerned.

In what is perhaps Alan Le May's best novel, *By Dim and Flaring Lamps*, men travel by mule through the murky forests and sticky mud of Missouri, constantly threatened, constantly alert, constantly aware that murder in the name of a good cause is easy. The book belongs to that category of semi-Westerns which use the turbulance of Kansas and Missouri immediately before the Civil War as their setting. *By Dim and Flaring Lamps* has a foreboding, haunting atmosphere which lingers long after the book has been put down. It is something quite different from the shimmering light of the wide open spaces, but it is a quality that conditions some of Le May's best writing, in *The Searchers* and *The Unforgiven*, better known books. It belongs peculiarly to that confused and bloody patch of history which was America's Civil War.

The Civil War as fought by Blue and Grey clad armies was not widely apparent in the West, although there were both Union and Confederate troops there and battles were fought in Texas and New Mexico. Most of the major battlegrounds were East of the Mississippi. The West saw something less murderous in its extent but grimmer and more vicious in its character—the Kansas and Missouri border raiders, pro- and anti-slavery irregulars who killed and sacked, burned and looted with what they regarded as official licence.

It is a territory of violence that has been much exploited in third rate fiction and which, in reality, nursed large numbers of outlaws and renegades. Quantrill's band, of Confederate loyalties, is the most famous, and it was with him that the teenaged Jesse James acquired the habits that were to make him famous. The summer of 1856 in Kansas, when things were relatively mild, saw the killings of two hundred men by border raiders of both factions plus the destruction of crops and property. Seven years later in January 1863 Captain Quantrill led his guerrillas in the well-known attack on Lawrence, Kansas. It is said that Quantrill's men killed a thousand people during 1863, preying on small detachments of Union soldiers, centres of anti-slavery feeling and runaway slaves.

The events that labelled Kansas 'bleeding' were perhaps an unofficial part of the Civil War, but it is arguable that their effects were, West of the Mississippi, more lasting. Many of the uniformed troops had no choice but to fight and no very strong allegiance to either side. But the raiders in Kansas and Missouri were voluntary killers. A man got used to violence. His own home might have been destroyed, his crops burned, stock stolen, parents, children, relatives, friends killed. When the War was over the difficulties of reestablishing an ordered and lawful way of life were immense, and many did not even try to begin.

Jesse James, his brother Frank, and the Younger brothers had all served a useful apprenticeship by the time the War was over, although it was not until 1874 that they really made their presence as outlaws felt. They operated in an atmosphere still tense with rivalry. Relatives and Southern sympathisers sheltered them; Yankees hated and feared them. Many of their supporters saw them as instruments of revenge for the South's defeat. They insisted that those in power in Missouri made it impossible for ex-Confederates to get back on their feet. But the State Governor denounced Jesse, and in a battle between the gang and a force of Pinkerton men Jesse's mother lost her right arm. 'So great is the terror that the Jameses and Youngers have instilled in Clay County that their names are never mentioned save in backrooms and then only in a whisper,' wrote one Missouri newspaper.[1]

Jesse's main targets were banks and trains. The St. Louis Midland

Railroad offered $25,000 reward for Jesse and $15,000 for Frank. As every schoolboy knows Jesse was finally shot in the back by 'That dirty little coward' Bob Ford in St. Joseph in 1882. The fact that he died by cowardice and treachery, shot by one of his own men, only served to enhance the legend. And the words 'Jesse James is not dead' were whispered in Missouri for many years to come.

The popular imagination has lauded Jesse as a folk hero. The banks and the railroads that he attacked were associated with monopoly and oppression (just as they were fifty years later in the days of the Depression) and felt by society's victims to be fair game. Frank James gave himself up and was cheered by crowds all the way to his native Clay County where he stood trial and was acquitted. He died in bed in 1915. Cole Younger, the last of the Younger brothers, died a year later.

The James and the Younger brothers have countless books, films and legends to their names. In most of these they appear as archetypal Western outlaws, occasionally presented with a degree of subtlety as social outcasts who had no choice but to do violence on society, sometimes seen as kind and courteous gentlemen who took up arms only against their enemies and distributed their wealth amongst the poor. In Fritz Lang's *The Return of Frank James* (1940) Henry Fonda's restrained portrayal of the outlaw is strangely convincing in spite of the expected glamorisation of the facts. Fonda's Frank is quiet, withdrawn and bitter. He has the manners of a gentleman—but he chews tobacco. He is a determined killer when he considers death to be just, but has a profound loyalty to those who are close to him. But, as happens so often in the Western, the character of the man is subsumed by the character of the actor, and the impression that lingers is of Fonda's expressionless eyes and his jaws working slowly over his tobacco quid. Frank James as a folk personality has very little to do with this memorable image.

The Jesse Jameses have been legion: Tyrone Power, Roy Rogers, Audie Murphy, Dale Robertson and Robert Wagner have all played him, to mention only a few. None of them bear much resemblance to the dark, heavily bearded man who was Jesse in real life, but he is a useful frame to be clothed in the raiment of the cowboy hero. In fact, the James brothers are probably less significant historically than the nameless hundreds who, disrupted by the ravages of war, helped to populate the far West. In *Bend of the River* James Stewart plays a man who had been a Kansas raider and is trying to forget his past. He cannot forget, but he can conquer his past by facing and overcoming a representation of evil in the shape of Arthur Kennedy, who raided for the South. He thus establishes himself as, still a killer, but a man of courage and principles as well. And incidentally implying that the Union cause was not only morally right, but its supporters superior.

In a number of Westerns, often some of the more interesting, the past, an earlier and more turbulent period of the frontier, is seen as a challenge to a more constructive present. The past troubles the hero, suggests that beneath the tough exterior there is a capacity for suffering. We see this in Richard Jessup's book *Chuka* (1961) which manipulates this particular kind of tough, troubled hero in classic fashion. Chuka is weighed down by his reputation and the knowledge he has a debt to pay off. He is uncommunicative and distrustful. People don't like him. He has no choice but to work out his own salvation. The hero must come to terms with the past and he does this most often by using the skills its violence has taught him to right a wrong, protect a community or to save a life. Chuka saves a life against extreme odds, and the woman he saves in turn helps him to make something less destructive of his own life. This is not so much a justification of violence as an individual's justification of his own existence. Young men who had known four years of war, whether guerrilla or regular, who had little or nothing to go home to, drifted West and tended to practice what the War had taught them. Young men whose earliest experiences were amongst violence and turmoil—Cole Younger was twelve when Lawrence was sacked—did not find it easy to recognise that authorised killing was at an end.

However, in one respect killing was authorised. In the years after the War there did exist a legitimate enemy: the Indian. Men who had fought to end the tyranny of slavery were now hustled westward to play their part in the extermination of the red man. Inevitably the men who stayed in the Army tended to be those who had nothing more worthwhile to do, or men (usually officers) who liked to fight. Young officers like Custer, who had made their mark in the War between the States but in fact had not much experience, went West itching for glory. There could be no glory without killing. Captain Fetterman, remembered like Custer for the circumstances of his death, was a perfect example of an officer impatient for personal triumph. Restive, and highly critical of the unaggressive policy of his commanding officer, Colonel Carrington, he enthusiastically led his men into massacre north of the Piney River and himself lost his life. Carrington was an unusual officer in his resistance to opportunities for slaughter, unloved by his superiors, criticised by officers of Fetterman's zeal. His career was an unhappy one.

The officer of more courage than commonsense is a frequent character in the cavalry Western. One such is Captain Loring in Luke Short's *Ambush* (1950), who is reluctant to accept the superior abilities of his scout. In reality the Army in the West depended heavily on scouts, Indian and white, but this is what Loring had to say: 'I've seen enough of these guides to know them. They're more Indian than white, and they've left a string of Indian wives behind them. They're dirty, untrustworthy ... purple liars and vain, and they're only interested in prolonging a campaign so that they can draw pay.'[2] Loring of course dies, having shown himself far from equal to the job, and the scout survives. In the Army Western it is very often arrogance that is the victim of poetic justice, rather than evil.

The Indians of course did present a problem. There could be no official beginning or end to the Indian wars. They were not an enemy whom it occurred to officialdom to treat in the conventional manner. Conventional courtesies and formalities were meaningless. Most soldiers, officers and men, were ignorant about Indians, about their tribes, their customs, their culture and their laws. There were a few exceptions. General Crook, one of the most active and shrewd pacifiers of the West, apparently respected by the Apaches, was one, but on the whole the authorities were unwilling to take the advice of those who knew and understood the Indians. It was one thing to rely on a scout who knew the way a certain tribe would behave in battle, quite another to take seriously this same man's judgement of Indians' expectations, of their morale or their wrongs. Apart from other considerations, it was a long way from the Black Hills or the New Mexican mountain ranges to Washington.

The conventional picture of the U.S. Cavalry is the wild, bugle-blowing charge to the rescue of innocent whites besieged by savages. For film makers it has been irresistible, but in spite of this the treatment is often perfunctory. It is frequently a gesture rather than a significant event in itself. John Prebble's novel *The Buffalo Soldiers* (1959) is a genuine attempt to portray the character of an undistinguished company of cavalry (black troopers, white lieutenant) precipitated with all its problems and rivalries into a situation of stark crisis. Lieutenant Byrne mutters ironically to himself the words of the manual on the cavalry charge when he is almost without hope: 'The charge is the decisive and most important characteristic of cavalry movement. The main conditions for its success are cohesion, rapidity, surprise and impetuosity and vigour in the shock.'[3]

The charge that Byrne then commands is no glorious and triumphant finale but a horrifying expenditure of effort in desert country which accomplishes very little. Byrne is new to Indian country, new to his officer status and new to the men whom he commands. But he quickly understands that the challenge the Comanche enemy embody is something the manuals have not anticipated. Both Byrne and his men are part of the aftermath of the Civil War. There was a fairly large number of black troops—the Tenth Regiment was composed of them—but almost all the officers were white. The soldiers in Prebble's novel are raw recruits recently freed (few writers have made anything of the fact that large numbers of freed slaves made their way West in one way or another) and Byrne himself has worked his way up from the ranks. Their situation is directly a result of the Civil War.

We can see the results of Civil War experience emerging in different ways. It is likely to make the trooper bitter, cynical, knowing, but no less scared than he ever was. He acquires certain techniques of daily survival, and cannot leave the Army because he knows no other way of life. The formidable O'Gara in Michael Straight's committed and informed novel *Carrington* (1961) reflects on his boots.

He looked down at his own boots, cracked and misshapen, stiff with dust and gathering more dust as they scuffed along. More than one man I killed for these old boots, he thought: back in Shiloh when the battery exploded and myself left for dead in the mud until a greyback roused me, heaving and tugging at my legs to get these boots off. Last pair he ever tried to steal. And yet, O'Gara reflected, there was no end to their thieving. A man died in the war and before his soul departed from his body his boots were gone. Instead of a pair of boots marching and wearing down for a man, it seemed as if a man lived and fought for his boots.[4]

Robert Penn Warren has a salient passage in *Wilderness* in which starving Confederate soldiers hunt in the pockets of the Union dead for bits of food. In the Indian wars soldiers were less likely to acquire something of value from the dead (unless from their own dead). Scalps, trinkets and feathers were usually all that an Indian corpse would yield, and none of these would contribute much to making life a little easier.

In most cavalry Westerns the hero, if he is not a scout, is an officer whose experience at West Point will not have taught him very much about boots. He probably finds life out West difficult and trying, the diet monotonous, an absence of women, except for one or two officers' wives, very likely a scarcity of pleasant company of any kind. This plus the normal rigours and dangers of service made for a very bleak life but, especially on the screen, we rarely get a glimpse of the sheer tedium of the soldier's frontier existence. The cavalry picture is generally in far too much haste to linger over the more prosaic details, which would give a rather different dimension to the kind of courage a soldier had.

Henry Sell and Victor Weybright give us a hint of the nature of army life on the frontier in their book on Buffalo Bill.

Sheridan's troops were a motley, poorly disciplined, badly paid rabble. The soldier's sixteen dollars a month did not leave him much, after deductions, for the whiskey on which he usually spent it. Most of them were lonely and bored and, like their officers, constantly bickering among themselves.[5]

In Ernest Haycox's *Bugles in the Afternoon*, a good, solid novel covering the Custer massacre, this boredom expresses itself in ritualistic fistfights between companies in which the well-bred hero also takes part with a great deal of satisfaction. Under circumstances of constraint the most infinitesimal dispute became a major point of honour, and had to be settled as such. If anything, the code of the frontiersman, that he must always be prepared to support his arguments by force, was exaggerated in the Army.

The U.S. Cavalry has provided the Western with many opportunities for character acting, countless robust, quirky figures like Straight's O'Gara. There have been sergeants of all descriptions, from Woody Strode's Sergeant Rutledge, in Ford's movie, to Robert Ryan's slightly simple Irish sergeant in Siodmark's *Custer of the West* (1967). One of the commonest is the stalwart, reliable, taciturn, fatherly and grey-haired character who is infinitely wise in the ways of the Army. He has advice for anyone who wants it. He may be critical of his superiors—he is almost certainly a great deal more experienced—but he does not voice his criticism. Irish immigrants provided the cavalry with more than their fair share of recruits and many of these fictional characters are Irish. As the Irishman has popularly been represented as a soak, a liar and a belligerent for many decades, perhaps centuries, he offers enormous scope to his exploiters. Of course, he does not always come out badly from this, and occasionally we come across a hero who has an Irish name (although usually not the traditional Irish characteristics). It is of interest to note that many more heroes, both in and out of the cavalry have Scottish names, descendants of exiled Jacobites, perhaps.

The Army has been treated in Westerns as a means of collecting men from varying ethnic backgrounds and exploiting their differences in accent and character. This can be a basis for comedy and minor feuding, but almost always the splendid moment arrives when all are united against a common enemy, and all differences are forgotten amidst acts of comradeship and courage. This itself becomes part of the post-Civil War great American theme. We see it in *The Undefeated* (1969), one of Andrew McLaglen's great American efforts, where the film ends with the welding together of Southerner, Yankee and Indian to the accompaniment of the sweet notes of the harmonica. The common enemy, as is almost inevitable in the great American theme, the Mexican. Precisely because the Western is about conflict does it lend itself so readily to themes of unity and reconciliation. But there has to be a common enemy. The United States survives by quelling the ignoble and the savage and offering a home for the brave. It is a theme that grows inevitably from the disparate nation trying to preserve a myth of unity and equality. The drawback is that someone, somewhere has to be the ignoble and the savage. In the last ten years it has not often been the Indian. It has frequently been the Mexican.

[2]

The bitter differences of the Civil War only made it that much more likely that the novel and cinema should find it necessary to celebrate 'the loving devotion of a free people', even though it is fairly clear that one of the last things to be expected from a free people is a spontaneous loving devotion. The Western also makes a great deal of precisely the opposite phenomenon, the hatred between Rebel and Yankee that often lingered for many years and motivated many feuds and many killings. The unifying factor was sometimes less glorious than war; it was sometimes crime.

It would be misleading to argue that there was no unifying process in the years after the War, for it was precisely on the frontier that shared dangers and common interests were most likely to bring people together. John Hawgood remarks on this, with particular reference to cattle raising. 'In the decades after the Civil War the spread of the "cow culture" up out of Texas helped to knit the divided country together again and keep the West "one society".' He goes on to say:

Men who had driven a herd of cattle all the way from the Rio Grande on to the Blackfoot reservation in Northern Montana .... could not but acquire a wide knowledge of their enormous country and an easy tolerance of sectional and local differences and idiosyncrasies. These differences sometimes caused trouble, for many of the cowhands were Confederate veterans, but the long drives tended to be a melting-pot rather than a tinder box.[6]

Even so, 'tended to be' is all that is ventured here. The evidence suggests that cowhands were widely tolerant of different religions and national backgrounds, tolerant of the negro 'in his place', contemptuous of the Indian and Mexican, and very often full of hatred for the Yankee or Rebel. There were exceptions: some white individuals respected individual Indians. Al Sieber, the famous scout in Apache country, could not have achieved what he did if he had despised his foe. Many white/Indian friendships appear in fiction. There have even been one or two white/black friendships within the Western genre. But on the whole the above is a general pattern which can be found both in memoirs and contemporary writings, and in fiction and the film.

Cattle raising did at least provide a focus for activity and aspiration.

It provided a purpose of some kind for many of the West's drifters, even if for most of them it would always be a dream. The growing cattle industry helped to produce at least the feeling of new beginnings on the frontier. The flow of immigrants during the war years was mostly bound for the far West, not for the prairie lands that were to become cattle raising country. The gold rushes drew a steady flow of fortune seekers into the mountains, but it was in the nature of things that these were not the men to bring solid settlement to the country. The Mormons steadily filled Utah with their families, bringing them West in highly organised immigrant trains. But the territories between the Rockies and Missouri were only being productively populated after the War, as men brought their wives and families and the railroad brought goods and Eastern newspapers and Eastern speculators of all kinds into the great void. Howard Fast, in his fictional portrait of Dodge City, gives some idea of what was going on.

The population came as if the news were carried on the wind. The place was big and high and handsome; there were no homes, but nestling shoulder to shoulder on the long line of Front Street were more saloons, honky-tonks, whore-houses, and gambling spots than any other city in the plains-country could boast. There was no night and no day; you rolled it together at Dodge. It was a junction. Driving up from the south along the Chisolm Trail, the Texas cattle came by the thousand to be shipped East on the Santa Fe Railroad: and the Texas hands by the hundreds fought the Civil War over. They brought hate with them and spewed it out in blood and broken bones. They mingled with the dregs of the plains, from Canada to Mexico. The buffalo hunters came in with their stinking hides, and the whisky pedlars made it their headquarters from which to sell guns and sugared alcohol to the Indians. Tourists found the West high and wide open at Dodge City. English lords and Russian grand dukes, they all had to see Dodge. To remember America. If they found nothing of men and women working and building, raising families, trying to make a future where there was no past, they still had enough to remember America by. They could hear the guns crackle and watch the funeral processions to Boot Hill.[7]

If Dodge City was not entirely typical in its extremities this passage does give an impression of the sheer bustle and energy, however disorganised, which frontier life generated and in turn helped to tame frontier life. Without such teeming centres of trade and entertainment the pioneering individual could never have survived. Or at least not in numbers that would make life in the country viable. It was the mining camps that first brought the speculators, men and women who hoped to profit from gold and silver strikes by being right there where it was taken out of the ground. The War itself barely affected them. But when the War was over they came in droves, the drummers, the real estate speculators, the girls on the make, ruined Southerners hoping for a break, the younger sons of European aristocracy looking for adventure. They made money illicitly, illegally, with cunning and sometimes through sheer hard work, or they remained broke and broken, and drifted through the Western territories with just sufficient hope on the horizon to keep them moving.

The money makers and the failures have populated the Western also, along with the hopeful strugglers and the precarious survivors. Although the Western is generally assumed to rely on stereotypes, it does legitimately contain a great range of personalities and occupations. In William Cox's *Black Silver* there is, as well as a rancher of substance and the usual cowboys and residents of a mining town, an Irish political militant, a Chinese cook of glowing reputation, a Jewish engineer, a Welsh union secretary, and the names of the three wives the central character has had add to the cosmopolitan flavour : Elizabeth, Inger and Marie.

One of the characters in *Black Silver*, not a particularly noteworthy Western but representative of some central aspects, is a Texan who fought for the South and spent some time in a prison camp. He is a careful portrait of a man who understands what his experiences have done to him but not how to cope with the aftermath.

Ever since he'd come out of that Yankee prison he had been getting into one thing and another that didn't pan out. It was as though a curse had been put on him by the blue-jacketed devils who had beaten him and starved him in Maryland. The whole damn thing was cockeyed, Maryland was suppose to be Rebel, not a place for a Yank prison camp.[8]

Sheer resentment and his grasp of the fact that the only thing to be done amidst such confusion is to make his own way regardless of others are responsible for this man's actions. His side-kick is an altogether more vicious customer as this exchange between boss and man suggests

'You don't just kill people,' Chalmer tried to explain. 'You try to figure out things.'
'Kilt 'em in the war. Kilt a million Yanks, more or less. Kilt some niggers in Texas, didn't we?'
'I keep tellin' you, that's different.'
'You keep tellin' me but I got a hard time believin'.'[9]

The psychology here may be crude but in essence this is what happened. If it was all right to kill Yanks and Niggers (and Indians) why scruple at any killing? The circumstances of killing mean nothing to Macedon, the character here. It is no worse to kill for gain than to kill as a soldier under orders. This is what the experience of killing has taught him. As a sharp contrast the book's hero finds it impossible to bring himself to pick off the enemy with a long range Sharps rifle. '"Like a turkey shoot"', his son comments.[10]

It is this dangerous lesson, that the victim and the circumstances do not matter, that is the distinctive feature of Sergio Leone's film *The Good, the Bad and the Ugly* (1967). The action of the film revolves around a hairsbreadth distinction between kinds of killing. It takes place during the confused, unhappy mess that was the Civil War in the West. Leone makes the most of this confusion, gives it an almost Buñuel-like illogic. His characters wander in and out of it, with loyalties to neither side—with loyalties to nothing and no one in fact, for each is concerned only for himself. They find themselves engaged in personal feuds in the midst of a Yankee bombardment. Later they are prisoners of the Yankees, at another point they actively engage in a battle against the Confederates. Conventional loyalty and conventional morality have no place.

Leone's film, vicious and amoral as it is, is splendidly anarchic in its scope and apparent intentions. It is much more than a story of the triumph of the 'good', who is himself only a bare degree better than the bad—although that degree is all important. It is a film about the grotesque disruption of war, and it is probably this that lingers most memorably. It decimates any idea of glory or heroism and comes very near to destroying any belief in the viability of simple, decent behaviour in circumstances where decency is being legitimately dislocated. And it makes us consider a root question: is it better to knife a man in the back or to kill men by the dozen with cannon? Is it better to kill for yourself or kill for your government? The question emerges in the film with some irony, and highly coloured by Leone's savage brand of humour. And it emerges surrounded with some doubt as to whether it has any meaning at all: Leone may be saying that killing, in such a totally violent and anarchic context, cannot be judged at all. We, the audience, make moral judgments based on the satisfaction on the face of Lee Van Cleef as he murders, and the impassivity of Clint Eastwood's expression as he does the same. There are some fumbled sequences, but there is a productive ambiguity in the movie which is much more satisfactory than Peckinpah's muddled attitudes in *The Wild Bunch* (1969).

The chaos and bewilderment that the West saw during and after the Civil War appears in Leone's film not simply as the result of lawlessness but as very much a part of the particular kind of amorality that licensed mass killing fosters. We see it in the Indian wars too. Because it was impossible to fight a conventional war against the Indians there were no reasonably decent standards of behaviour towards them. The Civil War had shown the vicious hatred that Yankees and Southerners were capable of. Hatred on one level, confusion and lack of commitment on another—it is hardly surprising that disappointed men from Senators to troopers, from dispossessed estate owners to immigrant peasants found in the Indians a handy scapegoat for all their difficulties. To have such an enemy was clearly disruptive of what morality the Army did contain. In a war that could not involve the conquering of territory—for it was the settlers, the ranchers, the miners and the railroads who did that—and could not involve the winning of cities—for the Indians had no city, only moveable, reneweable villages—all that was left was the extinction of the foe. If military men did not reason quite along these lines (there were much more calculating reasons for wanting the Indians decimated) instinctively they grasped the situation. Colonel Carrington's policy of simply maintaining a presence could not be satisfactory. In the war against the Indians the taking of life was not a means to an end, but an end in itself.

It would not be true to say that this is a murky point in which the Western avoids getting involved, for the Western has been continually involved in just this issue. There is a lot of avoidance and sidestepping, but it has been debated, accepted and condemned. It is almost impossible to escape it altogether. If there is no other reasonable justification for the continuing existence of the Western there is at least the point that it has not let us forget the Indian, in whatever guise he appears.

In some post-Civil War Westerns the Indian is as likely to be the salvation of the war-corrupted veteran as his ruin. Sam Fuller's *Run of the Arrow* (1957) lauded when it first appeared but embarrassingly overrated, begins with the last shot of the Civil War. Rod Steiger as a bitter Irish Southerner (that's a rich combination) goes West, encounters bad Indians and good Indians, marries one of the good ones, and sides with them against a stupid and unscrupulous Yankee cavalry commander. But in the course of this he learns that not all Yankees are stupid and unscrupulous, and lurking behind it all is the great American theme.

The figure who tends to get neglected in the Western's great American theme is the black. Generally at best he gets a condescending gesture. In the opening sequences of *The Undefeated* Rock Hudson as the Southern colonel, says farewell to his faithful ex-slaves (who are still on the plantation) and presents the oldest and most faithful with his father's watch. He then sets fire to the noble mansion which he cannot afford to keep himself and cannot bear to sell to carpetbaggers who appear as a sinister Yankee/black partnership. The colonel then goes West, leaving, we are to suppose, his faithful retainers basking in the flames. But many blacks went West too. A large proportion of Texas cowboys were ex-slaves. Some even became foremen, although this was usually further north as most Texans were too much Southerners to take to being bossed by a black man. In his book *Cattle Kings*, a study of the cattle empires, Lewis Atherton describes the situation like this:

Although Negroes and Mexicans constituted a sizeable part of the labor force in the Southwest, and could be found virtually everywhere in ranch country, they were subject to considerable discrimination. The caste system which handicapped them in the land of the self-made men traced back to the section where they were most heavily concentrated and to an earlier day, an evidence that methods of handling humans as well as cattle owed much to the influence of the Southwest.[11]

Texas of course had been a slave state. Even further north the black cowboy had his problems. In Dakota a Scots ranchowner, Lincoln Lang, was criticised for treating a black on his payroll as an equal. Some of his fellow white ranchers took it as a personal insult.

Not only has this been ignored as a theme by the Western, the very existence of the black cowboy has been neglected. There have been black cooks and black handymen and black servants but no black cowboys. The faithful negro is the usual character. Woody Strode, an actor of great distinction, has played his quota of devoted darkies, and few black actors in the Western context have an opportunity to do anything else. Woody Strode's most memorable performance in this line is in *The Man Who Shot Liberty Valance* (John Ford, 1961) where his constancy to John Wayne is above reproach. But most of us will prefer to remember him as Sergeant Rutledge, or his superb performance in Richard Brooks' *The Professionals*.

The other standby is the comic negro—Ernest Whitman in *The Return of Frank James* or Stepin' Fetchit (there's a name to remember) in *Bend of the River*. These are the men the patriarch's daughter can treat with great affection, something like family pets. Any idea of marriage would be as grotesque as mating with a cooperative burro. These characters are always treated with respect at least by the good white men, who are occasionally even prepared to risk their lives for a loyal darkie, but it goes without saying that the black man's position is always distinctly menial.

It is the black cowboy as an ordinary feature of the West's population that has not been recognised. There is a trend in conspicuous black heroes, as represented by Jim Brown, and Sidney Poitier has made his contribution to the Western, but our knowledge that these are in real life and a white world successful men takes the edge off the significance of their presence. It is not difficult to use black actors with sophisticated good looks in leading roles. What is much more impressive is the dry intelligence of Ossie Davis in not particularly heroic roles in *Sam Whiskey* and *The Scalphunters*.

The Scalphunters is a species of gothic comedy, with Ossie Davis and Burt Lancaster as runaway slave and hoary old mountain man respectively. It manages, without quite losing sight of the traditional hero, to present a series of reversals of conventional situations. The mountain man cannot take on the scalphunting outfit single handed and fumes impotently out of rifle range. The runaway slave, trained in habits of deference and servitude, becomes quietly yet effectively subversive. The film does not at all celebrate what has so often been a solemn feature of liberal fiction, the black/white friendship. Runaway slave and mountain man associate with constant contemptuous reference to each other's colour and condition. Ossie Davis does not play a Western hero who happens to have a black skin. He is not what we expect of a hero and the fact that he is black is pointedly emphasised. That is the signal feature of the film's success.

From using black actors in comic and subservient roles the Western has moved on to using them in heroic roles without making anything of the fact that they are black. This always contains the danger of becoming merely a gesture. Perhaps we can now look for Western drama that will take on the black Westerner in terms of his individuality, his difficulties, his jobs and the jobs that were denied him, the way he lived.

Like anywhere else in America problems of racial conflict were much in evidence in the aftermath of the War. They were not always seen as such. There was the Indian, non-white, non-civilised. Westerns probing Indian/white relationships have been frequent because in the frontier context the Indian's skills could make him a hero. In the last twenty years the Indian question is one on which the liberal conscience has been increasingly prone to expose itself dramatically. The Western cannot now do without the Mexican, if only as an easy target. It is curious that it has for so long been able to do without the black man except as a caricature.

It cannot be emphasised too greatly that the West during the period in which most Westerns are set was not just a vast uncharted territory of lawlessness and independence. It was an area that suffered in the Civil War's aftermath in the long run more drastically than many other parts of America. There was enough cohesive consciousness for Westerners to resent the added difficulties that the War created. As Lewis Atherton puts it rather sententiously: 'Nor did the West escape the general letdown in moral fiber that characterized the post-Civil War period.' [12] The 'letdown in moral fiber' gave scope for villainous activities of all kinds and the days that the West was struggling with its frontier were truly disturbing, confused and bewildering for many of the men and women trying to make their lives there. If it were not for the ready acceptance of the frontier myth (and the basis of reality behind the myth) the West after the Civil War might be remembered with the same bitterness as Reconstruction in the South, which encouraged the defeated states to nurse their rancour.

This frequently destructive turbulence does not always emerge strongly in the Western. It is often taken for granted, or appears to be already tamed with just eccentric vestiges remaining, or is merely stereotyped. But the stuff out of which the heroes mould their success is just this turbulence. It is there historically in all its variety and Western makers can select from it the ingredients they need. There must be villains. There must be unscrupulous cheating cowards. There must be overbearing bullies. There must be the weak and helpless. There must be a Lone Ranger. History can furnish them all.

THREE

Taming the Natives

These people must die out. There is no help for them. God has
given this earth to those who will subdue and cultivate it, and it is
vain to struggle against his righteous decree.

Horace Greeley *An Overland Journey*

[1]

In an early Western, James Cruze's *Pony Express* (1925), the unspotted
white buckskin of the Indians gleams in the unsteady black-and-white
of an old movie. The contrast with the shabbiness of the inhabitants
of Julesburg is distinctly in the Indians' favour. When they attack,
led by a treacherous half-breed whose appearance is much improved
when he abandons denims for feathers and paint, the bright white
splotches of their pinto ponies please the eye, by this time dulled by
the dust and drabness of the shanty town.

It is pretty certain that Cruze meant no symbolism here. The
Indians are surely savages, for they attack during a service in the
newly built church. They are swiftly despatched. The hero rides into
a group of three and is hidden by a swirl of dust from which three
riderless horses emerge; there are three bodies on the ground. The fact
that the hoof beats and the gunshots are silent makes it seem all the
more perfunctory.

In the nineteenth century, when noble sentiments and self-aggrandi-
sement were so often conjoined, some of the nation's literary figures
did not find it difficult to justify the extinction of the Indian. When
Horace Greeley announced that the Indians must die out he was
suggesting that the Indian belonged to an inferior race which could
not survive the demands of civilisation. His complacency is apparently
blind to the implications of what he says: he was in effect condoning
the mass killing of the Indians in order to make way for progress and
development. Fenimore Cooper meant much the same thing—and was
more direct—when he wrote the following: 'As a rule the red man
disappears before the superior moral and physical influence of the
white, just as I believe the black man will eventually do the same
thing, unless he shall seek shelter in some other region.'[1] This is a

quite extraordinary way of saying that the whites slaughter the Indians, and of endorsing its rightness. It does not say that the red man or the black man will be civilised by the 'superior moral and physical influence of the white': they will 'disappear'.

It is an alarming remark, as amazingly complacent as Greeley's. If progress is faced with an inferior race which cannot survive anyway there is little sense in having moral quibbles about killing it off: that is a slightly more generous way of looking at what Cooper says. But one cannot escape the statement of cause and effect contained in the sentence. That such opinions could be held by the urbane, the sophisticated and the sensitive makes it hardly surprising that soldiers and politicians did not find it difficult to recommend the mass slaughter of Indian men, women and children. But in most early films and in many later ones the Indians are simply a convenient enemy. They are generally an anonymous danger, and even in movies that present them with some fairness, such as some of D. W. Griffiths' or Thomas Ince's who did both attempt at times to give their Indians an identity and a living context, the masks are blank.

The stereotypes, both in looks and treatment, are easy to identify. There are close-ups of immobile faces streaked with paint, a cruel glint in the eye, then the sudden movement as the chief kicks his pony and the attacking horde streams towards the besieged white men. On this kind of level anonymity is almost a necessity, for the Indians are killed off in large numbers and frequently behave with such a great lack of commonsense—as in the famous chase in Ford's *Stagecoach* (1939) where, as Frank Nugent pointed out to Ford, the Indians neglected to do the most obvious thing, which was shoot the horses. Ford's reply—'if they had, it would have been the end of the picture, wouldn't it?'[2] is more than just a quip. Where would the Western have been without a species of sub-humanity that was dangerous yet dispensable?

In contrast to this is the treatment of the noble savage, who has been appearing regularly since the novels of Cooper (he gives their 'disappearance' a heroically romantic flavour) and has found a recent expression, transmuted, tormented, but still identifiable, in Abraham Polonsky's *Tell Them Willie Boy is Here*. This is one of Cooper's Indians.

The Tuscarora was one of those noble-looking warriors that were oftener met with among the aborigines of this continent a century since than today; and, while he had mingled sufficiently with the colonists to be familiar with their habits and even with their language, he had lost little, if any, of the wild grandeur and simple dignity of a chief.[3]

What Cooper does not add here, but which emerges as the plot unfolds (the novel is *The Pathfinder*) is that the Tuscarora is also treacherous and cunning. This combination of qualities very often appears in the Indian: nobility and low cunning, dignity and cruelty. It is suggested that familiarity with the white colonists would naturally diminish his grandeur and dignity. Cooper would argue that as the frontier cannot last, qualities that are rooted in the wild are doomed. The last of the Mohicans enacts this. There can be good Indians, but even the noblest are primitive, and Cooper was at one with his age in assuming that civilisation meant moral superiority.

Any treatment of the Indian in the last twenty years has been confused by a cultural guilt complex which has affected Western writers and directors in a number of ways. There have not been many successful attempts to achieve balance without artificiality in the presentation of the Indian. Some have tried very hard. Elliot Arnold's *Blood Brother* is a highly sympathetic and worthwhile novel, but the film version, *Broken Arrow*, which Delmer Daves directed in 1950, glosses the sombre tone of the book. *Willie Boy* is another careful treatment of the Indian, and jolted the critics into respectful acknowledgement, but there the backlash of the guilt complex is such that one is nagged by the small grain of romanticism that seems to be buried somewhere in the film's final sequences.

In *Blood Brother* Tom Jeffords, the hero (based on fact) knows and likes the Indians and their way of life, respects them without illusions, and hates the stupidity, selfishness and greed with which they are treated. Arnold is at times so determinedly factual as to be almost dull, but he does present with great clarity and method a highly convincing picture of Apaches and white men in Arizona. In this respect it is a better, though less well written, book than Paul Horgan's *A Distant Trumpet*, also concerned with white/ Apache relationships. Arnold's novel is a more authentic if less graceful treatment of its subject. Perhaps the most significant aspect of Arnold's achievement is the way in which he manages to delocalise the problem without losing touch with his chosen area of action. The angry Tom Jeffords says:

We talk about an Indian problem. This isn't an Indian problem. It is an American problem. It's not the Indians at all who are being tested, it's us. What good are we as a people—what good will we ever be—if we can't find a reasonable answer to all this? What have we learned? What do we know? What kind of men have we running our affairs? We fought four wars in less than a hundred years and what have we learned. We haven't even learned that we are not just a country, but an empire. We are an empire. This is a colony out here. It's the same as though there were thousands of miles of water around us instead of desert. And what lousy colonizers we are turning out to be! And what hypocrites.[4]

It is arguable that Jeffords showed remarkable insight for a rough frontiersman of the 1870s but this in the context is not important. The questions he asks not only delocalise the 'Indian problem' but present it in terms which are now relevant. Polonsky does something similar, for he sets *Willie Boy* in the twentieth century amidst a situation that still pertains, both in particular and in general. He shows us the terrible stagnation of reservation life, which has killed all but a few shreds of tradition and replaced it with nothing more viable than a white 'liberal' doctor who tries to educate her charges into civilisation. The white policy has been to decimate if not the Indians themselves, at least their way of life, and this has been achieved with horrifying success. The particular drama of Willie Boy, who tries to affirm his Indian identity and in doing so becomes unacceptable to white man and Indian alike, is most interesting for its implications.

Willie Boy has tragic dimensions because he has been a success in a white man's world, on the white man's terms. As a ranch foreman he has skills which are valuable. But the white man's terms include the demand that Willie should accept his inferiority even when his skills and intelligence make him perfectly capable of coping with civilisation. Willie can only reject the white man and desperately attempt to make the fact that he is an Indian meaningful. Willie with his Ghost Dance shirt and his rifle deliberately sets up his self-destruction. If he wants to be an Indian in any real sense it is the only thing he can do. The killing of Lola, the girl who shares his flight, becomes sad necessity rather than a vicious gesture, for her commitment to him involves her inevitably in his suicide: her death is a facet of his suicide. The shock that it gives us is the shock of understanding that there is no hope. Not only must Willie fail and die: the pulse of Indian life and tradition has failed and died.

It is in the final irony that the trace of romanticism is present. Only in death does the Indian become the equal of the white man. And only in killing does the white man, the unthinking sheriff, become the equal of the Indian. The final sequence is not a duel between heroes. The sheriff only reaches heroic stature when he allows Willie's own people to provide traditional funeral rites when he knows that Willie's body should be preserved for the purposes of the law. The Paiutes who have helped track Willie down prepare the funeral pyre and minutes later the law arrives in force and tries to drag Willie's burning body from the flames. The pathos and shamefulness of these last moments mean much more than Willie's grand gesture of allowing himself to be killed by firing an unloaded gun as the sheriff reached him.

The movie is satisfying because it is completely unequivocal. For the Indian there are two alternatives: a heroic, meaningless (because that kind of heroism is irrelevant) death in the old way or a stagnant, meaningless death-in-life on the reservation. We are shown the white man operating in an equally useless fashion. The fluttering liberalism of Doctor Arnold is dangerous for all her profound concern, for it seeks to lead the Indian into a rejection of his identity. Lola is being taught the accomplishments of a decent white woman. The dogged relish Sheriff Cooper has for tracking down his man—at last he can behave like a real Western hero and emulate his father, a renowned Indian fighter—is equally pointless. But at least Cooper has, ultimately some suspicion of this pointlessness, while Doctor Arnold shows no sign of change. We have finally more respect for Cooper, for all that he is nasty to his girl friend the doctor, and likes to win, sexually and in battle, than we have for the worthy doctor.

Willie Boy is set in 1909. Most of the Indian dramas that we see and read take place earlier than this, for by 1880 most of the tribes were effectively quelled. The treatment of the Indian in the Western was bound to be influenced by the fact that everyone knew the Indians had lost, and this could only encourage the squandering of Indian lives on the screen. (Something rather similar happens in most kinds of war films based on fact, especially where the enemy is not white. If 'they' lost it's all right for 'them' to die.) Some writers realised from the start that Indians could be of greater dramatic value if their status was elevated to something more than rifle fodder. Some directors were attracted by the idea of the Indian as a noble enemy. As early as 1912 Thomas Ince in his movie *Indian Massacre* tried to show the Indians as people rather than a faceless terror, and in so doing enhanced the sense of confrontation between Indian and white.

But directors felt no necessity to be consistent in their treatment. Ford, whose *Stagecoach* Indians have no identity, presents them with understanding and deliberate detail in *The Iron Horse* (1924), a much earlier movie. And of course his *Cheyenne Autumn* (1964), his most recent film, is one of the cinema's most persuasively sympathetic portraits. If it is not quite true that writers and directors in the first fifty years or so of the Western's life were not much concerned with presenting the Indian fairly, it is the case that it took that long for the Indian hero to emerge. In *Broken Arrow* we have an Indian heroine, but not until 1954, with Robert Aldrich's *Apache*, was there an Indian hero of some force—played by Burt Lancaster.

These days we do not often have a bad Indian, unless with suitable background and explanation, or as a foil to a good Indian. If he is bad, he is usually rejected by his own people, to make it quite clear that he is not typical. (This occurs in an episode of the television series *Hondo*, where an outlaw Apache is hunted by his own tribe as well as by the U.S. Cavalry.) A recent example of a bad Indian who is very much a loner and feared by his own tribe, who are far from being decently ordered by white authority as in *Hondo*, is Salvaje in *The Stalking Moon* (1968), Robert Mulligan's suspense Western. Salvaje is a figure of evil, mystery and terror. He is deliberately presented as a faceless, threatening creature. When we do catch a close glimpse of him we see only his eyes and the white paint on his face. Otherwise he is a shadowy figure in an animal skin whose movements merge with the trees and the mountains. It is only towards the end of the film that he appears at all. Earlier his progress is marked by the trail of dead he leaves behind him.

[2]

The real character of Indians we know a little about is elusive. The great chiefs, Cochise and Geronimo, Sitting Bull and Crazy Horse, the household names, have been described by contemporaneous whites respectfully, admiringly, contemptuously, dismissively, but the names have been absorbed into Western folklore with very little grasp of the personalities behind them. The lesser Indian is brought avidly to life. Salvaje is a sophisticated and intensified version of the animal heathen who appear frequently, described with scorn and abhorrence, in nineteenth century accounts. In these he is generally a worthless creature who certainly does not inspire fear. 'Squalid and conceited, proud and worthless, lazy and lousy, they will strut out or drink out their miserable existence, and at length afford the world a sensible relief by dying out of it,'[5] said Horace Greeley. John Finerty, a journalist of the 1870s, was another who had no time for the noble savage, although he did feel, and this was thirty years later than Greeley, that Indians constituted a serious threat.

The cruel disposition of the Indians is as much as part of their traditional education as of their fierce natures. It may be impossible to change, at this late date, their undeniable tendency to bloodshed and human torture.
   From infancy they are trained to endure suffering themselves and inflict it upon others. Generations of this kind of thing can plant a vice so deeply in the human heart that generations of milder teachings can hardly efface it. When next, if ever, the savages shout their battle cry, civilisation must meet them with a stern front and crush them relentlessly.[6]

At least this was quite straightforward. General Sherman, who was in a position to meet the Indians 'with a stern front and crush them relentlessly', was rather more devious. When agents of the Indian Bureau accused him of embarking on a war of extermination this is what he replied:

As to extermination, it is for the Indians to determine. We don't want to exterminate or even to fight them. At best it is an inglorious war, not apt to add much to our fame or our personal comfort; and as for our soldiers, to whom we owe our first thoughts, it is all danger and extreme labour, without a single compensating advantage. To accuse us of inaugurating or wishing such a war, is to accuse us of want of common sense.... The injustice and frauds heretofore practiced on the Indians as charged, are not of our making; and I know the present war did not result from any acts of ours.[7]

Sherman did not like fighting Indians, and to a certain extent he was right. The Army was under constant pressure to 'deal with' the Indians, whether to pacify them or remove them altogether was not always made clear, and it was often difficult for the Army to know exactly what was expected of it. However, in a letter Sherman made his real feelings rather less equivocal.

Either the Indians must give way, or we must abandon all west of the Missouri River and confess that forty million whites are cowed by a few thousand savages.... I have stretched my power and authority to help them, but when they laugh at our cordiality, rape our women, murder our men, burn whole trains with their drivers to cinders, and send word they never intended to keep their treaties, then we must fight them. When we come to fight Indians, I will take my code from soldiers and not from citizens.[8]

These are ominous words. Sherman never envisaged a situation of 'peaceful cooperation'. It was easy enough to make verbal gestures towards the Indians, especially as it was assumed that in dealings with Indians words meant very little.

There had been a long build up of public resentment against the Indians. During the Civil War they had taken advantage of the absence of troops. In the South-west the Apaches freely harassed settlers and miners, and in Wyoming the Sioux and Cheyennes were equally active. In 1862, dangerously eastward, the Minnesota Sioux, provoked by hunger, exploitation, and the whittling away of their modest allotment of land, perpetrated a series of ugly massacres. Reprisals, though a little slow, were unhesitating: execution (thirty nine Sioux warriors hanged simultaneously) and deportation.

The Government's efforts to deal with 'the Indian problem' were confused and blighted by the conflicting interests that simply could not all be accommodated. In 1865 a commission was sent out to report on the situation. At this time there were about 225,000 Indians between the Missouri and the Sierras and something like 400,000 white settlers. (Already there were almost twice as many settlers as Indians.) The railroads were pushing west. The stagecoach lines were doing good business. Every year meant that the white man had more to lose if the Indian were not controlled. No sooner was some sort of agreement reached with some of the tribes than back in Washington it was undermined by banning reservations in relatively well settled Kansas. This was typical of Government treaties with the Indians.

Gradually the Indians were defeated, killed where possible, and the rest shunted into reservations generally, as a matter of policy, at some considerable distance from their home lands. The Minnesota Sioux went to Nebraska. Recalcitrant Apaches went to Florida where they died in the swamps. The Northern Cheyenne went to Indian Territory, later to become Oklahoma, hopeless barren country where they died of starvation and disease. At intervals Indians, or small groups of young impatient warriors, broke out of the reservations and made defiant attacks on the white invasion. It got them nowhere. In 1878 the Cheyennes quietly left their Oklahoma reservation and set out on a trek that was to take the small proportion of survivors 1500 miles to their own country in Wyoming.

John Ford's film *Cheyenne Autumn* is based on this trek as described in Mari Sandoz's passionately committed book which reconstructs the journey through the eyes of the Cheyennes. Led by Dull Knife and Little Wolf about 280 Cheyennes, two thirds women and children, evaded capture and caused panic amongst settlers, soldiers, journalists and politicians as they made their way north. The affair acted as a tinder to public neurosis concerning the Indians. There were hysterical demands for action and retribution.

For the northern Plains Indians, who lived by hunting and were often on the move, who were superb riders and had a precise code of war, confinement on a dry scorched reservation hundreds of miles from their own territory, with no weapons and few ponies, was hard to bear. Much of Indian Territory was occupied by tribes that had been long established there: the Creeks, the Chickasaws, tribes which had been pushed west in the early days of the frontier to make room for advancing settlement. They were peaceful and settled, farmed as best they could—some had even owned negro slaves—and were relatively little trouble. They had their own police force and Indian crime was outside the jurisdiction of the U.S. marshals except where it involved white people. The Indian agents, many of them Quakers who hoped to convert warriors and horsemen into tillers of the soil, were baffled by what seemed to be the sheer heathen laziness of the newer arrivals. They would not tend their patches of corn; corn was not their food. The young men rode their ponies restlessly over the small area of land allowed them.

The Cheyenne left because they wanted to go home and live the life they knew. As they travelled through Kansas on their way north wild accounts of Indian depredations raged through the country. Edgar Bronson, sympathetic towards the Cheyennes, owned a ranch in Nebraska near which they passed, and was caught up in the swirl of rumour. 'Meantime, the Cheyennes were pushing forward day and night, stealing horses, ravaging the country, and killing all who came in their path.' [9] But in fact the Indians were taking pains to avoid areas of settlement and tried to avoid involvement with the whites. They did steal horses to help their progress and cattle to provide beef but, as was later admitted when the panic died down, they were responsible for very little loss of life.

The public was geared to equating Indian with depredation. Eastern newspaper accounts of Indian activity made the most of bloody events. Indians were seen as wild marauders, scarcely human, inviting their own destruction. The fearful emotion of just revenge was encouraged by Easterners shaking their heads over their breakfast newspapers and demanding that the West be made safe for innocent, hardworking, civilised whites. Revenge was all the easier to justify when the victim was savage. When the mad Colonel Chivington ordered the charge at Sand Creek in 1864—again the victims were Cheyennes—his men, in a scene described by one of his apologists, shot down children as if they were on a rabbit hunt. J. P. Dunn, author of the book *Massacres of the Mountains* (1886), whose whole object was to catalogue Indian outrages, defended Chivington with cool self-righteousness.

To the abstract question whether or not it is right to kill women and children, there can be but one answer. But as a matter of retaliation and a matter of policy, whether these people were justified in killing women and children at Sand Creek is a question to which the answer does not come so glibly. Just after the massacre at Fort Fetterman, General Sherman despatched to General Grant: 'We must act with vindictive earnestness against the Sioux, even to their extermination, men, women and children. Nothing less will reach the root of the case.' [10]

Dunn does not answer his own question. Chivington slaughtered Cheyennes, not Sioux. He slaughtered them at daybreak when they were still sleeping, camped on a spot that the Army had approved. Some of his own men were revolted by the scene, and at least one officer refused to carry out orders. The Sand Creek massacre was perhaps the blackest moment in the history of Indian pacification, but it was not unique. If America now feels guilty this does not disguise the disturbing nature of what is still her grossest fault: too often has she been in the position of aggressor when the colour of the victim's skin has not been white.

As far as the Indians were concerned fear, contempt, and sheer misunderstanding disrupted any good intentions the whites may have had. The Quaker agents were at least honest. They did not embezzle the funds or resell the cattle alotted for beef. In Thomas Fall's *The Justicer*, a novel set in Indian Territory, the Quaker agent is a model of integrity. In Howard Fast's *The Last Frontier* (1966), a novel based again on the Cheyenne trek, Quaker John Miles, who was in reality the Cheyenne and Arapaho agent, is baffled and weary but tries desperately hard to reach some kind of understanding of the Indians in his charge. Integrity did not necessarily mean understanding or achievement. An Indian agent had to know not just his Indians, but the devious ways of the Indian Bureau and the War Department also. Most of the time the agent was in an impossible position, and, however committed to the Indians' welfare, with limited funds and limited freedom he could do very little.

The end of the Cheyenne trek was, after a fashion, a happy one. The few that survived the battles (they were chased and attacked continually by the Army and civilians), the hunger, the treachery and the intense physical strain of the whole enterprise lived out their lives on a reservation created for them on the Tongue River, a tributary of the Yellowstone, in their own country. By 1879 public opinion veered round in their favour as some of the facts began to emerge and the excitement cooled. But public sympathy could not bring back the dead. Newspaper men took up the cause of the Cheyennes and those who were being tried for murder were released for want of evidence. It was the Cheyennes' last victory, and in the long run it did them little good.

Ford's celebration of the Cheyennes will perhaps be his final Western. If so it is appropriate that he should have devoted it to doing some justice to the people who have provided so many faceless dead in Western carnage. His camera lingers over the Cheyennes, barely clad and barely fed, moving north through the snow. His soldiers are frustrated and angry at doing a distasteful job. Ford's personal attitude to the Indians is uncomplicated. He wants to show them as dignified and real, as stoic in their suffering and proud in their defeat. It all has Ford's typical gruff romanticism. This is what he says himself:

... they are a very dignified people—even when they are being defeated. Of course, it's not very popular in the United States. The audience likes to see Indians get killed. They don't consider them as human beings—with a great culture of their own—quite different from ours.

If you analyzed the thing carefully, however, you'd find that their religion is very *similar* to ours.[11]

'Dignity' is an easy word to toss around when talking of 'uncivilised' peoples, but there is no suggestion that Ford is anything less than sincere. He is perfectly aware of Indian excesses. They did scalp, they did rape, they did mutilate. The accounts are numerous. In Ford's own *The Searchers* (1956) a family is slaughtered and John Wayne spends ten years tracking down the Comanches who did it. The characterisation of the Indians is respectful, but their savagery is not disguised. Illustrations of Indian cruelty are not hard to find. They are there in the newspapers and contemporary accounts; eye witnesses have got it all down on paper, and the details that reappear in film and fiction are authentic. Men are tortured with burning sticks and babies swung against trees. Most tribes methodically mutilated the dead to prevent them being a danger in the next world. White men soon picked up the habit (there is some evidence that scalping was introduced to the Indians by the Spanish). Scalping was encouraged in pre-Independence days when both the French and British paid bounty for the scalps of tribes assisting the enemy. Later, scalps were taken as trophies when proof of the kill was not required. The U.S. cavalry was not renowned for restraint when confronted with captive Indian women. Retribution spurred many white men on to savaging the bodies of their red enemies.

Alan Le May, author of *The Searchers*, has another book, *The Siege at Dancing Bird* (filmed as *The Unforgiven* by John Huston in 1960) in which the hostile Kiowa Indians are totally vicious. The lives of a family of settlers revolve around outwitting the Indians, knowing their habits, understanding their moods, anticipating their actions. Their survival depends on being constantly strained to breaking point, and the result is a tense and claustrophobic piece of writing.

[3]

The white man's guilty conscience became manifest at an early stage. Public opinion tended to fluctuate, but generally the Indians were regarded as an obstacle to settlement in the West which had to be removed. Some favoured more humane methods than others. There were a few individuals who sympathised with the Indians, amongst them some of the most experienced Indian fighters, but usually they had little influence. Occasionally the press voiced the opinion that the Indians were not being treated with fairness or honesty, but this caused at the most a short lived flurry of sympathy. It took something more drastic to stir the issue up effectively, and even then the actual results were minimal. In 1881, when Geronimo and his Apaches were still marauding, Helen Hunt Jackson published her book *A Century of Dishonour*, which describes the cheats and frauds and broken promises which cluttered the wake of the Government's negotiations with the Indians.

The history of the United States Government's repeated violations of faith with the Indians ... convicts us, as a nation, not only of having outraged the principles of justice, which are the basis of international law; and of having laid ourselves open to the accusation of both cruelty and perfidy; but of having made ourselves liable to all punishments which follow upon such sins—to arbitary punishment at the hands of any more civilised nation who might see fit to call us to account, and to that more certain natural punishment which, sooner or later, as surely comes from evil-doing as harvests come from sown seed.[12]

The tone throughout the book is bitterly reproachful. The sheer dishonesty in official dealings with Indians, the insult to their intelligence, the assumption that because they could not write, and could not speak English, words meant nothing, is indeed at times breathtaking. Treaty after treaty was agreed which were from the start quite unacceptable in a situation where Western expansion was being encouraged, land made available, railroads financed and gold discovered. With the settlement of the West coast the gap began to close with increasing rapidity. In a country that wanted men (white) and cattle there was no room for the Indian. Whatever a particular treaty might stipulate, everyone took it for granted that the Indians would have to give way.

Helen Hunt Jackson assembled the evidence and presented it with conviction. But it wasn't hard to discount it. The truth was not important; Indians, after all, were not the same as other people. The calm surface of complacency was not profoundly disturbed although there were some local storms. In the process of becoming legend the Indian slipped easily into the role of villain and continued to perform as the public expected.

Cooper of course established the Indian villain, and Western fiction had to create nothing that did not already exist in the public imagination. Present day fiction is more likely to concentrate on the Indian himself. Even those books in which the Indian is still the indispensable enemy he tends to have a face. He is likely to emerge as courageous, thoughtful, religious, strict in his morals, stern but loving, and if he scalps his foes he is kind to his horse. Thomas Berger's Cheyennes in his anti-heroic novel *Little Big Man* (1969) who are not of quite the same mould as Mari Sandoz's, are good natured and friendly, as well as smelly and brutal. There are exceptions of course. The drunken, broken Indian hanging round the saloons, the committed cruelty of Salvaje, Indians full of tricks and betrayal, they all appear at times. But we get plenty of white frontiersmen of the same species. Often the most balanced view comes in a run-of-the-mill Western which contains as a matter of course good and bad Indians and good and bad white men, rather than in an impassioned defence, however well written and researched, such as Mari Sandoz's *Cheyenne Autumn* or *Crazy Horse*. But there are times when we need the passion more than the balance, and there is no doubt that Mari Sandoz's books, and books such as Will Henry's *From Where the Sun now Stands*, which describes the battling retreats of Chief Joseph and the Nez Percés, fulfil an important need.

The Indians' real triumphs were few. They attacked wagon trains and the homes of isolated settlers, and they attacked those who ventured into territory they considered their own. But although this fed the outrage of civilisation it gained them very little except reprisal. Occasionally they successfully attacked a town—in 1865 the Cheyennes and Sioux combined to attack Julesburg (gorily portrayed in *Custer of the West*) but even attacks such as these could not stop the westward flow. Their infrequent victories over the Army, such as the Fetterman massacre in 1866 and Custer's defeat in 1876, only brought retribution on a massive scale. The Little Big Horn fight was the beginning of the end for the Sioux and Cheyennes.

George Armstrong Custer, the boy general, went West at the close of the Civil War. The Army was overpopulated with officers, promoted rapidly through the War, and there was nothing for him to do east of the Mississippi. He distinguished himself first by descending on a camp of sleeping Cheyennes on the banks of the Washita in the winter of 1868, only four years after Sand Creek. It was Custer's first real taste of Indian blood, and he backs it, in his own description, with lengthy accounts of Indian depredations. The Cheyennes, caught unawares, were slaughtered in great numbers, women and children inevitably, although Custer says he gave particular orders against this.

The Cheyennes did not forget Custer. In 1868 there had been a treaty guaranteeing the Black Hills to the Sioux 'for ever', one result of the Government Peace Commission that visited the Plains in 1867-68. In 1874 Custer himself led an expedition into Sioux territory to look for gold. (The search for gold had been going on there unofficially for much longer.) Gold was discovered, and it was at once inevitable that the Sioux would lose the Black Hills. Two years later Custer was defeated at the Little Big Horn by the combined forces of Cheyennes and Sioux. His own blindness and lust for glory—he disobeyed orders—were mainly responsible. But Custer should be remembered not because he rather stupidly lost his life fighting an impossible battle, but because this battle precipitated the events that led the Sioux to the reservation, Crazy Horse, the most famous of Sioux chieftains, to a treacherous death, and Sitting Bull to exile, surrender and his pointless death at Wounded Knee. They were less lucky than Geronimo, who lived to be photographed sitting unflinching at the wheel of a motor car.

Custer's attitude to the Indian—and we can be fairly sure that it was carefully cultivated for the purposes of publication—was paternalistic. His view was that although the Sioux and Cheyennes were not, of course, as intelligent as the average horse soldier they did have qualities which the cavalry could admire. While Captain Fetterman had dismissed his enemy as worthless, and through such arrogance got himself and his men massacred, Custer was careful to describe his foe with some courtesy, although he dwelt on details of their atrocities also, and still did not avoid massacre. It always enhances a victor if he can admire the courage and skill of his foe, and Custer did not lose much opportunity for self-enhancement. His writing is carefully geared to making his own achievements acceptable to public taste. But whatever his views on paper, he was determined to win a glorious victory. If it had not been for this the three-pronged operation carefully planned by his superiors might well have been a success.

One after another the tribes were trapped, defeated or cheated into reservations, and this is very often what Indian fighting in the Western is all about. In 1868 Kit Carson inflicted a final defeat on the Navaho, a nation not now thought of as warlike, and herded them in a tragic trek to the New Mexican reservation at Bosque Redondo. It was the end of a way of life for the Navaho; the humiliation weighed on them for decades. Reservations were the only answer the Government could produce for Indians who survived defeat. From the earliest dealings with Indians this was the solution. If the Government made the mistake of giving Indians good land they soon found themselves under pressure to take it back. If the Indians were allowed to go out on hunting expeditions to provide themselves with food and clothing, settlers complained that it was just an excuse for looting and killing. The only answer to this was that the Government should entirely support reservation Indians, but it was an enormously expensive business, and there was much resentment that the Indians had so much spent on them. Official calculations as to the necessary quantities of staple foods, flour, sugar, coffee and beef, were frugal. Widespread corruption severely diminished the quantity. It made things easier for everyone if the Government unofficially encouraged the attitude that 'the only good Indian is a dead Indian'.

The nation that evaded reservation life longest and most frequently broke out after confinement was the Apache. Until his surrender Geronimo raided in New Mexico and Arizona hiding out across the Border, which created problems with the Mexicans in any attempt to track him down. Film and fiction have had a long standing love-hate relationship with the Apache. He is portrayed as the cruellest and toughest of all Indians. It is the Apache above all others who employs torture and takes an avid interest in the suffering of his victims. Yet he is often the most unsentimentally heroic, and probably appears on the screen and in print more than any other tribe. The Apache has a strict code of behaviour, honourable, yet fiendishly cruel. He is devoted to children; he will risk any hazard in a cause he considers just. And he is usually clever.

However, the Apache chief in Paul Horgan's *A Distant Trumpet* is not very clever, nothing like a match for the combination of sensitive young lieutenant and devoted scout (also an Apache) that brings him in. The chief, perhaps intended to be Geronimo although there were many other famed Apaches, is not much more than a standard redskin type; the man who is irresistibly attracted by a new idea and simultaneously convinced that his own cunning will get him out of any difficulties. We know that Geronimo himself was intelligent and far from gullible, and it is hard not to feel that this fiction is something less than history.

Not that this would matter, but *A Distant Trumpet* is a serious novel by a serious writer, on the traditional grand American scale. It clearly intends to say something significant about the American character. It does show the Apaches getting a raw deal: after broken promises they are despatched into detention in Florida, including the loyal scout, which provokes the lieutenant into resigning his commission. Basically, however, it is irrevocably involved with the liberal conscience rather than with the Indians. Some lesser novels are more impressive, if only because they are unconcerned about conscience and want only to evolve a dramatic and reasonably convincing story.

Louis L'Amour's *Hondo*, not a particularly impressive Western in spite of the fact that it bears on its front cover the legend '"Best Western novel I have ever read" John Wayne', does contain a measured characterisation of the Apaches which is convincing. (The book has been the basis of two films and a feeble television series.) The book balances the dichotomy between cruelty and humanity with some understanding. The Apache chief is savage and relentless; that is a part of his personality and of his way of life. But he is not inhuman or illogically cruel. He is so impressed by the courage of a six year old white boy that he protects him and his widowed mother from molestation. The advantages of Apache protection may be dubious, but when we see Vittoro, the chief, in action he is restrained and honourable. He does torture, but he considers it a legitimate aspect of war, and the endurance of torture a part of a warrior's accomplishments. By conventional standards torture is totally evil (although they are standards that do not seem to have much bearing now), yet we do not see Vittoro as totally evil.

On the other hand, the savage must die. Vittoro, the good Indian, dies with suitable anonymity at the hands of the cavalry. Silva, a bad Indian with a perpetual evil glint in his eyes, is despatched by Hondo himself with much gory detail. An interesting feature of the book is that Hondo is half Indian. In this case being a half-breed means that he has the edge over both red and white. It is important that he has an Indian's skills and understanding of the terrain, but just as important that he has chosen 'civilisation'. He is fighting on the right side.

In *Hondo* the Indians are presented on their own terms and we are given the chance to judge them on their own terms. If the treatment is brief it is in many ways more welcome than the apparent conclusion of *A Distant Trumpet*, that the only good Indian is an Indian devoted to a white man, or at least devoted to the idea of the white man's ultimate victory. In Paul Horgan's book the relationship between red and white is inevitably paternalistic. In L'Amour's book they are equals. The 'fair' treatment of the Indian which we now take more or less for granted does not always discriminate between these two attitudes. Many of the most interesting Westerns in respect of this relationship are those which include Indian captives, half breeds and others with intimate knowledge of both ways of life, amongst their characters. These figures can be tragic, rejected by red and white, can be essential bridges between the two, and are sometimes both.

Many captured women and children became virtual members of the tribe that adopted them. Some were sold as slaves to other tribes. Many had no alternative but to become Indians themselves. Berger's Little Big Man cheerfully becomes a Cheyenne warrior and is stealing ponies from the Pawnees at the age of fourteen. In Will Cook's novel *Two Rode Together* (1959) the captive white boy recovered years later could have been born a Comanche. He has to be taken forcibly from the Indian camp, glowers savagely at the group of white settlers ready to claim him, and kills a white woman. In one of Dorothy Johnson's short stories a woman who was captured as a little girl is recovered and returned to her middle aged sisters. She is a squaw, mother of a chief. She cannot communicate with white people, her sisters find her repulsive, and she lives miserably and fearfully, thinking only of her warrior son, until she escapes and dies.

The half-breed is in a similar position. The half-breed scout in *The Stalking Moon* (impressive acting by Robert Forster) is a bitter young man who only by cultivating a skin of cynicism is able to take in his stride the inevitable taunts and insults that his Indian blood invites. There were many half-breeds. The mountain men, the French settlers in the north-west, ranchers and drifters had fathered quantities of half Indian children, and there were also the children of the captive white women. In many cases the children of Indian mothers were brought up in the tribe, where they lived as Indians and were generally accepted as Indians. It was more difficult for those of mixed blood who tried to make their way in the white world. Some prominent Wyoming ranchers had Indian wives, but they were generally discreetly left at home and did not appear in public. It was easier for the children if their father was wealthy and influential, but not all that easy. In fiction the situation can be romanticised. In *Warrior Gap*, one of the many Western adventure novels of Captain Charles King, the daughter of a settler in Wyoming and his Indian wife is sent East to school and returns a beautiful and cultured young lady. Here a touch of Indian blood is like an extra spicy dash of local colour. The girl is just a little bit exotic; not too much so, for that would make her unacceptable. She is just different enough to make her in the eyes of those around her unusual and fascinating.

But traditionally the half-breed is the villain. Now he is beginning to be regarded as a figure of psychological interest, but for many decades he has been a renegade combining the worst features of both races. He drinks. He is treacherous. Frequently he manages to betray both red and white. In Ford's *The Iron Horse* for instance a curious character who is either a half-breed or a renegade white— it is not clear—is the ultimate scapegoat. He incites the Indians, kills with malicious delight, and as if to emphasise that it is not the Indians themselves we should blame there is a brief and quiet shot of a little dog with wagging tail running up to investigate his dead Indian master.

The half-breed and the white renegade can always provide identifiable villains if the Indians themselves remain faceless. Nearly in the same category are the gun-runners, the whisky-sellers and the comancheros. They provoke, use and cheat the Indians entirely for their own gain. What they sometimes did not realise was that they themselves were as likely victims of Indian anger as anyone else. In Anthony Mann's *The Man from Laramie* the headstrong son of a rancher does not understand that if he sells rifles to the Apaches they are as likely to attack his father's ranch as anywhere else.

In reality the half-breed tended to get the worst of frontier experience. One or two writers have attempted to illustrate some of the difficulties of his situation. In Le May's *The Siege at Dancing Bird* the cause of Indian hostility is the fact that the adopted daughter of the Zachary family is part Kiowa. The Kiowas come to claim her. She has never been told that she is part Indian and is shattered by the discovery. Her instinct tells her that there is no place for her in the family or in society. And for a girl, she reflects, to be a half-breed outcast can lead only to the saloon and the brothel.

In Amelia Bean's book *The Feud* the hero is a half-breed. He has a sister, whose lover abandons her when her baby turns out to be only too obviously Indian. Because of his mixed blood the hero is a focus of suspicion, distrust and hatred. He has this to contend with as well as a range war; he is considered an animal by the mother of the girl he loves. The book is based on the Grant/Tewkesbury feud which took place in Arizona and is broadly accurate. The half-breed son of old Tewkesbury was the family's sole survivor of a bloody range war.

One of the most compelling treatments of the man who bridges two ways of life is Martin Ritt's film *Hombre* (1967). Paul Newman as a white man brought up amongst reservation Apaches who catch and tame wild horses for the Army has that relaxed intensity which we have come to associate with his style of acting. In this role it is particularly appropriate. Beginning with a sequence of obvious symbolism, a splendid rearing stallion finally corralled and calmed by Hombre and two Apaches, Ritt presents the Indians as having an ironic awareness of their inferior position and the fact that they are being continually cheated and defrauded.

Hombre himself, seen first long-haired in dirty buckskins, has all the skills and the independence of the Apache. But he also has an unshakeable coolness and confidence in his dealings with the white world, and when we see him later shaved and cropped and slickly attired no one would ever mistake him for an Indian. In spite of this he is inexorably an outsider. Deliberately he preserves his detachment, sophisticates his bitterness into cynicism, permits himself no feelings and no actions that will involve him with the white world on any other than business terms. In the white world Hombre is the archetypal loner and his only loyalty, to the Apaches, must be hidden. Thus, when Hombre risks his life to save the funds the Apache agent has embezzled he allows it to be thought, until the very end, that he wants the money for himself.

In the course of saving the money he saves and protects a group of fellow travellers not out of any Christian spirit but simply because he allows them to accompany him, making no concessions to their frailty. For them it is a gruelling test of survival, walking across the desert and going without water. For Hombre, the cultured but cynical savage, it is no more than doing what comes naturally. Endurance is no test for him. But his test does come, when he makes the decision to save the life of the fraudulent agent's wife, a silly and selfish woman, and in achieving this he loses his own. The point here is not that Hombre finally chooses the white world, for he does not. The little group he has been protecting are totally cut off from white society and are threatened by vicious (white) bandits. It does not matter who they are. What is important is that Hombre has knowledge and skills which they lack, and his final effort is an acceptance of the implications of his superiority.

It is a movie centred on a man's withdrawal from white society. It is very impressive, and all the more so for being kept firmly within a standard Western situation and for focusing on a man who has so many of the characteristics of a standard Western hero. His background gives these characteristics a special significance. Hombre does not combat evil, he combats weakness. The test that is undergone is a moral test as well as a physical test. Hombre is a man of *moral* stature, and this is reflected in the way he has come to terms with the terrain. We see him at one with his environment. None of the other characters are.

Hombre shares a great deal with the Indian in Milton Lott's novel *The Last Hunt* (1955) who has precisely Hombre's assurance underlied by bitterness.

One of the three was an Indian the others called Sammy, a man in his early twenties maybe, dressed as a white man in new expensive clothes, his hair cut short. He spoke good English and in his manner was assured and competent; but under his hard, polished surface Sandy sensed a defiance, a bitterness, a sadness.[13]

The white man as Indian, or the Indian as white man, is ultimately bound to be rejected by white society if he does not reject white society first. Countless Western heroes live as they do because civilisation cannot accept them. They are, very nearly, white men as Indians, and they are much the most satisfactory Western heroes. The, as it were, bourgeosified heroes, tailored for the purpose of social acceptance, are almost inevitably unsatisfactory figures in Western terms.

We still get comic opera Indians (as recently as 1967 there was a jarring example in *The Pistolero of Red River*, not otherwise a comic Western). Incidents of crude comedy tend to be offensive, as the Indians are amongst the most tragic of conquered peoples. They had a profound sense of their inevitable destruction by the whites, and it is this as much as anything that gives them the scope of tragedy. In 1832, Black Hawk, a chief of the Sauk tribe of Iowa, made a speech on his defeat in the attempt to resist the overrunning of his country by white settlers.

Black Hawk is a true Indian, and disdains to cry like a woman. He feels for his wife, his children and friends. But he does not care for himself. He cares for his nation and the Indians. They will suffer. He laments their fate. The white men do not scalp the head; but they do worse—they poison the heart, it is not pure with them. His country-men will not be scalped, but they will, in a few years, become like the white men, so that you can't trust them, and there must be, as in the white settlements, nearly as many officers as men, to take care of them and keep them in order.[14]

Black Hawk's understanding and foresight was of little use to him. One hundred years later Chief Standing Bear wrote this:

The white man does not understand the Indian for the reason that he does not understand America. He is too far removed from its forma-tive processes. The roots of the tree of his life have not yet grasped the rock and soil. The white man is still troubled with primitive fears; he still has in his consciousness the perils of this frontier continent, some of its fastnesses not yet having yielded to his questioning foot-steps and inquiring eyes. He shudders still with the memory of the loss of his forefathers upon its scorching deserts and forbidding mountain-tops. The man from Europe is still a foreigner and an alien. And he still hates the man who questioned his path across the continent.[15]

In a sense the Western hero is the only American who successfully forgot Europe. He is the nearest white America got to producing a native. Her genuine native heroes, although they have gained places in the legend, still await proper tribute to their own and their descendants' reality.

FOUR

Settlement

On the whole the settlers were a pretty good lot. But most of the boosters, speculators, and land agents who tolled them in were the lowest class of vermin that ever infected a good country.

John Leakey *The West that Was*

Don't ever get the impression you can ride your horses into a saloon or shoot out the lights in Dodge; it may go somewhere else, but it don't go there.

Andy Adams *Log of a Cowboy*

[1]

The savage land could be tamed by ownership. Land hunger drove thousands westwards, hopeful that they would come on some luxuriant Garden of Eden which would sustain and enrich them. But ownership of the land was the profound need. When the 1862 Homestead Act made land free for those who cultivated the same claim for five years and brought the immediate purchase of land within the scope of many immigrants there was an excited response amongst the land hungry. For land on the public domain an initial payment of $1.25 an acre bought 160 acres per American adult. But for some it meant trouble. No longer could a man go out into the wilderness and assume ownership on the basis of cultivation. Someone else might come along with a legitimate claim registered in the proper way and get the benefit of all the hard labour. Many people were caught by sheer ignorance of the Act, and many people abused it. Ranchers built up their acres by claiming quarter sections in the names of men who never intended to take up their claims. A familiar Western theme concerns the settler bullied out of his legitimate claim by a more powerful neighbour, or the squatter, unaware that he suddenly has no rights, forced to abandon his painfully built home.

The open range on which the cattlemen depended became dotted with fenced off quarter sections. The ranchers saw land to which they felt they had a natural right become inaccessible. For all the vast expanses of empty territory land rivalry caused many of the West's bitterest feuds. Land was of little value without water; he who controlled water controlled the land. If the water was fenced off the surrounding land was useless. Timber was also important for housing and fencing, but most claims in the plains country were without timber. The standard dwelling in the great treeless areas was the sod house, often little more than a hole dug into a slope. The sod house was warm, but it was also dirty, dusty and, when it rained, muddy.

In 1862 it seemed as if land could not possibly run out. Twenty odd years later the open spaces were beginning to look crowded. The good land appeared to have gone. Millions of acres could not be cultivated. Vast stretches of desert were useless. The mountains could not be ploughed up. If cattle had changed the nation's attitude to the prairies, 'the great American desert', it was not until the coming of the oil rigs that attitudes to the land would change radically again. The primal question always was, what would the land produce? The settler moved west with primitive tools and primitive ideas about cultivation. Although a dream of riches led him on he was concerned with subsistence farming, not with cash crops. He had to be, for he was there before the towns and before the transport that could carry his produce back East. Even when the railroads were busily transporting cattle the small homesteader lagged behind in seeking eastern markets. He did not operate on a large enough scale. He was lucky if he had anything to sell. It took perhaps twenty years for him to catch up, twenty years before he tore himself away from deep ploughing, planting corn and raising hogs to thinking in terms of dry farming, grain crops, sugar beet and so on in proportions that were to grow to the monolithic.

The small farmers' difficulties were partly the fault of the Homestead Act itself. The acreage allowed was in most cases unsatisfactory, too large for the subsistence farmer, who had neither the means nor the labour to make the best of it, and ludicrously small for raising stock on an economic scale. Ludicrously small, too, for raising cash crops on a large enough scale to make the difficulties and the cost of transport worth while. Labour and transport caused problems that were to continue to plague the farmer for decades. In some parts of the West the lack of water made even 160 acres insufficient to support a family.

Although by the 1870s there were movements afoot to improve the lot of the homestead farmer basic attitudes did not change. It was not until 1904 that legislation began to make changes in the number of acres a homesteader could acquire, and much later that dry farming, which could make the best of the rapidly exhausted soil, became extensive. There were many barriers to improvement. Whatever the acreage attitudes to subsistence farming were not likely to change as long as settlers were on the move with such frequency. Many did not stay long enough on their claim to perfect their ownership. Five years was a long time to stay in one place when there was the hope of something better further west. The popular image of the stalwart homesteader opening up the wilderness encouraged the westward movement. In Kansas only 35% of settlers who entered in the years between 1854 and 1860 remained five years later.

By the second half of the 1880s there was an increasing clamour for more land. Eyes turned to reservation land. In 1889 Indian Territory was thrown open to a chaotic competition for claims between thousands who thought that this would be their very last chance. The Oklahoma landrush has featured in a number of Westerns, most notably perhaps in the two movie versions of Edna Ferber's *Cimarron*, the first directed by Wesley Ruggles in 1931, one of the earliest sound epics, and the second Anthony Mann's in 1960, probably his least impressive Western. Both responded to the challenge of filming a sequence that involved hundreds of horses and vehicles in a desperate race for land. For those who took part in the real thing it was a grim struggle. Everyone thought that this really was the last frontier, and the dreams of land ownership would fade for those who failed this time to make a claim. This was not strictly true, but those who massed on the border of Indian Territory and waited for the stroke of noon, April 22, 1889, thought it was.

More than fifty thousand joined in the race. In twenty four hours every corner of land had been snapped up. The Indians, from whom the Government had purchased the land at $1.25 an acre, had nothing. Most of the land that became available in the next few years came also from the Indians. Ironically, for in 1887 the Dawes Act had given Indians the right to own land on the same terms as whites. The reservations, very often situated on highly undesirable land in the first place, were divided up, and the land that was left over, not an inconsiderable amount, became open to white settlement. It was a cynical, but not final, means of depriving the Indians of yet more land. The land that remained to them was often worthless.

Land was needed for a great deal more than cultivation and stock raising. It was needed for towns, for building—hotels, stockyards, town halls, cemetaries—and for the railroads. Space was needed for the elaborate machinery that more sophisticated mining methods brought West. Space was needed for schools and colleges. As civilisation, forced into rapid growth by western impatience and western money, expanded so did the land shrink. And so, in many cases, did the economic resources of individuals, for local government and schools needed money, and even if a settler owned his land and could feed himself and his family cash was hard to come by.

The land that John Clay writes of, intoxicatingly free, populated with buffalo and antelope, did change. Its ruthlessness was not softened, as the blowing dust of the 1930s was to remind everyone, but many of its delights disappeared. By the middle of the 1870s the buffalo were getting scarce. An eastern passion for buffalo hides brought the buffalo hunters in force and left stinking carcasses and whitening bones scattered over the plains, and hungry Indians wandering further and further afield in their search for meat. The riches of the West were exhaustible. The soil was exhaustible: farmers often moved on because there was no nourishment left in the earth. The rivers ran dry: the 1890s saw five years of serious drought. The lodes were worked out: crumbling ghost towns showed where the metal had once been.

The movement was not always westward. Many came back, disappointed miners, homesteaders who had given up. As one cowhand put it:

Farmers are allus goin' out there in times like these, and comin' back when it gits dry. Take me. I went—and I'm comin' back. Y'know, you kin tell by the remains of their camps which way they're goin'. Goin' West, they leave cracker boxes and cans about; comin' east, all they leave is rabbit hair and fieldlark feathers.[1]

The country took its toll in deaths and failures. If any homesteader had chanced upon Thoreau's remark—'It would be some advantage to live a primitive and frontier life though in the midst of an outward civilisation if only to learn what are the gross necessaries of life and what methods have been taken to obtain them'[2]—he would have seen in it a terrible irony.

And yet the idealism and the romanticism lingered. The depressing history of the Great Plains after the end of the frontier has not affected the glowing picture of pioneer times. In the 1880s, although farms were beginning to be worked on a large scale and with modern machinery, the situation had not changed much for the farmer who might have been in the country, if not always on the same spot, for twenty or thirty years. And in spite of the indications of the Oklahoma landrush by the end of the century there were many thousands of acres of public land which had never been taken up. Government land is still being advertised for sale. Fred A. Shannon comments: 'By June 30, 1890 only 372,659 homestead entries had been perfected, granting 48,225,736 acres to supposed settlers—an area less than that of the state of Nebraska and equal only to 3.5 per cent of the total territory west of the Mississippi River.'[3] He points out that more than four times as much land had been granted to the railroads. And four times as much land was homesteaded after that date.

So the end of the frontier did not mean that the West was filled. To many homesteaders it meant very little. They could not afford modern machinery, labour was scarce in spite of unemployment further east, shipping costs were exorbitant. It did mean, for some at least, the fading of those idealistic hopes that had sustained their westward movement, the hopes of taming the wild country and bringing self-improvement. The only way to revive them was to move on, and this restless mobility persists.

If the vast, open territories appeared to shrink with improved communications and more direct links with the East for many of those stalwart homesteaders, 'the true pioneers—those who subdued the West',[4] it remained unchanged. Life was just as hard. The Indian threat had gone, but the natural threats remained. There were few available comforts. The home and the family, the church, and the nearest town, which could be fifty miles or more distant, provided such as there were. A gathering place was of some importance.

Perhaps the religion of the West is best described as spiritual hunger. Gospel meetings offered the frontier people opportunity for much-needed companionship. The church became a haven from loneliness and isolation and supplied a means of releasing pent-up frustrations caused by the strain of hard work, the vicissitudes of life, adverse experiences with the Indians, and open warfare with elements of nature ...[5]

The isolation enforced by vast empty spaces, so appealing in other ways, made its imprint on the character and outlook of the people who settled them. In many parts of the West the emptiness has not been filled and perhaps never will be.

[2]

The towns were the life-lines. They were the centres that enabled an area, sometimes immense, to form itself into something like a community. Towns meant markets, money, pleasure and relaxation on however small a scale. The towns were the clearing houses for staple foods and cotton cloth, weapons and ammunition, liquor and women. In the Western the town most often means activity, bustle, noise, above all people who can throw up action out of the coming and going and pinpoint the Western hero as effectively as the emptiness of open country.

Whatever its relevance the town itself does not vary greatly. Whether a one-horse dead end or a rapidly growing metropolis the Western town usually has certain distinctive features. Any quick glance at old photographs will identify them: a dusty main street, false-fronted buildings with the saloon and the general store in prominent positions, hitching rails, a livery stable. In the south-west the buildings are of adobe, with low, dark openings, and there is almost certainly a church. On the screen there are a few decorative Mexicans, dozing with hats pulled over their eyes, women making tortillas or suckling babies. The cantina replaces the saloon, and tequila replaces red-eye.

Towns in the Western often appear to be no more than random communities with no obvious use other than to provide the drifting cowboy with a drink, a woman and a fresh horse. The Hollywood-built main street appears repeatedly with no sense of the town's origin, its growth or its function. Sometimes there is a railroad coming through, or a stage-coach once a week, a bank to be robbed, but no solid reason for the existence of any of these. And in fact many towns in the West, whatever their origins or original purpose, were destined to a lingering half-life, existing only because everyone did not leave. On the screen we see an example in the little town in *Bad Day at Black Rock*. The railroad does come through, but as no one comes and no one goes the train rarely stops. People do make a living there: there is a local rancher, a hotel, a garage, a doctor—but the town as a community is dying on its feet.

The little town squatting in the middle of nothing that we see briefly in *Will Penny* (1967) directed by Tom Gries, or the town in Burt Kennedy's *Killer on a Horse* (1967), in both cases a handful of forlorn buildings, inspire no confidence in their survival. Like Firecreek, Kennedy's town is populated by people who know they are failures, who don't care any more. Part of the effect of *Killer on a Horse* is the way the town appears so totally cut off, remote. Yet just such towns were centres for scattered ranchers and settlers, who would have to come many miles for their flour and beans and coffee, and havens for the cowboy who spent his money on other but for him equally basic commodities. As long as the settlers and cowboys had money to spend, the towns would survive.

In many cases the origins of a town were haphazard apart from the fact that like any other frontier establishment they needed water. The whim of an individual, or simply the response to emptiness, could situate a town. Space could make people want to huddle together rather than plant themselves in the middle of nowhere. But the towns that grew fastest were the towns that grew around mining strikes, railroad construction camps, trading posts, or forts. They were natural pauses on the frontier, natural points of congregation. If people were already there a town built itself around them. Even if the Westerner was not dependent on the towns, and he did not strictly have to be, these conglomerations of humanity were almost bound, at times, to hold an irresistible attraction. It did not matter how shoddy or ramshackle or temporary they were. They still meant people. In the Western the town is there to liberate the protagonists from the limitations of the lonely West. In the town there can be anyone, any type, any occupation, ranging through all degrees of respectability, race and appearance, and anything can happen.

The famous towns were the towns with the most people, most bustle and most business, such as Abilene, the first of the great cow towns, which flourished not because of cattle, but because of the fortuitous conjunction of cattle and the railroad.

Abilene may be defined. It was the point where the north-and-south cattle trail intersected the east-and-west railroad. Abilene was more than a point. It is a symbol. It stands for all that happened when two civilisations met for conflict, for disorder, for the clashing of great currents which carry on their crest the turbulent and disorderly elements of both civilisations—in this case the rough characters of the plain and of the forest. On the surface Abilene was corruption personified. Life was hectic, raw, lurid, awful. But the dance hall, the saloon, and the red light, the dissonance of immoral revelry punctuated by pistol shots, were but the superficialities which hid from the view the deeper forces that were working themselves out round the new town. If Abilene excelled all later cow towns in wickedness, it also excelled them in service—the service of bartering the beef of the South for the money of the North.[6]

The character of the cow town is a part of the Western legend. The cowboys after long days in the saddle whooping it up and shooting off their pistols at nothing in particular, with nothing in particular sometimes producing a corpse or two. The red light district situated on the other side of the tracks from the business part of town. The famous marshals, Hickok, Wyatt Earp, Bat Masterson, Luke Short, Tom Smith, patrolling the streets and the saloons. The Western constantly imitates this, and the lesser towns constantly imitate the greater, the cowboys riding in from the surrounding ranches for their Saturday night jollifications with Sunday to sleep off the hangover.

If the cow towns provided a commercial service essential in the West's development, they also provided services which the cowboys considered of equal importance. John Clay's description of Dodge City, the most famous of them all, suggests what these services were.

Dodge was some town then. It consisted of one main business street running parallel to the Santa Fe Railroad. The great bulk of the business houses were saloons. York, Parker and Draper had a big outfitting store in the midst of this medley of thirst parlours, gambling rooms, and pimp houses. Cox had a hotel at the east end of this street. It was about the most rough-and-ready place it was ever my luck to stay in. It was so well populated there was scarcely room for you. An ordinary cow camp was a palace in comparison for comfort. In Cox's hotel you expected much and got little. In the camp you expected little and got a great deal.[7]

Even so cowboys who had been long on the trail were glad to get to Dodge, whether it was their final destination or just a pause on the way further north.

Howard Fast's fictional description in *The Last Frontier* sets Dodge in a different light. This is not the gay, boisterous, raucous Western town of the screen.

As they neared Dodge, coming over a rise and down towards the town, it rose up out of the short-grassed prairie like a rickety mirage. The long line of unpainted, leaning, clapboard shells faced the railroad on Front Street ... it made no pretence of being a place where people lived. There were no houses or outlying farms, with this as the central business section; it was a blight, a blot, a lumped scar up out of the belly of Kansas. It hadn't grown from the beginning, not even the terrific unpaced growth of a frontier town. One day there was nothing, and then the railroad came and with it Dodge City, hurled together, flung up, populated.[8]

The inhabitants of Dodge existed to provide pleasures for a rough and transient population. Saloon keepers, bar tenders, gamblers, prostitutes, and their helpers and hangers-on made up the bulk of the permanent residents. Most of the men who paused in Dodge they would never see again, or if they did would not remember. Even the permanent residents' permanency was only relative. Sooner or later they were likely to move on too.

Fast's description of a Dodge interior continues to emphasise the grimness rather than the gaiety. This is the Alamo saloon, Dodge City's most renowned.

The bar ran the length of the Alamo, forty feet, merging into a tinny, upright piano. A small, bald man rocked on the stool, playing the same jig tune over and over again. A line of sticky glasses tinkled to his playing, and there was half a pitcher of headless beer waiting within reach. The tables sat in sawdust the colour of mud, making a sort of fence around a sawdust-streaked dance floor. Two doors at the end of the room bluntly told the ladies and the gents where to go, and an unpainted board stairs rose into obscurity between them.

There were half a dozen men at the bar and a dozen more sitting in two card games. At the further corner a roulette wheel and a dice table waited for night. At another table a red gown, stringy yellow hair, and puffed arms lay in the wreck of an overturned whiskey glass. The smell was thick, rancid, unspeakable.[9]

The customers could not afford to be choosy, and everyone knew it. In some establishments pains were taken to provide lavish decoration and expensive furnishing, but they had few customers who took any trouble over themselves. On the screen we often see a degree of elegance and glitter in the furnishings of brothels and hotels. In Van Cort's cryptically violent book *Journey of the Gun* (1966) the young hero enters the Carter House—'On either side of a door stood a huge fan palm in a bucket. There was a carpet on the floor, a room with a desk in the bay of the curving stairway, and to the right a wide doorway leading to a dining room which actually had white cloths on the tables.'[10] Behind the bar are paintings of 'large voluptuous, brazen nude women'[11]. But the tart he takes up with is a sad wreck of a girl.

In *Hang 'Em High* (1969), directed by Ted Post, Marshal Cooper spends a night in the 'bridal suite' of a lush establishment run by a refined, plumply well-dressed, middle-aged woman. It is profuse with carpets and curtains, and cheap perfume to kill the range smell of her customers, and the Marshal himself is provided with a jolly, wholesome redhead. Downstairs there is an elegant bar, and the whole place is run with taste and strictness. The girls behave like pretty, giggly schoolgirls under the charge of a firm but benevolent headmistress. In *The Pistolero of Red River* Angie Dickinson runs a homely establishment with herself unquestionably a cut above her girls and able to rise with dignity above any slur on her reputation. Although the store keeper refers to her as 'trash' the movie itself presents her as nothing of the sort. The fact that she has a consistent relationship with one man, and that this relationship is presented in an aura of soupy sexlessness (only Hollywood can put a man and woman in bed together so passionlessly) helps to dispel the impression that this woman is anything less than elegant, beautiful and virtuous. She runs her establishment with the assistance of a black couple who enhance the homeliness by filling the traditional roles of devoted service. The girls eat a homely big breakfast in a homely kitchen just as if they all belonged to one big family.

In the early days of the frontier at least such establishments were few and far between. The needs of a whisky-starved, woman-starved cowboy were pretty straightforward, and he didn't need the frills in order to satisfy them. The classier outfits were a part of the civilising process that grew with the towns. There was more money to spend, more money to import luxuries from the East. A well appointed saloon, dance hall or whore house was a sign of prosperity, and in them customers were of course expected to spend more money.

Drinking was as important and time-consuming an occupation as fornicating, but for many gambling was an even stronger attraction of the towns. Small time poker games were to be found everywhere. The camera rarely gives us the interior of a saloon without showing us a card game in progress. The Alamo in Dodge had its roulette wheel, but this was likely to be found only in the larger towns. Most major Western towns attracted their share of professional gamblers and many saloons, even small ones, had a resident gambler who operated with the management. Crooked establishments were widespread, but you had to be pretty sharp to spot them, and even if you did it was often more than your life was worth to make your opinion known.

In the Western the professional gambler is instantly recognisable. His black coat and ruffled white shirt distinguish him from the average Westerner. His character varies: he is sometimes an evil man, with a surface gloss of the gentleman but underneath an unscrupulous cheat, or he can be a real gentleman providing a significant contrast with the rougher elements of the West. Such is Bret Harte's John Oakhurst, probably fiction's first professional gambler, who, despite his dubious profession, is a gentleman through and through. The gambler in Ford's *Stagecoach* is more equivocal. He fancies himself as a ladies' man, and his attentions to the officer's wife are not unwelcome, and yet there is an unpleasantness about him which breaks through the polite veneer.

The gambler as Western hero is fairly common, but more usual is the Western hero who gambles, and is a canny gambler up to all the tricks of the trade. Not, of course, that he himself practises them, but he is able to recognise and combat them. George Peppard as the hero of Arnold Laven's *Rough Night in Jericho* (1967) is a professional gambler, among other things, and wears the uniform black until the final sequences call for other skills and the more appropriate garb of buckskin. His coolness at cards is equally applicable to gunplay. Cape Wallace, the hero of William MacLeod Raine's novel *Glory Hole*, is a professional gambler resident in a Leadville saloon. 'His white shirt was immaculate, his Prince Albert broadcloth coat well pressed, and his custom made boots polished to a looking-glass shine.'[12]

One of L'Amour's heroes, Fallon, is also a gambler, a cynical man aware of the limitations of his existence, but also a fairly successful man. His success has depended on his very intimate knowledge of cards.

Now, Fallon was a man who could do things with cards. He could, while shuffling, run up a top stock or a bottom stock; he could shift the cut, deal from the top or the bottom, or second-deal; he knew all about slick aces, marked or trimmed cards, shiners, mirror in pipe-bowls or match boxes, and the tiny pricks on finger rings for the purpose of marking cards.

Sleeve or belt holdouts were no mystery to him, and he knew all about the man who brings drinks or sandwiches to the table with a cold deck held underneath the tray ready for a switch. In short, Macon Fallon was a professional; and although usually honest, he was not above cheating the cheaters if they invited it.[13]

The gambler's success depends to some extent too on his quickness on the draw. He must be able not only to spot cheaters but to take action. In Westerns it is generally accepted that a man could justifiably kill a cheat, and countless have been killed to prove it. But the professional, and others too, considered it perfectly acceptable to fleece an inexperienced card player and poker debts brought many a young man to a bad end. Without the inexperienced the professionals would have found it hard to make a living.

The legend of the gambler as gentleman clearly goes back to the Mississippi steamboat gambler who fed on the sons of rich families rather than the lean earnings of saddle tramps. Many of the Western's gamblers are pointedly Southern in accent and gentility. Card playing is a perfectly respectable and totally classless pastime. It was done everywhere—in the bunk house, by the camp fire, in scruffy little cantinas on the edge of the desert, in the railroad construction camps, anywhere that men had a bit of spare cash and not much to do in their spare time.

For the hero there is a gambler's code as clear as the gunman's code. The way a man played cards could be a test of his character, and many card games on the screen seem deliberately set up to illustrate this. They have their own kind of tension. A poker game between pros can become an irresistible centre of interest. The man who can win or lose coolly and without emotion is someone to be reckoned with. The winner who does not give the losers a fair chance to recoup is regarded with distrust.

In *Rough Night* the town rivals assess each other through their card game. It is one of the rounds in the competition and both recognise it as such. Often we are shown hero and villain facing each other across a card table as a rehearsal for some more deadly contest that will take place later. They assess each other, and what they learn will come in useful. In what remains of frontier society in the United States and Canada this practise of character assessment over cards still operates. A young man's initiation into poker is still often seen as a test of manhood. He has to learn how to conduct himself.

The gambler as hero tends to be more than a gambler. Usually it is only one of his many skills. His coolness and his ability to judge character are useful in the employment of his other skills, in gunplay, or business. William Cox's Duke Parry, in his book *The Duke*, has all the qualities of the Western hero. Along with these 'Even the range clothing he wore was custom-made, though subdued in hue. He ate the best, smoked Havana cigars, walked with the mighty in the western capitals. He lacked not for women, wine, or song.'[14] He is kind, gentle and understanding with no loss to his toughness. He is at home in the city and on the range. But equally easily the gambler can be villainous. The black and white garb can suggest the sinister as well as the courteous. Turquoise in *The Lone Wolf* (1967) by W. C. Tuttle, a delightful writer, is flashy and double-crossing. Gamblers are inevitably associated with shady joints and cheating deals, and even the good gamblers cannot quite escape this. They are a part of the semi-underworld of city life. They share the sordid locale of the prostitute and the drunk even when they rise above it.

Parallel to the Western town's reputation for entertainment, and probably directly nourished by it, came the growth of a self-conscious sense of community and civic responsibility. As citizens became increasingly aware of the essential nature of the services they provided they also became concerned with the moral solidity of their status. Sometimes this implied a fair measure of hypocrisy. Appearances become vital, but the man who is loudest in voicing his abhorrence of the brothels is sometimes the man who is a regular secret visitor. More prosaically, no man with the town's interests at heart would be anxious to get rid of the town's greatest attractions. And so, paradoxically, but with no great sense of wonder at the paradox, there grew side by side more splendid and lavish brothels, and schools and churches and town halls. The more flourishing and aspiring the town, the more likely was this to happen.

The paradox appears in many Westerns, taken for granted generally as a slightly comic indication of the West's unique character. A righteous churchgoing population and killing on the streets: a flourishing community supporting worthy institutions and nourishing the drunk and the prostitute: a handsome town hall, but primitive sanitation and streets knee deep in mud. Chicago, in its time the most contradictory frontier town of all, reveals the contrasts.

Chicago, a city of thirty thousand people in 1850, contained eighty thousand five years later, and one hundred ten thousand at the close of the decade. It had become a cosmopolitan metropolis, the commercial clearing house of the upper Mississippi valley. In 1854 seventy-four trains a day tapped the Northwest. Its grain trade handled twenty million bushels that year; Chicago had already become the greatest primary wheat depot in the world. But even in Chicago, while the pioneers themselves had passed, frontier conditions had not.

The drains in the streets, the alleys, the casual heaps of refuse in the vacant lots, reached to high heaven. A 'Gehenna of abominations', newspapers christened the Lake Shore. Cows settled themselves for the night's rest on the sidewalks of the city. Surrounding massive public edifices and hotels, handsome churches and imposing business-houses, were wooden shanties and sawn-wood cabins.[15]

Chicago contained contrasts on a scale that most Western towns could not match (although they may have wished to) but it was generally true that civic consciousness was less concerned with cleaning up than with looking good. Moral cleansing was something else: ladies' committees attacked drink and whores with gusto. Purity was more significant than cleanliness. A grandiose building looked much more impressive than a modest clean street. The town hall could be a symbol of progress that no one could miss. Some of the implications of this desire to appear progressive at all costs are present in *Death of a Gunfighter* (1969), a movie directed by Alan Smithee sustained by the irresistible seediness of Richard Widmark in the leading role. Here a town still threatened by frontier violence gets rid of the sheriff who, they feel, too obviously belongs to a previous, barbaric age. The men who kill the sheriff are on the surface models of responsible citizenship. He dies on the street and they, with their rifles smoking, are ready to greet the twentieth century. They have upheld the respectability and reputation of their town.

The fictional Western town generally has its quota of homely and solid citizens, the blacksmith for instance, often dispensing cracker barrel philosophy to his customers. If the town contains its villains these are easy to spot. The store keeper is a mild man with a wife and family, the doctor genial though perhaps overfond of the bottle, the lawyer and the newspaper editor are sometimes hooked in with the baddies, but if they are straight they are decent. There is at least one obviously decent woman to be seen on the street probably with a decent kid or two, and quiet respectability is as strongly present as any other character of the town.

But not all towns were rapidly developing and driven to ostensible civilisation by a civic consciousness. There were the backwater hamlets, avoided by the railroads, neglected by finance, forgotten by progress, that struggled just to survive. There were towns where men who might normally have been pillars of the community, if there had been a community of any substance to uphold, were warped and wasted, lawyers irrelevant to the law, doctors drowning a dead-end professional existence in drink. There were towns propped up by a straitlaced respectability that were in fact rotten at the core: any serious disturbance exposed the rottenness. Hard Times in *Killer on a Horse* is an example, whose force is not impaired by its melodrama. Totally destroyed by a single maniac killer because it does not have the backbone to resist the few survivors are horribly exposed to their own realisation of failure. The film itself has an unpredictable gothic intensity which gives it some distinction. The town survives, or rather reawakens, not so much through the emergence of an all-American hero but through the irrational determination of a man to revive the burnt-out shell. His attempt to make the community meaningful, even when it has ceased to be a real community, is an attempt to justify its past existence.

There is without a doubt a gothic quality in the West's dying towns. The ghost towns, the town stricken with cholera in *Day of the Evil Gun* (1968), an almost surrealistic interlude in an average Western, the little hamlets that hang on by the skin of their teeth to the surrounding country, these have a curious isolation, a curious irrelevance. They are cut off from human and social contact. The corrupt towns share some of these qualities. They exist irrespective of law and society, of the territory beyond, of responsibilities to the nation. Jericho in *Rough Night* has an outward prosperity but is not really alive. Fear corrupts it as much as the domination of a single powerful man. Fear and lack of communications allow the domination to continue. The same is true of Black Rock and the towns in Howard Hawk's *Rio Bravo* (1959) and *El Dorado* (1967). They are easily terrorised, without a moral centre that might sustain resistance. In this type of Western fear and cowardice are at the very heart of a town's rottenness. In Lewis Patten's novel *No God in Saguaro* (1966) it is fear and weakness that prompt the killing. In this case, in the context of the Western hero, fear generates evil.

Civic fear could be a counterpart to civic responsibility. The town could nourish a desire to improve the community, but it could also encourage a wish to become lost in a crowd. Responsibility meant conformity. It was no part of the Western hero to be inconspicuous but this was not necessarily true of the Western citizen. Conformity can suggest weakness. The city Western often dwells on this: the hero is a man prepared to draw attention to himself, prepared to take risks. The fact that his heroism renders him conspicuous is a reflection of the town's inabilities.

The city Western is often about a community facing a threat, not necessarily a rotten community, but usually a scared community. *High Noon, Rio Bravo*, even *Shane* where the links between town and outlying community are of great importance, pivot on this theme. This kind of Western, above all a community Western, widens the heroic theme, relates the hero more directly to a society of some kind, and ultimately to the nation. This is not to say that they are intrinsically of greater worth; they can too easily become the vehicles of unhelpful platitudes. The above three are obviously exceptional, not so much in that they avoid platitudes but in that they avoid putting them across in a hammer-fisted way.

The community Western is frequently about a balance of power. Power tended to concentrate in the towns. That was where the money was. The towns rivalled the cattleman's domain and this was frequently the direct cause of feuding, for the power in the towns was often provokingly exploitive of the land and the cattleman. The big rancher tended to distrust the towns, while the small farmer was more reliant on them. He needed the community, its sustenance and its institutions, while the rancher was usually more self-sufficient. In the Western the farmer is generally represented as a family man, more dependent on a conventional society, while the rancher is ruler of his own empire.

City power in the Western tends to be more sinister than ranch power. The city villain, the crooked lawyer or corrupt mayor, is a nastier character than the outlaw on horseback, although often it is the latter who does the dirty work for the city villain. The crooked schemer has very little to redeem him, while a horse and some rough country make the outlaw more acceptable. At times the town dictator has a ranch nearby to feed his strength in the town. There he can stable his men and store his ammunition, and the ranch existed too as a symbol of wealth and success in Western terms.

There are Westerns whose entire action takes place within the confines of a town and some of these are amongst the classics. *High Noon* is the obvious example. Tension concentrates in a single street as the just-married hero awaits the threat in the shape of a notorious outlaw with a grudge whom no one else will face. *The Man Who Shot Liberty Valance* (Ford, 1961) has only brief out of town moments, as has *Death of a Gunfighter*, not a classic but a movie that illustrates the kind of intensity restriction to a town locale can produce. *Rio Bravo* is another. If the Western had never utilised a town locale for anything else it would have established its unrivalled importance for one event —the walk-down. Out of town gunfighters have their attractions but the main street walk-down is in a class of its own. There must be a street. There must be an audience, even if that audience is safely hidden behind locked doors. There needs to be a suggestion of suspended activity, a sudden pause, a sudden hush as the rivals confront each other.

There has been an immense variety in town gunfights, and in every case the significant factor is that there are people around, people going about their business who are suddenly caught up in a battle, liable to be hurt, and helpless in the face of erupting violence. The saloon brawl that ends in death, the bank raid, the jail break, gun battles in churches, cemeteries, livery stables, shots from rooftops and doorways, all these have the extra dimension of a populace. The brilliant opening sequence of *The Wild Bunch* gathers a south-western town's citizens into an obscure, confusing and for this reason wholly terrifying gunfight. Frontier violence was not necessarily a confrontation in elemental surroundings. The towns bred violence, fostered it, even demanded it, and without the towns the Western would lose a vital dimension. Ultimately this was what settlement meant: more people thrown together in a smaller space, less scope for action, less room for movement, more friction with encroaching law and order. In the Western this often means more intensity in the presentation of its archetypal themes.

FIVE

Home on the Range

The range country, sir, was never intended for raising farm-truck. It was intended for cattle and horses, and was the best stick-raising land on earth until they got to turning over the sod—improving the country, as they call it. Lord, forgive them for such improvements!

from Merill G. Burlinghame *The Montana Frontier*

[1]

The cattle business in the Western states developed to its climax with astonishing speed. Although there had been cattle in the south-west since the days of Cortez, 1867, the year that the railroad reached Abilene, is the significant date in the history of the beef bonanza. 25,000 cattle went through the Abilene market that season. Four years later 300,000 cattle were driven from Texas to Kansas. Twenty years later the production of beef had suffered some drastic experiences, and the West of cattle and cowboys was already changing. Westerns that are about cattle, cattle empires and cattlemen are usually set in these brief years of promise.

In 1884 a gentleman from Scotland, J. S. Tait, published in Edinburgh a pamphlet entitled *The Cattle Fields of the Far West*. It was designed to attract investment in Western ranching from Britain. In it Tait wrote:

The cattle fields of Western America extend with slight interruption from Montana to Southern Texas, north and south, and from the Mississippi Valley to the Pacific, east and west. On the vast plains or prairies embraced in this area, cattle roam all the year round, foraging entirely for themselves, and with the expenditure of a minimum of care and outlay on the part of the owners.[1]

The possibilities for cattle raising seemed boundless. Tait added, 'The whole future of the trade is clear, and luminous with promise.' And indeed in 1884 it appeared so, in spite of serious drought the previous summer which had done some damage. But in fact the beef bonanza was already in its final act, and Tait was a little late on the scene. Certainly by 1877 word of the amazing profits to be made from cattle had spread east and across the Atlantic. In that year *The Scotsman*, Scotland's major daily newspaper, had sent out a representative to investigate the livestock situation in the West. In 1880 Britain was so concerned at the competition from American beef (refrigeration was in use by this time) that a Royal Commission was set up to report on the subject. But this did not deter British speculation in American cattle, for by 1882 it was reckoned that something like thirty million dollars worth of British money had been invested in Western ranches and, interestingly, much of this had its origins in Edinburgh and Dundee. By the early 1880s vast numbers of Western cattle were owned by people whose familiar domain was the streets of New York or Boston, London or Edinburgh.

The world of speculation, stocks and shares seems a long way from the well-known scenes of working the cattle. In fact, although many of the cattle owners would have recoiled from a Western cow pony, it was not only money that bridged the gulf. The owners had their managers, their representatives and their go-betweens, and some of these were involved in the less palatable aspects of cattle raising. As we shall see, a representative of Scottish interests, John Clay, became involved in one of the last large scale manifestations of range war, and many lesser known men indulged in practices which were not always to the advantage of the brand.

The Western has made us familiar with the cattle owner and his loyal men struggling against odds human and natural to build up his herd and bring it to market. Less in evidence are the features of absentee landlordism which at times dominated certain areas of the range. Enthusiastic companies thousands of miles away would buy virtually non-existent herds, and when the following spring's calf count came would be dismayed to discover that the 'herd' had dwindled radically. Pamphlets like Tait's only encouraged this kind of thing. Judicious rustling on the part of less than scrupulous managers helped it along.

Themes of this kind have not emerged strongly in the Western. Corruption, rival financial interests, corporation politics, yes: but the cow saga has been presented with some consistency in terms of individual ownership, of the intimate relationship between owner, cattle and land, and above all of the virtues of these things. There are cheating managers of course, and gullible owners, but they exist for the most part to emphasise the intrinsic worth of the man who owns and cares for his own cattle on his own land.

In fact the cattleman brought together two American characteristics held very dear. He was a pioneer. And he was a man of property. His property may have been on the hoof and vulnerable, but for a time it was considered as solid in cash terms as a string of hotels in a capital city. It was the cattleman, backed up by the railroad, who played the most important part in civilising vast acres of wild country.

It was the range cattleman who broke the spell; who made these great areas his own; who, in his search for grass, crossed every divide, rode into every coulee, and swam every stream. The solitude of the desert passed, and men began to realise that this, our last frontier, was not a barrier between the river settlements and the mining communities in the mountains but an area valuable in itself, where men might live and prosper.[2]

The fact that the cattleman was an explorer and an adventurer, that he risked his life and carved his own way, and did these things in an atmosphere of money-making potential, at once gave him his place in the American tradition of frontier success.

The cattle trade on a large scale was a post-Civil War phenomenon. It begins with *Red River*, the seeking of a market for the cattle that had multiplied during the years of war but were worth nothing in Texas, their home state. Charles Siringo describes returning to Southern Texas after the War and rounding up wild cattle in the brush. If you could find a market you could make a fortune, for these were unbranded cows there for the taking, although roping wild cattle out of the brush and getting a brand on them was no work for greenhorns. But it could have its rewards. Shanghai Pierce sold his herd of maverick cattle for one hundred and ten thousand dollars. Siringo comments, 'That shows what could be done in those days, with no capital, but lots of cheek and a branding iron. The two Pierce's had come out there from Yankeedom a few years before poorer than skimmed milk.'[3]

Many of the Texas cattle empires began in this way in the unsettled years following the War. John Clay hints that a number of the biggest Wyoming outfits had similiar origins at a later stage. But without the railroad fortunes could not have been made. Before the railroad reached Kansas only two men solved the problem of what to do with the cattle the Civil War made unmarketable. In 1860 Oliver Loving and Charles Goodnight trailed their cattle through incredible hazards of drought and Indians to Colorado where the gold rush was and men needed beef. When the War was over the two men made an even more hazardous trip in 1866 to New Mexico, where cattle were needed by the military and by Indian reservations. The route they charted became known as the Goodnight/Loving Trail. Loving lost his life on it. Meanwhile, in 1865, Jesse Chisolm made his first drive to Kansas, and the Chisolm Trail became famous in song and story.

The railroad moved west and the shipping points moved west with it. They are names that feature in Western after Western: Abilene, Ellsworth, Hays City, Dodge, Wichita. Their saloons, their marshals and their outlaws have been woven into the Western myth. They are towns all associated with Texas cattle and Texas cattlemen, but their heyday did not last long. The further the railroad spread the less important they became. Further north the Union Pacific was pushing westwards across Nebraska and into Wyoming. Later the Northern Pacific gave easier access to the Dakotas and Montana. But the northern ranges did not wait for the railroad.

The first cattlemen of the northern ranges preceded the Civil War, for they raised cattle on a fairly small scale to sell to the emigrant trains. Later the Montana mining camps and reservations created a demand for beef, and that beef came from Texas on long, slow and arduous drives up what was to be known as the Western Cattle Trail. At first the cattlemen from Texas came only to sell, but the lush, empty ranges of Wyoming tempted them. In Ernest Haycox's *Free Grass* (1928) father and son are moving their herds from Texas to a chosen parcel of open range in the north. Haycox makes this a satisfying story of competition and revenge.

In the 1870s Texas was already getting crowded. Cattle were spreading northwards to Wyoming, Montana and the Dakotas, filling up Nebraska, Kansas and Indian Territory (where they occupied range leased from the Indians), moving westwards into Colorado, New Mexico, Arizona and Nevada. Land which at one time had been dismissed as desert and unprofitable became dotted with cattle. Grass and water were the treasured raw materials.

Countless narratives of the cattle trade have centred on the primacy of these two materials—narratives of travel, trail breaking, range war and all kinds of rivalry. They are narratives full of hardship, suffering, courage, bloodlust and viciousness: but one feature emerges from all of them. It was a noble struggle. The cattleman emerges in myth as a man of substance and superiority. To own cattle is a noble aim in life. Alongside this, though not, so far, emphasised strongly enough to challenge the central myth, are two more humble pictures. There was the life of the cowboy, a man possibly like Will Penny in Tom Gries's movie, illiterate and homeless at the age of fifty, who has never owned a cow in his life and probably never will. And there was the life of a ranchman like John Leakey, starting out as a young cowboy in the 1880s, struggling and failing to make something of his own ranch through the Depression, and in 1952 drifting nostalgically over the old cattle trails.

When I headed south again I picked up the old Chisolm Trail at Dodge City, Kansas. For a long time I had been wanting to see the layout of that famous old cowpath; and I followed it, as near as a fellow can in an automobile, to San Antonio. And by the lay of the country, fairly level, with good water spaced about right most of the way, I could see why it had made trailherd history in its day. Of course it was all farms and towns by the time I first set eyes on it, but I could imagine how it must have looked near a hundred years ago—when it was just good, grassy cattle country.[4]

Even in the midst of his worst troubles John Leakey's relish for the old days emerges richly. He does not need the Western to encourage his faith in the value of cattle days and cattle country, and yet he is keen to nurse his own nostalgia by probing back. For us the Western is doing this all the time. We may not recognise the nostalgia as such, but part of our response to the Western is that perpetual dream of all humanity that the old days were somehow better.

The trail drive is of special significance, as it features the cattleman totally dependent on the country, which may offer something unpredictable each day. On the trail the cowboy is protecting cattle against the widest variety of threats. From the earliest days the Western has made the most of the trail drive, and its essential features do not vary. Every trail drive has its stampede, its thefts, its Indian attacks, its encounters with Kansas raiders or rustlers, and probably its conflicts with a rival outfit. When in 1923 Emerson Hough conducted the heroine of *North of 36* through the hazards of the trail they varied little from the adventures the heroines of *The Last Sunset* encountered nearly forty years later. The multiple stampedes of the earliest Westerns, very often the same footage used repeatedly, hardly differ from the latest in this vein the cinema has to offer. But even without the hazards there is something magnificent about the great stream of moving cattle, the rising dust, the lively cow ponies, the nightly camps, and it is this picture of steady animal movement that illuminates the attraction of the myth.

Large numbers of Westerns go nowhere near a cow. With the exception of Dick Richards' muted *The Culpepper Cattle Co.* there has not been a trail driving picture since *Red River* in 1948. When one sees the sheer beauty of a mass of cattle in early morning that Lucien Ballard's camera gives us in *Will Penny*, or the tantalising lyrical glimpses of cattle grazing in *Sam Whiskey* it is hard to understand why in so many Westerns, even many based on ranching, the treatment of the cow is so perfunctory. There are typical shots of driving, roping and branding cattle but much of this has been present to exhibit the skill of stuntman or cowboy star rather than to provide an insight into what handling cattle really involves. When Broncho Billy turns a stampede or Roy Rogers twirls a rope this has little to do with cows.

Of documents describing cattle country, and working with cattle Andy Adams' *Log of a Cowboy* is well known and highly respected. In it he describes a trail drive that began on April 21st, 1882 from Texas to the Blackfoot Agency in Montana. In a number of other books, some fictional, some repetitious, Adams describes the life and work of the cowboy, but *Log of a Cowboy* is the freshest and most vivid. In it, for instance, he relates the advice of the foreman before setting off.

Boys, the secret of trailing cattle is never to let your herd know that they are under restraint. Let everything that is done be done voluntarily by the cattle. From the moment you let them off the bed ground in the morning until they are bedded at night, never let a cow take a step, except in the direction of its destination. In this manner you can loaf away the day, and cover from fifteen to twenty miles, and the herd in the meantime will enjoy all the freedom of the open range. Of course, its long tiresome hours to the men; but the condition of the herd and saddle stock demands sacrifices on our part, if any have to be made.[5]

Adams himself comments, 'Our comfort was nothing; men were cheap, but cattle cost money.'[6] Douglas Branch quotes an old cowboy in his book *The Cowboy and his Interpreters*. 'The next spring I would have the same old trip, the same old things would happen in the same old way, and with the same old wind-up. I put in eighteen or twenty years on the trail, and all I had in the outcome was the high-heeled boots, the striped pants and about $4.80 of other clothes, so there you are.'[7]

Yet for all the prosaic routine, a life with cattle was a life if not of romance certainly of a dauntless quality which appealed to many men and many writers. Eugene Rhodes, a writer of Western stories characterised by an intimate balance of humour and drama, fills his writing with the everyday details of life in the New Mexican cow country, but all the time is convincing us that it was a good life. Ernest Haycox writes with a flare for rich description and manages to suggest the profound appeal of raising cattle.

Onward they travelled. North, always north. Sunrise and sunset. Beans and coffee in the starlight. Night after night with the infinite heavens for a canopy and the yellow firelight playing upon Quagmire's twisted, solemn visage. Twenty-five hundred cattle trampling a broad trail across the lush earth, Roman Nose plodding to the fore, wise with years. Hot sun beating down; swift spring rains pouring out of the sky, flooding the coulees and vanishing as quickly as they came. And again the hot sun playing on the wet prairie and the steam rising up. Five miles a day, eight miles a day, sometimes fifteen miles a day. They crossed the ford of the Smoky Hill, they crossed the Saline and the Solomon. Kansas was behind, and the plains of Nebraska beckoned them north—level, limitless.[8]

The appeal lies not so much in the cattle as in the country, and the way the country moulds and colours life. It is not even so much what is done, the tasks that caring for cattle and horses demands, that matters as the flavour these activities have.

To a great extent it is the vast outdoors that creates this distinctive impression. The sense of exposure to the elements is very strong in Haycox's description. The elements determine the nature of the journey —floods, drought, thunder that might stampede the cattle, dust storms, The elements seem to be in alliance with the land itself, and the two provide twin forces which the cowboy has to combat.

Some aspects of these forces ingrained in the characterisation of the cowboy. Hunched under his slicker in the rain, his hat brim pulled down against a rising dust storm, manhandling cattle across a swollen river, struggling painfully across waterless desert: these pictures of the cowboy have become intregal parts of his personality. And they have become, inevitably, deeply associated with our impressions of cattle raising.

Cattle country too, despite the association of conflict, suggests peace. Grassland dotted with grazing beasts has for centuries suggested a calm accord which growing crops do not. Crops cannot grow without the plough. They cannot grow without man attacking the soil, cutting it up, spreading it with chemicals, changing its nature. Cattle feed on what grows naturally, and if undisturbed they graze with an unhurried purposefulness which emphasises tranquillity. It is a fine antithesis. But often on the screen, in seeking to make the most of the more dramatic events, stampedes and Indian raids, this other aspect of working with cattle is forgotten.

[2]

By the end of the 1870s the northern ranges were flowing with cattle and towns such as Cheyenne and Ogallala were becoming centres of the cattle trade. By the middle of the 1880s the northern ranges were crowded, and bigger ranchers were trying to keep out cattle that were not their own, sheep and small farmers. By 1881 there was a bonanza in sheep and cattlemen considered this a serious threat. The beef bonanza still seemed to be at its height. Cattle were shipped east to Chicago in their thousands where the stockyards and packing plants processed them into cans.

By this time it was not the scrawny but invulnerable Texas longhorn going into those cans but stock that was being constantly improved by shorthorn and Hereford and later Aberdeen Angus blood. Andrew McLaglen's film *The Rare Breed* (1966) showed, with a certain amount of whimsey and imagination, the introduction of a prize Hereford bull to the Texas longhorn. The Hereford was scorned and derided, but the result was a blockier, weight-carrying animal and better beef. The herd of rustled cattle in *Hang 'Em High* was pretty, square-faced black and white. No longhorn was ever like that. John Wayne's herd in *Red River*, years before a Hereford ever crossed the Mississippi, was suspiciously tainted with the familiar white blotched faces of that attractive breed of cattle. In fact the Western prairies of the screen are almost entirely populated by Hereford cattle and there is no doubt that they are much easier on the eye than the ferocious longhorn.

Herefords were scorned at first for, as J. S. Tait makes abundantly clear, half the fun of raising Western cattle was that they required a minimum of care. The wild longhorn and the tough work ox had survived winter snowstorms and summer drought without so much as a handful of hay or a bucket of water. But these pampered English cows had not the backbone let alone the intelligence to paw through snow to reach a few withered blades of brown grass—or so it was felt. As a cattleman says in Thomas Sturgeon's 'book-of-the-film' *The Rare Breed*: 'this is a country where beef, two thousand in a bunch, has to trail sometimes a thousand miles. How would a polled Hereford do over fifty miles of desert, without water for three days? And no horns—why, out on the range they would be picked like plums by the wolves and the cougars; and I dread to think what would happen the first time one of your bulls met up with a tough old longhorn maverick!'[9]

This was 1884. Even then weight and the quality of the meat were becoming increasingly important. There was a growing concern with breeding good beef. If it was possible to raise an animal that ate no more than the longhorn but sold for twice as much it was worth having a try. One or two ranchers even attempted to set up their own packing plants to combat the dominance of Chicago and save the cost of shipping, but this was a failure, and increasingly cattlemen were at the mercy of the railroads and the stockyards.

The habits of bonanza died hard. It took time and some hard lessons before cattlemen realised that cows could not be left to fend for themselves on the open ranges through the winter. Two vicious winters in succession, those of 1885-6 and 1886-7, the second worse than the first, rubbed in the lesson. Many ranchers lost everything. The blizzards pushed the cattle southwards up against the nearest fence where they died in heaps. It was the end of the road for large numbers of small cattle owners and many of the larger ones only survived because they could borrow money. Cowboys in the winter line camps attempted to ensure that the cattle did not stray too far off the home range and kept the fences under repair in the days of barbed wire. But there was little a man could do in the face of blizzards that swept down from the Arctic and lasted unabated for days on end.

Wyoming, now the supreme cattle state, suffered drastically. Even in Texas the effects of these cruel winters were felt. In the end of the 1880s the cattle business on the northern ranges had become a complexity of lending and borrowing, of intensified rivalry between big man and small man, of bitter conflicts sparked off by an enormous increase in rustling and the unflinching belief amongst the long-established cattlemen that their occupation and their land gave them a natural supremacy.

The big men struggled to recoup their losses after the disastrous winters in spite of predictions that the range cattle industry would never recover. The little men were in many cases forced to sell out, thus making the big men bigger. The initial reaction when the spring of 1887 revealed the dead and the terrible condition of the living was horror and despair. Granville Stuart, a prominent Wyoming cattle-man, wrote later, 'A business that had been fascinating to me before, suddenly became distasteful. I never wanted to own again an animal that I could not feed and shelter.' [10] A contemporary journal pronounced, 'The fact that we have now to face is that the range of the past is gone; that of the present is of little worth and cannot be relied on in the future. Range husbandry is over, is ruined, destroyed, it may have been by the insatiable greed of its followers.' [11]

These experiences and the large scale rustling that followed provoked bitterness and violence which is not entirely forgotten today. The fact that utilisation of the open range was decreasing—although in 1890 eighty per cent of the state of Wyoming was public domain the whole system of ranching was beginning to change—did not deter the rustlers or help the strugglers. The big men combined to combat rustling. They had recovered sufficient faith in cattle raising by the end of the decade to feel that cattle were pre-eminent, that Wyoming in particular was a state in which there was room for nothing else. The cattle kings were bitterly hated by those who were less successful, and such remarks as the Secretary of the Board of Live Stock Commissioners let drop hardly helped: 'there are too many people here now—too many people and not enough cattle.' [12] Stock detectives, Pinkerton men and armed individuals swarmed the Wyoming ranges and provided bloodshed enough to satisfy the most avid admirer of the 'realistic' Western.

The days when it was possible to make a quick fortune out of cattle were over. Even the most solidly established ranchers felt vulnerable to rustling, rivalry and encroachment on their range. By 1890 rustling in Wyoming had reached a disturbing peak, and it was this that caused the gradual eruption of the West's bitterest feuds. Range war on a fairly small scale is a staple theme of the Western, but the Johnson County War was of proportions that dwarf the average screen ruckus. It is all the more disturbing for the fact that the real truth of this strange affair still escapes careful historians.

Wyoming is still touchy about the affair, which involved a number of her leading citizens, and even now there are reputations to be lost. Although a number of Westerns have clearly drawn on the Johnson County disturbance, none have used it specifically and by name in the way the Lincoln County range war has been used. There are a number of fiercely partisan accounts of this classic confrontation, between the Wyoming Stock Growers Association and the small homesteaders. The big cattlemen, with Cheyenne as their base, planned an invasion of Johnson County, in the Powder River country of Wyoming, to exterminate rustling. For years rustling had been endemic in this part of the state and for some months prior to the invasion suspicion and distrust had been rife. There had been unexplained killings, threats, homesteaders shot in the back on lonely roads.

The Stock Growers Association accused the homesteaders of pilfering from their herds. It was fairly easy to put a brand on mavericks or slaughter the odd stray. But there was big time rustling too in which, the big ranchers felt, the small men were implicated. After a long period of piecemeal reprisal fifty gunmen moved in, many of them hired gunslingers of dubious reputation from outside the state. They made their way across country in a closed train and they took with them a list of eighty suspected rustlers. They led their horses from the train, rode through the night and killed, finally, two men. But they had to lay siege to a small cabin from dawn to dusk in order to accomplish this. They were then flouted, first by a posse of homesteaders and townspeople led by Sheriff Angus of Buffalo, then by the Army who arrived in time to save the invaders from almost certain slaughter.

The two men were added to the list of fatalities amongst suspected rustlers but, as with the other killings, no one was brought to court. Johnson County could not afford to hold and prosecute the fifty men. And the law was nervous of the fact that men of standing and influence had ridden with the company, and even more had worked behind the scenes. Leading witnesses mysteriously disappeared; kidnapping was suspected. The court was not able to function properly, and the whole affair fizzled out. The fact that, rustlers or not, two men could be killed, their murderers known and apprehended, and nothing done, had no significance. It was just another in that long series of similar episodes that made up frontier history.

The case was dismissed. After all, it was argued, the men accused of murder were only protecting their property. The way in which John Clay, one leading citizen who was fortuitously absent when the invasion took place but nevertheless was seriously implicated through his close association with the instigators of the plot, sums it all up is revealing.

It cost the cattle owners around $100,000. They responded freely, although it was the panic year of 1893. But money counts for little when placed beside nobility of character, of patient self-denial, of loyal friendship—the strong supporting the weak morally and financially. From this fiery furnace of trial and tribulation came pure gold, no tawdry counterfeit, but the real stuff, represented by splendid examples of courage, honesty, and everlasting belief in the justice of their cause. Against this there were a few cattlemen, some of them old-timers, who failed to support their friends, who before the raid were far from silent critics of Wyoming's tardiness in punishing the rustlers. They were absent at the hour of need, and among their fellow men they were despised and a black mark put against their names. Politics was the cause of some retreating, cowardice and self-interest influenced others. But sufficient for the day is the evil thereof. Today Wyoming is a better state to live in, so far as property rights are concerned, than it was twenty-five years ago.[13]

'Courage', 'honesty', belief in justice matched against 'cowardice' and 'self-interest': one inevitably reacts with suspicion to Clay's complacent acknowledgement of moral victory. The small homesteader who considered himself bullied and harassed by the big men got little satisfaction out of the business. The courage of Nathan Champion—who may well have been guilty—one of the two men besieged by fifty until he was finally burnt out and riddled with bullets, was the desperate courage of a bewildered man. He left a diary of his last hours, often quoted and apparently authentic.

It is now about noon. There is someone at the stable yet, they are throwing a rope out at the door and drawing it back. I guess it is to draw me out. I wish that duck would get out further so I could get a shot at him. Boys, I don't know what they have done with them two fellows that staid last night. Boys, I feel pretty lonesome just now. I wish there was someone here with me so we could watch all sides at once. They may fool around until I get a good shot before they leave.[14]

Clay has nothing to say of the dead men and it is unlikely now that it will ever be possible to apportion the guilt justly. With total confidence, and a superb example of historical metathesis, Clay asserts that Wyoming is 'a better state to live in', thanks to the invasion. He slides into that hideously dangerous hindsight justification of violence that plagues progress in America. The comment of another upstanding citizen of Wyoming, who was directly involved, is perhaps more pertinent. 'It never has been any trouble since to convict a cattle thief in Johnson County.'[15]

The Johnson County War has clearly been an indirect influence in a number of Westerns, although the whole incident, excepting Nate Champion's heroic defence, takes us right away from the rugged Western qualities we expect to find celebrated. The war was a victory for big business, and if the background of the battle was characteristically Western the nature of the struggle as a whole was significantly American. David Lavender, an historian of the West, writes:

The fierce confrontation that arose in the 1890s between entrenched capital and solidifying numbers of poor men was of course a national, not just a Western, problem. But in the West .... Conflicts took on an elemental directness, as witness the cattlemen's invasion of Johnson County, northern Wyoming.[16]

'An elemental directness': this could be the stuff of epic, and frequently was. But there was something so unsavoury about the reality of this incident that it would not translate well into the traditional mode, unless it could be converted in some way into a triumph of the individual over immense odds. The unsavoury quality is due not to the killing itself, but to the association of killing, and killing of a most unheroic nature, with the political manipulations of property owners.

The association of business with guns is a very American phenomenon. Many Westerns have drawn big business into their sphere. In some big business is represented by a kind of benevolent dictator —television's version of the Judge in *The Virginian*, for instance— who resolves his conflicts with the small men by absorbing them into his domain. The Western hero can become a limb of the establishment, but he must preserve the gestures of independence, and he must convince us that the establishment is benevolent. At other times big business is tyrannous, dishonest, dirty and destructive. It is often presented as the stranglehold of monopoly which can starve out the struggling settlers whose Western brand of resistance makes no impact on the business machine. But in most Westerns of this kind there will be a frontier hero who *can* meet the challenge of the unscrupulous, ruthless business man, and destroy him.

In Peckinpah's *The Wild Bunch* it is the railroad, its representative and the man he hires who are the villains, merciless, destructive and paradoxically acting in the name of progress. The steam locomotive is a symbol of inhuman power rather than of growth, which at other times it can be. In *The Wild Bunch* the railroad's maw gapes and from it leap the cannibal-like horsemen sent out to destroy their fellows. This essentially modern symbol of capitalist enterprise appears again and again in various forms throughout the Western.

The carnivore is not necessarily the machine. It can be the trust, the bosses, the monopoly. In Alan Le May's book *Gunsight Trail* (1931), not one of his best but usefully illustrative, we have a modern range war, set in the flivver period, in which the classic Western contests, between hired killers and homesteaders, big men and small men, landowners and townspeople, do not appear. Instead we have two old-timers facing each other, early settlers who have built up their own ranch empires, men who feel that their right to the country has been proved by their own staying power and courage. Behind one there is nothing but his total commitment to the land. Behind the other there is a complex network of moneymaking schemes unscrupulously backed by the State's politicians, an oozing corruption that reaches out to taint sheriff and lawyer, National Guard and Governor.

Le May very likely had in mind the Johnson County War and similar incidents. His twentieth century range war, where guns still have the final say but cowboys move speedily in cars, bridges the old frontier and more modern gangsterism, and reveals the continuity of the gun culture. It is the old time Westerner, without the trusts and the politicians behind him, who wins, but a lot of men have been killed and no one is going to hang for that. The point here is that the true Western hero can have no truck with big business. Oliver Major is a better man than Earl Shaw because his clean frontier spirit survives. He has presented his independence, preserved the old ways —including a good old-fashioned walk-down—and will not submit to the pressures of business even when these are also the pressures of progress.

Similarly, the only possible hero of the Johnson County invasion is Nate Champion. It is almost impossible for a gunslinger hired to kill by an anonymous trust to be heroic. The unconventional gunman in *Invitation to a Gunfighter* (1964), directed by Richard Wilson, is an unusual screen version. The tradition here brings us right into the world of Hammett and Chandler, and from there to the gun-toting heroes of the 'sixties played by Lee Marvin, Steve McQueen or Richard Widmark, in their various anti-system roles. The conflict of the individual against the power of linked influences and interests has become an American myth which recent Westerns and thrillers have reinforced.

In Le May's *Gunsight Trail* it is the backing of the system that makes an otherwise equal fight a big versus little affair, and thus brings us back to a classic Western theme. Of course, little must win, and thereby prove itself big. Little wins in *Gunsight Trail* because the system is exposed. Without this all the old-fashioned Western qualities would have achieved nothing: it is through the astuteness of the young hero that the system *is* exposed. This is an interesting yet perhaps an inevitable development, that the Western hero becomes a shrewd exposer rather than a lightning shot. (The present day imitation 'Western' hero, whether private eye or hard boiled cop, is usually both.) There is a traditional gun battle and a traditional duel at the finish of Le May's book, but this does not conceal the fact that it is moving with the speed of a Model T Ford away from the old Western values.

Throughout this version of feuding there is sensed an ominous threat from the cities. It is from the cities that the political forces emanate. 'Cities' suggests the East and it is hinted in *Gunsight Trail* that the range patriarch's fight represents the West's battle for independence. Even rustling, as opposed to the casual branding of mavericks, was an evil sustained by the cities, for it was there that the stolen cattle found buyers. This theme of the danger from the cities, of East versus West, often runs just under the surface of Westerns that attempt to characterise outlawry in terms of business pressure. It is present in Bob Obets' story *Rails to the Rio* (1965), a railroad Western set after the Spanish-American War, and in Luke Short's *Western Freight* (1941) set in a Colorado mining town. In both these there is the suggestion that growing business, growing prosperity, a growing community, inevitably bring with them a kind of corruption which is hard to challenge in the orthodox Western manner. In both the plot is manipulated in such a way that the climax is a matter of guts and guns, and this is the usual pattern. It is the only way the Western hero can get his chance.

[3]

The straightforward—and historically earlier—range war theme is generally simple and usually isolated. The power blocs are self-reliant. Being concerned with range land the cities do not encroach. Ernest Haycox's splendidly solid *Free Grass* and, less successful, *Riders West*, or Alan Le May's *The Smoky Years* indeed involve elemental contests. The contest is a fight for range rights or, crucially, for water. In *Free Grass* two outfits race from Texas to the newly opened northern ranges. In *Riders West* one big outfit attempts to take over the range of several smaller ones. In *The Smoky Years* two giants do battle with each other. The struggles here are elemental not only because they involve grass and water, but also because they are untainted, on one side if not on both, by the corrupt tentacles of the business octopus. The characters in these stories are men who have their roots in the West, and in fighting for grass and water are fighting for survival.

The phrase 'free grass' became symbolic of rights in which Westerners believed, but the era of free grass was short lived. As early as

1862 the Homestead Act allowed settlers to claim rangeland the ranchers considered their own. But it took quite some time for the homesteaders to impinge seriously on the ranchers' consciousness. When that happened struggles between cattlemen and homesteaders became unavoidable.

The attitude of the cowboy to the sodbuster is articulately expressed by one of the characters in *Riders West*. ' "I never had any use for a nester, missis. Far as I'm concerned, you ain't even people." ' And the barn is fired. A sign is left: 'NOTICE TO ALL NESTERS: LEAVE THE VALLEY BY DAYLIGHT OF THE FOURTEENTH OF THIS MONTH. NO EXCEPTIONS AND NO EXCUSES.' [17] The rancher, confident in his superiority, was convinced that no one could take seriously the laws made back east.

The Western has few sodbusting heroes. Repeatedly the homesteader is presented as a caricature, or a near caricature, like the spluttering, angular old man in *Guns of Wyoming* (1963, director Tay Garnett) who is won over by the cattle king hero. The typical nester is an earthbound individual with a milk cow and a grim faced wife in a sunbonnet and barefoot children. The knights of the range regard him with scorn and resentment. Something of this attitude is conveyed in John Clay's grudging remarks.

You can fight armies or disease or trespass, but the settler never. He advances slowly, surely, silently, like a great motor truck, pushing everything before him. He is cringing in distress, automatic in prosperity, and yet he is a builder, a great Western asset, peopling a childless land, planting schools by the side of cattle corals, preaching in their practical way the new salvation that is coming to the arid West. The old-timers thought their work was a flash in the pan, but it remains a luminous light over the valley and divide.[18]

Rancher/settler antagonism spread right through the West, and the arm of Washington was not long enough to protect the homesteader. The very fact that the settler was so ready to move on, helped the rancher win. But of course, in the end, the rancher lost, and as Clay accepts with obvious reluctance it was the sodbusters who brought the schools, the churches—and the women—to the West, and who transformed the frontier for better or worse.

The settler had some assistance. In 1873 barbed wire was patented, and that virtually marked the end of the open range. It died slowly, for there were bitter wire-cutting feuds, but the end was in sight when the first fence posts were driven into the earth. Those who resisted fencing were fully aware of what it meant: the end of limitless access to grazing land and the beginning, some felt, of monopoly. A notice posted in a Coleman, Texas street announced:

Down with monopolies! They can't exist in Texas and especially in Coleman County. Away with your foreign capitalists! The range and soil of Texas belongs to the heroes of the South. No monopolies, and don't tax us to school the nigger. Give us homes as God intended and not gates to churches and towns and schools. Above all, give us water for our stock.[19]

Undoubtedly God was for white Texans and against fences. But many small farmers considered barbed wire a means of defining their ownership, and of keeping the big ranchman's cattle off their narrow strips of grazing land.

Some big ranchers were not slow to see the advantages of barbed wire, and in their anxiety to collar for themselves as much grazing land as possible unlawfully fenced vast acreages. Alexander Swan, a most respected figure amongst Wyoming landowners, was prosecuted for fencing eleven sections of federal land in 1883. The *Wyoming Sentinel* remarked, 'Some morning we shall wake up to find that a corporation has run a fence about the boundary line of Wyoming, and all within the same have been notified to move.'[20] Often the fences ran across roads and cattle trails, cut off water, completely surrounded isolated homesteaders caught in the middle of a cattle company's domain. The cowboy reaching down with his wirecutters and clipping the parallel strands of wire is a familiar scene in the Western, but often it was not merely a question of fence cutting. The feuds could be involved and bloody.

Barbed wire meant for the cowboy line-riding rather than cow-herding. The pattern of stock raising began to change. The Western tends to be haphazard in its details of ranching, though some novels have a quantity of authentic detail and information about cattle raising which is of real interest. It is a pity that there is not more, especially on film, as one of the Western's most attractive achievements is its linking of the authentic with the dramatic. Ranching in the late '80s and '90s was a different proposition from the rough and ready business of raising cattle immediately after the Civil War.

The changes did not halt rustling and even after the Johnson County War rustling in Wyoming was a large scale enterprise. The famous Hole in the Wall gang, Butch Cassidy's outfit, was responsible for shifting hundreds of head of cattle between Wyoming and Utah and had an almost impregnable hideout in the upper reaches of the Powder River. George Roy Hill's film *Butch Cassidy and the Sundance Kid* (1969) does not concern itself with the gang's rustling activities, and rustling baddies do tend to be anonymous, frequently caught with the branding iron in their hands and gunned down on sight. William Wellman's *The Oxbow Incident* (based on Walter Van Tilburg Clark's classic novel) is an exception, *Hang 'Em High* another.

The significant point in both is that cattle stealing is considered a hanging business.

In most cattle states stockmen's associations were formed as a means of protection. Stock detectives were employed to hunt down rustlers. One of the most famous of stock detectives—or infamous, depending on which version of his career one accepts—was Tom Horn. As a teenager Tom was hunting Apaches, but by early middle age he was in Wyoming and winning some renown in the employ of the big cattlemen. By some he was considered a ruthless murderer, by others an expert and conscientious frontiersman. He was convicted of killing a young boy in cold blood and was hanged in Cheyenne in 1903 protesting his innocence. The century's last ten years in Wyoming were no less tumultuous than early frontier days although civilisation had ostensibly taken a firm hold.

In a story based on fact which John Clay includes in his memoirs Tom Horn appears as the archetypal frontiersman.

... he kept under cover, shunning the divides, slipping up ravines, diving into canyons, reaching his point by tracks known only to himself. You never knew his movements, and yet he always turned up at the right moment. A strange, incomprehensible being, with sinews of steel, nerves of iron, the cunning of a fox, the pertinasity of a hound. Add to all this the craft of the red man, and you have a dangerous combination either in love or in war.[21]

The story tells how Tom catches redhanded a homesteader who steals and slaughters other men's cows one by one and sells the carcasses to the local butcher. Clay provides a neat illustration of the tyranny of the smallholder, chipping away hundreds of dollars worth of beef from the big herds. There is a similar episode in television's *The Virginian*, only there the Virginian himself moderates and tragedy is averted. The homesteader, instead of being hanged or driven out, comes under the paternalistic wing and all is well.

More vicious probably than the cattleman's wars were the bitter, savage feuds between cattlemen and sheepmen. One of the most bloody of these occurred in the Tonto Basin, Arizona in 1887, between the Tewksbury and Graham families. If there was any form of humanity the cattleman despised more than the nester it was the sheep herder, a man alone, on foot, with only his dogs and his 'stinking woollies' for company. Sheep came to the ranges after cattle were established. They seemed unnatural, trespassers, and did not fit in with accepted methods of stock raising. It was widely believed that sheep destroyed the range and made it useless for grazing cattle. In the cattleman's eyes the sheepman was an even greater threat to his livelihood than the nester.

There have been a number of accounts of the Tewksbury/Graham feud, the most extensive of which is Earle Forrest's *Arizona's Dark and Bloody Ground* (1936). There have also been novels based on the feud—Zane Grey's *To the Last Man*, Dane Coolidge's *The Man Killers* and Amelia Bean's *The Feud*. There have been two film versions of Grey's book, one in 1923 directed by Victor Fleming (who was many years later to direct *Gone with the Wind*), the second in 1933 by Henry Hathaway with Randolph Scott starring. The story clearly held great fascination. Around twenty men were killed. Sheep were shot, driven over cliff edges, and a Navaho herder was killed and beheaded. It was a vicious business sustained by personal grudges and rivalries.

Jack Schaefer has a story, *Miley Bennet*, which illustrates starkly the cattleman's hatred for sheep. Miley is a sheep herder. He is warned by ranchers to get off 'their' land, in fact public range, and when he refuses to go this is what happens.

All three of them pulled high-powered rifles from their saddle scabbards and started towards the sheep. The first shots took the dogs. Then the bullets began ploughing into the flock, tearing through two or three bodies at a time. The sheep screamed their terror and scattered, running their short spurts and huddling in groups, and the bullets followed and ploughed into them. The rifle barrels were hot when the last shells were used and the men came for their horses and rode after the scattered remnants, trampling them as they could ...[22]

Miley takes his revenge by killing some of the men responsible, and later kills himself after being given a life sentence on the grounds that he was crazy. It is a restrained story. Miley, a total outcast, has a blind commitment to his responsibilities and a courage that no one expected of a mere sheep herder. When he tries to reply in kind to a ruthlessness he does not understand he destroys himself. The theme reverses one of the great Western themes. Here the lonely individual far from redeeming the West is destroyed by the West.

Range rivalry has become an issue in many different kinds of Western plots. In the West land has always been a symbol of power and of independence. The control of land means the control of individuals as well as wealth. The range itself becomes a major character. The mystic resonance of phrases like 'free grass', 'virgin land', 'open range', even 'quarter section', contribute forcefully to the land's personality. Land becomes property, but it is also space and freedom. Land becomes politics, but it also nurtures beasts and grows crops.

The full scale range war with all its political implications, that moves far beyond a personal or even local feud, is not often found in the Western. In such a situation it is hard to celebrate the traditional Western hero. A range war can be manipulated for this purpose, and frequently has been (see McLaglen's *Chisum* for the grossest example) but the ugliness, the anti-frontier spirit—the overreaching of the frontier spirit—does not blend easily with the conventional Western. The implications of range war have been avoided. A Western about land hunger in all its brutality and greed, in all its corruptibility, would challenge, much more directly than the present trend in anti-heroic Westerns, many treasured aspects of the myth.

The range cattle industry lived out its last days of glory as it had begun, in struggle and violence. The mighty kings survived, and many still do, but the heyday was over with the sinister events in Johnson County. Cattle raising soon became a matter of fences, jeeps and airplanes, although there still had to be men to care for the cattle and there were still jobs that had to be done on horseback. The contours of the country have not changed nor has the character of the cow. The cowboy earns a bit more and watches television in his leisure hours, but the nature of the work he does has not changed radically.

Neither are the vicious toughs an extinct race. Lee Marvin in *Bad Day at Black Rock*, Newman in Martin Ritt's *Hud* (1963) remind us. The modern version of the Western range war is the union, the company, the land rivalry of today, and hired killing remains a feature. Clyde Barrow operated in the same territory as Jesse James. In the 1930s many ranchers lost their last range war to the Depression, and ironically with their property they lost a way of life. The acute awareness of a not so distant past continues to ache like an old wound.

But these are not our readiest associations with cattle country. The prairies and the cattle on them still have their magic, a magic that suggests an intimacy between man and land, between man and the whole generative cycle that caring for stock implies. The fact that the cowboy's revolver is as ready a tool as his rope adds the appeal of a warrior race. The very nature of the job was full of movement and continually suggestive of violence. The rope and the branding iron, the quirt and the spurs, the power of the horse: these mean not only action but aggression, and legitimate aggression in a business that is noble, profit-making and nation-building. In the early frontier days the massiveness was inspiring and built many of the nation's heroes. In the twentieth century progress has converted much of this into something less attractive, tainted with vulgarity, megalomania and sophisticated violence. Instinctively the Western preserved the original myth.

SIX

Pas de Cheval, Pas de Cowboy

A Western without horses would be as intolerable as one with a
cowboy wearing oxfords instead of boots.

Frank Dobie *The Mustangs*

Fenimore Cooper's Leatherstocking is a frontier hero on foot. He has
a certain distrust of horses. In the New York forests a man can go
where a horse cannot, and a canoe is a handier way of getting about
than a quadruped. But Washington Irving points out that the horseman has something which the frontiersman on foot lacks. 'A man who
bestrides a horse must be essentially different from a man who cowers
in a canoe.' [1] For Irving the later phase of the frontier has a much
greater appeal than the early days of exploring the rivers, lakes and
forests of New York, and this is largely because of the strength and
speed of the horseman.

The equestrian exercises ... in which they are engaged, the nature of the
countries they traverse, vast plains and mountains, pure and exhilarating
in atmospheric qualities, seem to make them physically and mentally a
more lively and mercurial race than the fur traders and trappers of
former days. [2]

Leatherstocking and his Indian companions regard riding almost as
a sign of weakness. In most of Cooper's Leatherstocking novels only
women and, usually inexperienced, Army officers ride horses, and
very often, as in *The Last of the Mohicans* where Hawkeye and
others are trying to escape the vengeance of the Hurons, horses are
a liability. One of the most significant attributes of the early frontiersmen was their ability to travel many miles on foot, swiftly and silently.
The soundless step of the Indian is part of the legend, and the crack-
ing stick is as dramatic as the pistol shot. But this does belong more to
the eastern forests than to the plains of Nebraska, where it is replaced
by the thunder of hoofs.

By the time the legend has moved West the man on foot is, usually
but not always, a debased character. The unhorsed cowboy standing
precariously on his high heeled boots has been deprived of half his
power and several feet of his stature. The cowboy on foot is as vulnerable as the colonel's daughter on her thoroughbred pushing her way

through dense undergrowth in which unseen Iroquois are lurking. But alongside this there is the man who, like Hondo in Louis L'Amour's novel or Randolph Scott in *Western Union*, shoulders his saddle when his horse is shot and walks several miles under a desert sun.

Even Hawkeye predicted that it would be the cavalry that would bring victory over the Indians and the French. And if the cavalryman was ignorant of the terrain over which he waged war he has always had a lustrous attraction. The horse soldier has always been regarded as superior to the foot soldier, from the time when it was a sign of class and status to bestride a horse to the time when illiterate recruits were sent West to get on a horse for the first time and go out and fight Indians. The horseman is taller and faster than the man on foot. But there is more than this in the difference. The horse transforms the man, adds something to his personality and his presence as well as to his stature and his speed.

The horse also provides a means for the man himself to show his power, and even grace and beauty. Here Mrs. Custer describes her husband.

Horse and man seemed one when the general vaulted into the saddle. His body was so lightly poised and so full of swinging, undulating motion, it almost seemed that the wind moved him as it blew over the plain. Yet every nerve was alert and like finely tempered steel, for the muscles and sinews that seemed so pliable were equal to the curbing of the most fiery animal.[3]

An exhibition of fine horsemanship is a splendid sight. The fluidity and control are aesthetically pleasing. But the power and the incipient cruelty of bit and spur are an essential part of the appeal. The horse is bigger, stronger and faster than the man, and if the man can make the horse obey him he has conquered. It is a delight to watch, in reality or on the screen, a relaxed and quietly authoritative rider, in spite of the fact that we know that in the making of many Westerns and large-scale epics hundreds of horses are gratuitously killed.

The excitement lies in the mass charge, or in this kind of thing:

Mr. Oakhurst, a good rider after the Californian fashion, did not check his speed as he approached his destination, but charged the hotel at a gallop, threw his horse on his haunches within a foot of the piazza, and then quietly emerged from the cloud of dust that veiled his dismounting.[4]

A familiar moment, described here with gentle irony by Bret Harte. A man can conquer a horse through sheer strength plus a certain amount of cunning, but it is important that the rider victorious should not cancel out the horse itself as a symbol of power and freedom. Man masters the horse, but he masters it in order to make use of its energy. Man must understand the horse; it is the only way he can tame its behaviour without taming its spirit. There are many moments in Westerns when this understanding between man and horse is reached, and many stories concerned with this process.

There are stories too which feature the indomitable stallion, the most splendid symbol of freedom. The symbolic value of the horse is immense, whether it is the rearing untamed stallion at the beginning of *Hombre* or the Lone Ranger's Silver. The step from the horse as symbol to the horse as hero is a short one. Roy Rogers' gentlemanly Trigger could just about make an arrest single-footed. On the other hand Burt Lancaster's mount in *The Scalphunters* found it hard to distinguish between good and evil and served its master in a far from well-mannered fashion.

On the screen Hopalong Cassidy rode a handsome white horse, alert and well behaved. But in Clarence Mulford's original story Hopalong, not at all the elegant well-dressed screen version, rode a certain Red Eagle whom he addressed in these friendly terms.

'You ugly old wart of a cayuse!' he cried, fighting it viciously as it reared and plunged and bit. 'Don't you know I can lick four like you an' not touch leather! There, that's better. If you bite me again I'll kick yore corrugations in! But we made 'em hit th'trail, didn't we, old hinge-back?'[5]

Of course, swearing at a horse—and Hopalong's language here is mild, if colourful—is a normal part of the relationship. The good Westerner cares for his horse, shares his last drop of water with him, and relies on him. The working cow pony is no longer Trigger, although just as clever at his job. The most admired working beast might well be scrawny and evil-eyed, but he would know his cows, and the relationship between the cowboy and his pony is breathtaking. Although it was as often the rider's savage handling as the mount's voluntary co-operation that produced this impressive partnership.

There was usually no time to be gentle with an unbroken horse. A rider had to take the shortest route to getting the animal to do what was needed, for the horse in the West was far from being the pre-requisite of the leisured classes. The fine-looking, well turned out horse is not in the West a symbol of class and status as we meet him repeatedly in the nineteenth century literature of the Eastern States and Europe. An admired horse is just as likely to belong to an Indian, a hired hand or a gambler as to a gentleman of the eastern variety, and he is likely to be admired for his cleverness and his endurance rather than for his looks or his good behaviour.

The partnership between Western horse and man has often been celebrated, and it is when we are presented with an everyday working relationship that it is at its most impressive. Much of the time we take it for granted, but in a novel such as Walter Van Tilburg Clark's *The Oxbow Incident*, for instance, there emerges a suggestiveness which is not sentimental, but gentle and strenuous at the same time. Art Croft, who narrates the story, on his horse Blue Boy, a horse in no way spectacular, responds to every change in the horse's movement as second nature. He gauges every increase and slackening of effort and adjusts himself to it automatically, and this is described in a subdued, matter-of-fact manner. It is not the way he looks on a horse, so often emphasised by Western writers, but the way he understands which muscles are working and to what end that is important. Care for the horse and understanding of the horse become second nature when the horse is an essential feature of life and livelihood.

Art Croft is just an ordinary man on a horse. He's no hero. But a lot of his personality has to do with his horse and the fact that he is a cowboy who does most of his work on horseback. In general the horse has a great deal to do with the personality of the Western hero. Why is it that the rancher considers himself superior to the farmer? The farmer's job is the more essential of the two. Why is Shane the drifter more attractive than Joe the provider? Why is it that Coogan on a motor bike or even Chandler's Philip Marlowe, whose relationship with his car is reminiscent of the Western hero's with his horse, can never match the romance of undersized, smallpox marked Charles Siringo, Pinkerton detective on horseback?

The horse is certainly part of the picture. On the screen the glowing chestnut of Shane's horse is an inseparable part of the initial impact, although in the book the focus is entirely on the man, and the horse is not described. Only at the end of the story, when Shane rides off into the night for the final showdown, does the horse come into its own, 'a dark and powerful shape etched in the moonlight drifting across the field straight to the man.'[6] And this is appropriate for it is only now that we see the real Shane, and the horse is merged into the whole picture.

He was tall and terrible there in the road, looming up gigantic in the mystic half-light. He was the man I saw that first day, a stranger, dark and forbidding, forging his lone way out of an unknown past in the utter loneliness of his own immovable and instinctive defiance. He was the symbol of all the dim, formless imaginings of danger and terror in the untested realm of human potentialities beyond my understanding. The impact of the menace that marked him was like a physical blow.[7]

Joe the farmer will never be this. His mastery over the earth, always doubtful, will never be so spectacular as mastery over horses and cattle.

And although mastery over machines may appear spectacular, although the motorised Coogan and Marlowe need skill and courage, there is something lacking. A machine can't fight back. A machine has no intelligence. And a machine is powerless without a man to turn it on. A fast car may have a certain grace, but it is nothing like the animal grace of a loping horse.

The sodbuster, celebrated pioneer of the American soil, who risked and endured as much as any man on horseback, does not stand a chance against the cowboy. Even though in fact he won the battle that *Shane* represents, in general if not in particular Wister's 'last romantic figure' was indeed the horseman, and no one, not the racing driver nor the astronaut nor any other hero will make him redundant in our imaginations.

The transformation can occur as soon as a man places his foot in the stirrup. The sheriff in John Sturges' *The Law and Jake Wade* (1958), played by Robert Taylor, is a tediously respectable character in white shirt and string tie driving out to visit his fiancée. But when events put him on a horse he is transformed. When Kirk Douglas leaves his horse in *Lonely Are the Brave* he at once becomes vulnerable. When he regains the saddle we are almost convinced that he really can defeat the machines that are closing in on him. The cliché opening of a lone rider emerging from the landscape is guaranteed to make a certain impact. Hero or villain, his character is broadly defined even before he approaches near enough for us to see his face.

The kind of horse, too, is important. The screen hero is not likely to ride just any old pony. He is going to be partly identified by his horse. Roy Rogers' palomino or the Lone Ranger's grey could be spotted miles away on the black and white screen, so one knew that rescue was at hand even without the surge in the music. The Appaloosa stallion in Sidney J. Furie's *Southwest to Sonora* (1966) was a striking accompaniment to Marlon Brando's understated hero. Not that the horse was pumped full of personality, but the eye-catching freckled spotting of the Appaloosa breed and the need the hero had for the horse gave it visual and dramatic impact.

It is only if the significance of the horse is understood that we can appreciate the full poignancy of a story like Arthur Miller's *The Misfits*, published in 1957 and filmed by John Huston in 1961. Gay and Perce in Miller's story are twentieth century cowboys: they earn a living of sorts by capturing wild mustangs and selling them for meat. They capture horses by using a plane and truck. Here is the debasement of the Western horse. In fact, capturing the horses requires skill and experience. The horses fight back. Gay and Perce are exultant as they swing their ropes from the back of the weaving truck. Their battle with each horse is a test of strength and manhood. The brown stallion fights half-strangled by a rope and with blood trickling from its nostrils.

The stallion's head shoots up and it backs and stands, listening. The moon makes a yellow disk of one eye as Gay comes in from the side and grasps its neck rope in both gloved hands. The horse bares its teeth and gouges for his shoulder, and he slips his hand further down along the rope, murmuring to it, but it suddenly swerves and gallops. Gay wraps the rope around his arm and runs behind, trying to dig in his heels. A quick burst of force yanks him about and he falls. He is being dragged on his side, the talc blinding him. The rope suddenly slackens; he scrambles to his feet and the shoulder of the horse hits the side of his head as it gallops past, and he is pulled to the ground again. He sits up, swinging his boots around in front of him, seeking the clay with his heels. The stallion coughs and wheels, and for a moment stands facing him where he sits. The noose, he knows, is not tight enough to make it wheeze as it does, and he again wraps the rope around his arm digging his heels in and preparing in his mind to roll away if it should charge him there.[8]

Gay defeats the stallion; man's archetypal victory over horse. Perce, earlier on, is thrown by a horse in a rodeo. It's part of his job. Miller, in his story about misfits, three men and a woman fighting for a meaningful existence, handles the two parts of the horse's significance in the Western, the horse as work and the horse as symbol. The horse that throws Perce, a bucking belt pressing against its testicles to guarantee some excitement, is both, and so is the stallion that Gay captures. When Gay, in the end, cuts the stallion loose, this does not undermine the power of the battle, or the fact that in twentieth century terms it was nothing more than a test of individual guts which has meaning only on a personal level, not on the more suggestive level of myth.

The modern Western is bound to be concerned in some way with just this: the disintegration of the individual's value as myth. And the horse is bound to be important here, because whatever else a modern Western may be about it is inevitably concerned to some extent with the fact that the horse is obsolete, or nearly so. The bucking broncho is still a money-making spectacle, and the market for horsemeat continues. The cowpony still has some uses and there have to be mounts for the dude ranch. But the horse's significance as an important factor in myth-building has in the twentieth century shrunk immeasurably.

For this reason the Western horse is all the more likely to go on existing. The power of a myth that has its origins in the past increases as the possibilities for recreating the myth diminish. Of course there have been horseless, or virtually horseless, Westerns. *High Noon* and *The Man Who Shot Liberty Valance*, already cited as highly successful town Westerns, are almost by definition nearly horseless. Their effect relies to a great extent on the limitations of a small town. There is a sense of menace, of being unable to escape.

In *High Noon* the absence of horseback hero or villain characterises the film. Although the gunmen arrive in town on horses, their leader comes in on a train, and Gary Cooper as the sheriff, dressed in black for his wedding, walks the town's dusty street. The measure of his journey, from main street to the railroad station, is significant. No wide open spaces here. Gary Cooper's determined tread with its air of heavy responsibility is memorable, and it is a reminder that the most classic of all Western situations, the walk-down, takes place on foot.

This and a number of other classic westerns are dramas of the gun rather than of the horse. Still, the horses are there, as part of the scenery. A glimpse down main street shows them tied to hitching rails, an occasional rider loping past, a team pulling a buckboard. They are a feature of life even if we don't actually see the hero astride one. Very often the Western's environment is more heavily populated by horses than by people. Even in the turn-of-the-century Western *Death of a Gunfighter* the sheriff mounts his horse, with some weariness, and patrols the streets of the town every night. The horse is an essential part of the sheriff's profession. The mayor's bright yellow automobile will scare it out of its wits, but the horse is as constant a factor in the sheriff's life as is the gun.

The movie's attitude to the obsolescent sheriff is equivocal—it is not a very satisfactory movie partly for this reason. But if there is one thing that does doom the sheriff to dying with his century it is his horse, and the kind of life his horse represents not his gun. Although progress can do without the horse the gun remains essential.

The horseless Western deprives us of the chase on horseback which is in some ways an even more obligatory feature of the Western than the walk-down. The bark of a pistol mingling with the thunder of hoofs is a pattern of sound we all recognise. It hardly matters that the chances of hitting a moving horseman with a pistol fired from a galloping horse were highly remote. The chase is wholly absorbing and not without variation. The posse pursuing the outlaw, Indians after the Pony Express rider, the gang of thugs on the sheriff's tail, or the duel between good man and bad: the speed of horse over landscape is in itself enough to make these enduring situations.

It is the combination of horse and gun power that contains the unshakeable appeal. The attraction lies in the speed, the force and the deadliness. The Indian comes into his own here, for he is the expert at horseback killing. From the end of the eighteenth century the horse was an essential part of his mode of warfare. The screen Sioux can kill with rifle, arrow or lance from his galloping pony guiding the animal only with his heels. The U.S. Cavalry were much less versatile. They might discharge their pistols, but the cavalry charge traditionally relied on close quarter fighting with the sabre, if indeed it was possible for the men to halt their crazed horses when they encountered the enemy.

The charge rivals the chase in excitement. The flow of Indians in feathers and warpaint from the crest of the hill is a splendid sight, and very often too much for a director to resist. The bugle call and the massing of blue uniforms to the rescue has a similar appeal. One horse may transform its single rider, hundreds of horses can achieve a multiple, dazzling magnificence. It does not matter whether it is a Cheyenne, a Teutonic knight or a Tartar riding the horse. The effect is the same, as so many screen epics have illustrated, movies which often owe a great deal to the Western style.

The charge means battle, death, heroism. General Custer with sabre raised and golden locks flying at the head of the Seventh Cavalry. The impetuous, frantic movement of the horses is enough to suggest violence and terror even if no one is actually killed. The striking of the hoofs and the shaking of the earth and the accompanying yells are sufficient noise of battle without the explosion of revolvers and cannon. With the cavalry charge the boiling excitement of battle is present, which is impossible in the trenches of later forms of warfare.

Captain Fetterman galloped off from Fort Phil Kearney in pursuit of the Sioux as if he were on a fox hunt. Having a good gallop on a powerful horse becomes mingled with bloodlust. The enthusiasm may be boyish, but the intent is murderous. There was nothing like a full-scale cavalry charge to make it easier to kill.

'Charge!' came the word of command, and Rostov felt the droop of Rook's hindquarters as he broke into a gallop.

Anticipating his horse's movements, Rostov became more and more elated. He had noticed a solitary tree ahead. At first this tree had been in the very centre of the line that had seemed so terrible. But now they had crossed that line and not only had nothing terrible happened but on the contrary it was all jollier and more exciting every moment. 'Oh, won't I slash at them!' thought Rostov, gripping the hilt of his sabre.'

This is no Western, but Tolstoy's *War and Peace*, describing a battle in Austria when the Russians were fighting Napoleon. It describes both the elation and the curious unreality of the charge.

'Hurr-a-a-ah!' roared cheering voices.

'Let anyone come my way now,' thought Rostov, driving his spurs into

Rook and allowing him to go full gallop so that they outstripped the others. Ahead the enemy were already visible. Suddenly something like a wide birch-broom seemed to sweep over the squadron. Rostov lifted his sabre ready to strike, but at that instant Nikitenko, the trooper who was riding in front of him veered aside, and Rostov felt himself as in a dream being carried forward at an unnatural pace yet not moving from the spot.[10]

Again the horse transforms the man. It is hard to be a coward in the midst of a cavalry charge, and the impetus is likely to make it that much easier to be brave, or cruel. Would Custer have killed so many women and children on the banks of the Washita in 1868 if he and his men had been on foot?

The distant ring of the bugle sounding the charge and the appearance of the U.S. Cavalry galloping over the horizon is a familiar, and these days usually ironically greeted, moment. It is hard, though, to find a really stirring description in the literature of the West, a description that communicates successfully the mass surge of power. Custer himself at times attempts to do this in his autobiographical *My Life on the Plains* (1874) but without much impact, though he may well have been a better writer than general. In both occupations a confident flamboyance is much in evidence. There is no doubt that here there can be little competition between the movie and the written word, unless we are dealing with a writer of the solid visual imagination and working sensitivity of Tolstoy. To see and hear the massed movement of horses, even larger than life and in glossy technicolour, tells us more than all but the very best written descriptions.

This is one reason why the horse confirms the necessity of the screen Western and why, conversely, the screen Western is prolonging the life of the written Western. Whatever we read we can translate into terms of the screen image. Our imaginations are irrevocably influenced by what the cinema shows us, and it is the celluloid image of a man on a horse that gives an extra dimension to the written word rather than the man on a horse that we may occasionally see. As Frank Dobie says:

The horse dilated the imaginations of the Indian as it had dilated the imaginations of millions viewing him horsed. It elevated him in pride and put motion into his spirits commensurate with that of his mount galloping over grass through which he had once crawled up to his game. It put him on a par with the Tartars, the Parthians, the gauchos, the cowboys of the open range and all the other free riders of remembrance whose very names stir the gasolined and the seated towards a life of movement, freedom and spaces.[11]

It is the movie above all that presents to us the tantalising vision of 'movement, freedom and spaces'. The Indian adopted the horse as, perhaps, we would all like to adopt the horse. The trans-Mississippi Indian became an expert rider and was proud of his horses. Horse racing and horse stealing were major activities. The horse seems to be a natural extension of the Indian, and he rides in the same sinuous, effortless manner in which he moves on foot. Unlike the cowboy, the unhorsed Indian is not deprived of half his manhood. The Indian hero has a cool dignity on foot, and although the horse is necessary to him, he does not seem to need the horse to complete his personality.

Both Indian and white man could treat their horses with great cruelty. The horse had to be as tough as the man, and although the Spanish ponies of the West were toughened by hardship they also had to accustom themselves to bit and spur and long endurance. If a pony was worked to death it was not hard to get hold of another. A cowboy could buy a decent animal for forty or fifty dollars, an unbroken one for ten. The gear and equipment would probably cost him rather more. Charlie Siringo paid twenty seven dollars for his first saddle, but a fancy tooled and silvered affair might have cost him a hundred. A Plains Indian would make his own saddle of wood and rawhide which was not at all comfortable for the horse. At the time when Siringo paid his twenty seven dollars he was earning fifteen a month, so it was a substantial outlay.

A handsome saddle and bridle of tooled leather gleaming with silver inlay is a part of the glamorous version of the cowboy's style. The horse's trappings, in the same way as the man's dress, are an important part of the complete picture of the Westerner. The heavy thirty pound saddle, the bedroll and slicker tied on behind, the rifle scabbard, all these contribute to the overall impression of tough, reliable masculinity. The flat Eastern saddle just does not have this kind of suggestiveness, apart from being wholly inappropriate. The wide rings of a snaffle bit suggest a gentle creature that would never need rigorous checking while the hanging metal of the Western spade bit indicates a horse of spirit and toughness.

To ride for many hours over rough country and under a baking sun required endurance in the rider as well as in the horse. Many Westerns are centrally concerned with the ability simply to last out under difficult conditions. There are many tests for the young initiate: to stay in the saddle for hour after hour, to go without water, to go on foot to rest the horse, and specific testing situations which have to be faced. They are all part of the battle for survival, in which the horse plays so vital a part.

Charlie Siringo, whose book *A Texas Cowboy* (1885) has for many years been an established classic of Western memoirs, writes of his horses, especially of his favourite Whisky Peet, with a canny affection. Some of the others were Croppy, Comanche, Last Chance, Creeping

Moses, Gotch, Damfido and Beat-and-be-damned. A splendid roll call. Beat-and-be-damned was 'shot full of arrows because he wouldn't hurry while being driven off by a band of Indians who had made a raid on the camp.' [12] It's hard to imagine a suitable fate for Creeping Moses. Siringo writes of his horses in exactly the same way as he writes of the men with whom he worked. They were clearly just as, or perhaps more, important.

Whisky Peet was a race horse and won his owner several fat prizes. Sam Bass, the young outlaw from Indiana famed in song and story, was a racing addict too, and raced his mare Jenny in Texas and Indian Territory. She was a good horse and it was a profitable business, but he soon moved on to more challenging enterprises. Both Siringo and Sam Bass raced their horses against Indians, who were fanatical horse racers. For Sam Bass it was a useful apprenticeship for his later activities. For Siringo it was a handy way to make a quick dollar when he was broke.

So the speed and prowess of the horse was important, and the rider could share in the horse's glory. Literature and art have always treated the horse as a noble animal, and part of the reason is that the nobility sheds so readily onto the rider. The warhorse raking its forehoof on the ground reflects the courage of the soldier. The white horse of Napoleon or the black steed Walter Scott describes as the mount of 'Bonnie Dundee' reflect the ambition and generalship of their riders. The superbly stylised shining beasts that Stubbs painted reflect the ordered conventions of the eighteenth century English gentleman. Noble horse was owned and controlled by noble man. The Western horse takes us right through the spectrum, from the horse as a kind of gentleman's gentleman to the horse as a version of the noble savage, akin to the romantic, plunging creatures of Géricault and Delacroix. But even Stubbs' horses suggest an air of tolerance, as if the horse had consented to be tamed but not been forced, and rarely, if ever, does the Westerner's horse lose his wild potential.

If the horse is an intrinsic part of the Western, and of the epic, he is also a highly important feature of historical fiction of all kinds. This the masters of the historic novel, such as Scott and Tolstoy, recognised, and the writers of second rate historical romance continue to recognise. If the hero is on a horse he is half way towards convincing the reader of an irresistible manliness. If he is a cavalry officer, even better. (It may seem ludicrous to associate Scott and Tolstoy with such crudity but it is certainly true that they both use the horse to its fullest advantage, and with great knowledge, and the effect is essentially the same.)

Regardless of what the horse can do for a man's masculinity, and also for a woman's authority, the horse looks good. On the screen, patterned against a landscape that is itself stunning, the horse can look even better. Most of the strikingly memorable visual moments in the screen Western involve the horse, the horse in movement in relation to a static landscape. John Ford trails his horse soldiers in silhouette against a darkening sky in *The Horse Soldiers* (1959), a corny shot perhaps, but still magnificent. Robert Mulligan positions dark horses in geometric relationship against a burningly pale desert in *The Stalking Moon*. The black and white ripple of Indian ponies patterned the silent screen in a manner scarcely less striking.

The movement of horse and rider over a land that man must conquer suggests that the horseman has already won a private victory. Riding into the sunset when the drama is over, or riding out of the wilderness when it opens, has its own appropriate symbolism. When near the beginning of Elia Kazan's *Viva Zapata!* (1952) we see one man on a white horse and everyone else on foot we don't need any further clue for our indentification of the hero. That is him, in spite of his peasant garb, on a horse and in swift motion. His transformation later into an authoritative figure in tight black pants with silver conchos, wielding rifle and pistol, is merely the fulfilment of the inevitable. When Joseph Conrad's Nostromo rides through the streets on his white horse he does not need to act in order to prove his superiority. The horse has already done this for him.

SEVEN

The Law of the Gun

'My court can kill as thorough as your guns when killing's the proper answer.'

Jack Schaefer *First Blood*

We killed a few of the worst bad men
For the pleasure of seeing them kick.

'The Cowboy'

[1]

The gunfight has become a feature of the Western landscape, as natural to the hills and prairies as the cow or the horse. A man needs a gun to protect himself against the hazards of the country, and in order to live off the country. By implication a man who does not carry a gun is a man who is not able to fend for himself or cope with natural dangers. The idea that the gun is a vital tool necessary to every true Westerner has never died. It is still present in the twentieth century version of the Westerner, it is still present in that type of hero we associate with Hemingway, the hunter who knows and loves the country, who can live off the fish he catches and the duck he shoots.

The implications of the gun are self-evident. Every man who carries a gun knows he is carrying a weapon that can kill, and sooner or later he is likely to find a situation in which he can use it. If such a situation cannot be found, it may well be manufactured. We learn to distinguish the good man with a gun from the bad man with a gun, and this distinction is crucial to our enjoyment of the Western. According to the mythic code the bad man will crouch behind a rock, rub dirt on the barrel of his rifle so that the glint won't betray him, and shoot a man in the back. The good man will face his enemy and make sure his enemy is facing him. He will call out to warn him before he draws and fires. These are the rules of the game. It is a clear-cut code which provides a fair-minded, gentlemanly licence to kill. In the West killing in self-defence, even if you provoked your enemy to draw on you, was always justifiable homicide. 'You dirty, lying Yankee,' says the quick tempered Southerner in *Shane*. 'Prove it,' says Wilson, the hired gun. They both draw and fire and the one-time Rebel is dead in the mud. With a smile of satisfaction Wilson turns away. Self-defence.

America resists the anarchy of her past. The great days of the frontier, when people were filling up the territories and law and formal government lagged far behind, were days of vigorous independence. And independence, a word used so often by those who extoll the frontier period as the most significant in the development of the country's character, is very often only a euphemism for anarchy, while anarchy itself covered much that was vicious and violent as well as creative and determined. As fast as the West moved into the era of automobiles and oil wells the man who killed was woven into the tapestry of the gun culture. The frontier gunman is now regarded as a craftsman whose actions were governed by a strict and noble code. The anarchic violence of the West, where to be able to kill was to be able to survive, has been encompassed and to some extent tamed by etiquette. We have been schooled to understand that the man who takes up his Colt in the cause of civilising the West is not the same as the vicious killer of criminal mentality who exploits the frontier's lawlessness.

The code owes much to the Southern gentleman, to the young men who, in antebellum days, inspired by the novels of Sir Walter Scott, rode in imitation medieval tournaments. The sword and the duelling pistol were a part of the Southern gentleman's equipment, and the delicate question of honour was near to his heart. When these proved to be inadequate for the purposes of winning a war many Southerners took them West. The Southerner's sense of honour was almost certainly more influenced by conditions in the West than the West was by Southern chivalry, but nevertheless it has provided a basis for our twentieth century conception of the Western duel. 'Prove it,' says the gunfighter. He plays on a Southerner's concept of honour. An insult must be backed up or shot down. As the protagonists have their revolvers to hand (and the code says you don't shoot an unarmed man) they don't bother with seconds and meeting at dawn—which would anyway be unnecessary as this is a fair fight, within the law such as it is, and if a man dies it won't be murder.

In Stephen Crane's story, *The Bride Comes to Yellow Sky*, Jack Potter the sheriff encounters his ancient enemy Scratchy Wilson. Scratchy has been bolstering up his courage with a few drinks and is all set for the final showdown. But Jack is in a suit, without a gun, and with a young lady on his arm. With some embarrassment he explains to Scratchy that he has just got married. Scratchy is glum. 'I s'pose it's all off now,' he says.[1] The quiet humour of Crane's story is a long way from those legends of the sheriffs and marshals of the rip roaring cow towns and mining camps, where the mortuaries were always crowded and the lawman wasn't expected to last more than a week.

In the earliest days of the Western only the bad and the bullying were actually killed and the tradition of poetic justice was fulsomely present. In fact in the early novels there wasn't a great deal of shooting. The villain was as likely to be vanquished in a fist fight as by a six-shooter. There are often hints that this method is in fact more manly, certainly more civilised, like having a work-out in the Y.M.C.A. gym. It was closer to the experience, or at least the more immediate longings, of the average dime novel reader. But while thousands of readers back East were devouring a tame version of the West—Ned Buntline, who transformed Buffalo Bill into the West's first hero for Eastern consumption, went West in 1868—the frontier itself was moving towards its climax of death by violence, treachery and cunning.

The quarter century that saw the rise of the dime novel, the firm entrenchment of the Westerner as a cultural hero and the progress of Buffalo Bill's Wild West show through the eastern states saw also Indian depredations, vigilante hangings, bloody range wars and the West's most famous gun battles. Not that it was so very tame back East. The same period saw some of America's most violent industrial disputes, the activities of the Ku Klux Klan and the assassination of two presidents. There was an ugliness in this period of progress, and the ugliness did not miraculously vanish with the dawn of the new century.

The excesses of particular lawbreakers, against a background of uncertainty as to what the law actually was, did not appear so remarkable. Clyde Barrow, galloping through Texas on four wheels in the early 1930s, killed and died horribly, but he was carrying on the tradition of the Western outlaw. He robbed banks in the same way, and was trapped and shot down by Texas Rangers in 1934 just as Sam Bass was trapped and shot by Texas Rangers fifty six years before. Most of the West's famous gunslingers met their ends through traps or trickery. Wild Bill Hickok was shot in the back. So was Jesse James. Billy the Kid was shot in the dark when he was probably unarmed and did not even have his boots on. No lawman was going to rely on a fast draw at high noon to despatch a killer.

No one in fact was likely to be anxious to object to the manner in which these men met their deaths. The most civilised of the West's residents calmly upheld the most dubious methods of manslaughter. John Clay writes of a suspected cattle rustler: '... some victim had bored a hole in him with a Winchester bullet and left him alone in some solitary arroyo. The moral stickler of the East would call this murder. Knowing the circumstances, I call it retribution—well merited at that.' [2] Retribution, vengeance: these were essential in the Westerner's unofficial code. The refined version of the code that popular culture has fashioned elevates the seeking of revenge to a noble pursuit. When there was no law, or the law could not be relied upon, a man had to be his own instrument of justice. While the trigger finger tightened or he adjusted the noose under the left ear he was the equal of the Supreme Court. For nearly a century the Western has celebrated the man-hunt and the man hunter. The man who with courage and skill tracks down an outlaw is one of our most constant heroes.

This man should be, and sometimes is, the sheriff. He is the man with the star, with the license to hunt and kill men. But there wasn't always a sheriff where and when he was needed and frequently the individual citizen had to take, or did take, the law into his own hands. And even where there was a sheriff he was often no match for the individual citizen, especially if that citizen had the support of his fellows and did not like the way the sheriff handled things. Many a Western has featured the sheriff who owes his position to the backing of a strong local outfit or, another breed, who protects his prisoner against the fury of a mob demanding instant justice. Jack Schaefer's story *First Blood* (1954) ends with a young deputy killing, in defence of a prisoner of whose guilt there is little doubt, a man whom he has adulated as a hero. The judge refuses to hasten the trial, insisting that it must be carried out with the proper formalities. Without these the law is worth nothing.

Schaefer is a writer who can be relied upon to illuminate but not destroy a rich ambivalence. Race Crim, the deputy's hero, is killed in the name of the law. The law protects a known killer. Crim says, ' "If people around here had the right kind of guts they'd grab him and the other one and swing them quick." ' [3] Guts versus courts. Independent courage versus stale, convoluted legality in which there were so many loopholes that a clever lawyer could get a guilty man off on a technicality.

It did happen. Nowhere is the law foolproof. The context in which the law was struggling is revealed here.

According to Clabe Robinson ... more than forty men were killed in or near Oakville during the ten years following the Civil War. Oakville had a population of perhaps a hundred people; its population has not grown much since. 'During the decade of these murders,' says Mr. Robinson, 'exactly two men were arrested for serious offences and put in the Oakville jail. These two were strangers in Oakville and were charged with an offence in another county. While they were in jail a party of men shot through the window and killed them.' [4]

The gun of the independent hero appears a cleaner force than the sickening hysteria of mob action or the casual killing of the trigger happy. We do have the Western hero who tries not to shoot, or at least not to kill. But we must believe he can shoot if he has to. Ideally we have faith in the healing power of his gun. However, too often the situation was such that the lone individual simply had not the power to mount a single-handed cleaning up operation. For it was not so much a matter of bringing a single desperado to justice, as of changing the habits of the populace. And the hero himself reflects these habits. He becomes the Western's focus partly because he embodies the most appealing form of aggression.

This helps the hero to become independent of the law. Formal law as an instrument of the state or even of the community had at times made only rare appearances in the Western. Even when our hero is a sheriff or marshal he usually becomes an instrument of an emotionally conceived justice rather than the arm of statutory law. His significance does not normally extend beyond the community. The famous sheriffs of the West were men not very different from the men they brought to justice—or briefly despatched. Wyatt Earp, Bat Masterson and others of that ilk tended to be on the right side of the law through convenience rather than conviction. Their function was more to keep a town under some kind of order than to track down seasoned criminals. It was the Texas Rangers, the Pinkerton men, the range detectives and the bounty hunters that were chiefly concerned with the latter occupation. The habitual criminal was frequently dealt with by citizens. The denizens of Northfield, Minnesota opened fire on the Younger gang in 1876 and foiled an attempted bank robbery, and those of Coffeyville, Kansas killed four of the Dalton gang when they tried to rob two banks simultaneously in 1892.

Bob Ford shot Jesse James in the hopes of a two thousand dollar reward. The bounty hunter is one of the most despised actors in the Western drama. Lawman of a kind, his profession is hunting men for a reward, and although he may be as useful to the civilising process as the sheriff or the Lone Ranger he is often presented as a lower form of humanity. The cold-eyed Wiswald in T. T. Flynn's novel *Two Faces West* is as weasely as his name. The hero also hunts and kills men, but the two cannot be compared; Wiswald does it for money. The bounty hunters in *The Wild Bunch* are virtually sub-human, swooping down on the dead like the vultures that so aptly descend as the movie closes. The Pinkerton men, paid, skilled and often ruthless, were in a different category from the town sheriff, known to the community, though much of the hatred directed against the Pinkertons resulted from their strike breaking activities rather than from their man hunting.

The Pinkertons were a highly organised outfit. But a man's life for money cheapens a code in which vengeance is a noble pursuit. However distasteful they were and are now portrayed the bounty hunter and detective had all the skill and determination of the frontier hero. The most impressive sequence in *Butch Cassidy* is the chase, directed with a brilliant and sinister simplicity. The anonymous detectives pursue the two heroes. Their faces remain pale blurs in the distance. But they threateningly convey their presence as men cunning and dedicated in pursuit. 'Who *are* these guys?' Butch and the Kid ask each other. They come on and on. We see the demonic lights of their torches in the darkness. We hear the ominous thud of their horses' hoofs and then, as it fades, the pathetic jingle of the bit of the horse Butch and the Kid are sharing. There are only these intermittent sounds of hoofs, a chinking bridle, a blowing horse, a minimum of terse dialogue, and these increase our awareness of an oppressive silence. Not a single note of music disrupts the perfect tension here.

This is the lawman as the faceless hunter, the anonymous threat, no longer the symbol of virtue in a clear-cut black/white clash. We sense their heroic qualities but we never see them in close-up. They remain distanced, fragmented by the dazzling sun, and unrelentingly dangerous. Because we never see them clearly they are never quite the dubious bounty hunters, but nor do they ever achieve, quite, the legendary quality in this portrayal:

Chivalrous, bold and impetuous in action, he is yet wary and calculating, always impatient of restraint, and sometimes unscrupulous and unmerciful. He is ununiformed and undrilled, and performs his active duties thoroughly, but with little regard to order and system. He is an excellent rider and a dead shot.[5]

This is the Texas Ranger, who fought Mexicans, Indians and outlaws with singular determination. Not everyone was enthusiastic about the Rangers' activities: it is clear that there was a fair amount of irresponsibility and carelessness in their actions.

The stereotype of the good man with a gun that the Western has most thoroughly established is that of the individual as the instrument of a just retribution. He has been there from the earliest appearance of the fictional Buffalo Bill to some of the more sophisticated Westerns of the 'sixties. If he has changed in outward form from the Boy Scout-like Young Wild West through a long series of slick hombres from Tom Mix to television's Virginian to the unwashed masculinity of Marshal John Wayne in *True Grit* (1970, directed by Henry Hathaway), deep inside the pure bright flame of the just man still burns.

This makes the poignancy of movies like *Ride the High Country* (1962), so thoroughly Peckinpah's best, or *Bandolero!* (1967), easily McLaglen's best, helped by the superb music, all the more attractive. Lurking behind the two middle aged gunmen in Peckinpah's film, Randolph Scott rakish and unscrupulous and Joel McCrea more or less respectably employed, consorting in a busy, bursting town with automobiles on the streets, is the shining image of the just man. When in the climactic battle the camera looks up at the two men looming tall and splendid, fighting at last in a just cause and for a younger generation, the superb transference from the scruffy and outdated to the finely heroic owes its impact to this image that flickers through the movie.

In *Bandolero!* the stalwart sheriff, force of law and civilisation against the casual disruptive invasion of outlaws, destroys the two attractive, rootless brothers. Dead and bloody in the dust of a deserted Mexican town death makes them heroes: there is a kind of justice in it. They are victims of the necessity to eliminate all that is untamed and nonconformist. George Roy Hill's Butch Cassidy and Sundance owe a great deal to movies that have presented outlaws as restless misfits, with their own kind of loyalty, their own kind of charm, who are doomed in the face of organised law and encroaching conformity. McLaglen's heroes have something of the same boyish, almost innocent quality that Newman and Redford impart to Butch and the Kid. Dean Martin and James Stewart as the brothers share also the sadness and the bewilderment of the later film, though the reasons are different. They have been betrayed by the past, their roots destroyed by the Civil War. Butch and the Kid are hounded by the future. There are twenty years or so between them. In *Bandolero!* the future is a solid citizen, the honest lawman, and the heroes must die. In *Butch Cassidy* it is a more sinister faceless power, the posse thundering on like a machine, the ranks of anonymous troops whose unnecessary volleys kill the two individuals who have a pathetic faith in their own private skills. The heroes must die, and as they die the camera freezes and bears them out of slaughter into immortality. In neither case do the lawbreakers die at the hands of a glamorous symbol of justice, but the necessity of their deaths is nevertheless subsumed into a larger and deeply satisfying throb of poetic justice. It is the more conventional pattern reversed. Instead of evil being duly destroyed by the just man, the just men destroy themselves because they are superfluous. We would rather they died than became bank clerks or sod busters.

The role of the hero as an instrument of justice lives on, often crudely. He is the man whose whole personality is moulded by his dedication to the cause of retribution, the individual's or the community's. It can be a kind of martyrdom, as it is in Alan Le May's novel *The Smoky Years*. The man must become of steel not through choice but of necessity. Zane Grey's output is densely populated with instruments of justice, men with an aura of dedicated loneliness surrounding them. Grey's heroes usually get their girls, but the mysterious stranger who rights a wrong and rides off is one of the Western's commonest instruments of justice. The very fact of his ambivalence in relation to formal law enhances his romantic value.

[2]

'A gun is just a tool,' Shane says. The tough young actress in Louis L'Amour's *Heller with a Gun* (1955) echoes this. ' "Out here a gun is a tool. Men use them when they have to.... Where there's no law, all the strength can't be left in the hands of the lawless, so good men use guns too." ' [6] The catch is of course, that a good man who kills is no more lawful than a bad man who kills. King Mabry, L'Amour's good man, knows this. He knows too that for a man with a reputation as a gunman the hardest fight of all is to keep on the right side of the law. Another character in the book, Griffin, has lost this particular battle. 'What kind of a man had he become? Once he would have shot a man for even suggesting that he hire his gun. Now was he ready to take money for murder?' [7]

L'Amour is a sophisticated writer who does not caricature the distinction between good and bad. This is no case of the smiling, smooth faced, white hatted Roy Rogers opposed to the bristly, frowning, black hatted villain. Mabry as a hero is sympathetic, Griffin contemptible, but the distance between them is not so very great. The distinction, however, *is* vital. The whole ambience of the Western rests on this distinction. The so-called debunking Westerns of recent years have still relied on it.

There is nothing romantic about a gun or a gunman, Schaefer and L'Amour seem to be saying. And yet simultaneously they both reveal for us superbly romantic figures whose tough, realistic, demanding environment helps to etch their romantic qualities more sharply. Their skill with weapons is a part of their romance. A gun may be a tool, but give a gun to a man who knows how to use it and the result is power.

The gun is not necessarily a serious matter as Mark Twain, probably the first to write in comic vein about the West, reveals. He has had many imitators, and it has always been possible to laugh at guns, shooting and killing.

I was armed to the teeth with a pitiful little Smith & Wesson's seven-shooter, which carried a ball like a homoeopathic pill, and took the whole seven to make a dose for an adult. But I thought it was grand. It appeared to me to be a dangerous weapon. It only had one fault—you could not hit anything with it.[8]

A gun in the hands of the inept or the ignorant is good for a laugh and Western comedy has made a lot of this. In *Roughing It* (1872), from which this passage is taken, Twain recounts similar experiences with a horse and other peculiar institutions of the West. The fact that he himself is so often the victim of his mildly satiric pen blurs the reality that when he made his trip to the Nevada mining camps he was indeed in dangerous country.

Mark Twain could laugh at his Smith and Wesson and find killing —'a dose for an adult'—a subject of humour, but for most Westerners the gun was as essential to survival as the horse, and for fiction's cowboy the gun is as necessary a part of his dress as his pants. Without his gun he is naked. The gun, like the horse, has its effect on the man's presence and personality. To return once more to Shane:

> The tooled cartridge belt nestled around him, riding above the hip on the left, sweeping down on the right to hold the holster snug along the thigh, just as he had said, the gun handle about half way between the wrist and elbow of his right arm hanging there relaxed and ready.
>
> Belt and holster and gun.... These were not things he was wearing or carrying. They were part of him, part of the man, of the full sum of that integrate force that was Shane.[9]

The gun is an adjunct of the body. The description is purposefully physical, and by implication sexual. The gun is an essential feature of the man's manliness. The screen cowboy, his gun resting on his narrow hip, is inviting an awareness of his sexuality. His horse contributes to this too, for while the gun becomes part of the man's sexual apparatus words like mount and ride are ubiquitous in their sexual connotations. But it is the gun that is the most overt symbol of masculinity.

This suggestiveness clearly facilitated the cowboy's appeal at a time when the cinema refrained from explicit sex. Amongst writers the gun as a sexual symbol becomes evident earliest in a writer whose treatment of relationships between the sexes is usually sickeningly coy—Zane Grey. In *Riders of the Purple Sage* Grey dwells continually on his hero's 'dark apparel and the great black gun-sheaths'. The following passage hardly needs comment.

> For answer he unbuckled the heavy cartridge belt, and laid it with the heavy, swinging gun-sheaths in her lap.
>
> 'Lassiter', Jane whispered, as she gazed from him to the black, cold guns. Without them he appeared shorn of strength, defenseless, a smaller man. Was she Delilah? Swiftly, conscious of only one motive—refusal to see this man called craven by his enemies—she rose, and with blundering fingers buckled the belt round his waist where it belonged.[10]

The cowboy unhorsed is vulnerable: the cowboy unarmed is de-sexed. The lady reprieves the gunfighter from impotence. Earlier on

Lassiter has said, ' "Gun-packin' in the west since the Civil War has growed into a kind of moral law. An' out here on this border it's the difference between a man and somethin' not a man." ' [11]

With most Western heroes of the screen the gun is a symbol of at least masculinity, if not of explicit sexuality. In *The Magnificent Seven* (1960), directed by John Sturges, the line-up of gunfighters who defend the Mexican village has an aura of potency that is not only death dealing. The Western would fail in its appeal if it were not continually suggesting a creative force. Of course, in many Western situations life depends on killing. But there is more to it than this. The frontier must not only be tamed but be populated. The man must not only be skilful with his weapons he must be virile—and, conversely, the woman must not only be an attractive diversion, she must be able to bear sons to carry on the struggle. The Western has until quite recently bowed to propriety in matters of sex, but this is hardly important when the audience can rarely be in doubt of the protagonist's sexuality.

There are exceptions of course. The activities of Robert Taylor, hero of *Guns of Wyoming*, in both love and war suggest nothing more exciting than bourgeois sterility. The dramatic moment when he straps on his gun for the final showdown fails to ignite any sparks, and the shooting itself is as if Robert Taylor had indeed said 'Bang, bang, you're dead' and the bad man had obediently tumbled to the ground. A victory for the property owners of Wyoming rather than for lusty manhood.

Lusty manhood is much in evidence in Van Cort's novel *Journey of the Gun* (1966). Within a few pages Clay Rand, the book's young hero, makes love to his first woman and kills his first man. ' " ... that gun of yours ... don't you ever get rid of it ...?" ' murmurs the prostitute. Then, later: 'The gun smoked in Clay's hand. He did not even recall firing it; had not felt the jump of steel as the deadly leaden bullet smacked its way out of the barrel and at its target.' [12] The two experiences blend to confirm Clay's manhood. Clay Rand the killer is the same as Clay Rand the lover, and it is quite clear why women admire him.

This partly explains why the gun is a significant counter measure to the loneliness of the long distance rider. Men may want to kill him but women admire him. Even those who fear or despise him realise what the gun stands for. In *Liberty Valance* Hallie (Vera Miles) fully realises her love for the lawyer from the East *after* he has supposedly killed Valance. She may love him because he represents a civilised, educated life, but he still must prove that his manhood can match up to the demands of the old West. The real man of the West is John Wayne as cowboy Tom Doniphon. He is the cool, tough, but funda-

1 *Above:* The real Wild Bill Hickok, 1873 *(Photo: The Mercaldo archive)*

2 *Above:* Emma Hickok, famous Wild West show rider and stepdaughter of Wild Bill *(Photo: The Mercaldo archive)*

3 Kirk Douglas in *Lonely are the Brave* (*A Universal Picture. By courtesy of the distributors Cinema International Corporation*)

4 *Above:* Jesse James in death. This picture was taken just before he was placed in his $500 coffin. *(Photo: The Mercaldo archive)*

5 *Above:* Roy Rogers, one of the many stars who played Jesse on the screen

6 *Above:* 'The mysterious stranger with the hint of an unacceptable past'. Scene from *Shane* starring Alan Ladd. *(A Paramount Picture. By courtesy of the distributors Cinema International Corporation)*

7 *Below:* 'Tension concentrates in a single street'. Still from *High Noon (Amanda Films Ltd/NTA Inc.)*

8 *Above:* A real-life marshal, Wyatt Earp, 1885 *(Photo: Copyright Stuart N. Lake)*

9 *Below:* 'Marshal' John Wayne in *True Grit* *(A Paramount Picture. By courtesy of the distributors Cinema International Corporation)*

NAME, GEORGE PARKER, alias "BUTCH" CASSIDY, alias GEORGE
CASSIDY, alias INGERFIELD.

AGE, 36 years (1901).	HEIGHT, 5 ft., 9 inches.
WEIGHT, 165 lbs.	BUILD, Medium.
COMPLEXION, light.	COLOR OF HAIR, flaxen.
EYES, blue.	MUSTACHE, sandy, if any.
NATIONALITY, American.	OCCUPATION, cowboy, rustler.

CRIMINAL OCCUPATION, bank robber and highwayman, cattle and horse
thief.

MARKS, two cuts scars back of head, small scar under left eye, small brown
mole calf of leg.

"BUTCH" CASSIDY is known as a criminal principally in Wyoming,
Utah, Idaho, Colorado and Nevada and has served time in Wyoming State
penitentiary at Laramie for grand larceny, but was pardoned January 19th, 1896.

10 *Above:* Pinkerton Detective Agency's mug shot and wanted poster for the real Butch Cassidy

11 *Below:* Still from *Butch Cassidy and the Sundance Kid* starring Paul Newman and Robert Redford *(By courtesy of Twentieth Century-Fox Company Ltd)*

12 and 13 *Above left:* Calamity Jane, 'Crude, frequently drunk and unparticular about whom she shared her bed with' *(Photo: National Archives)*. *Above right:* The chocolate-box heroine. Bardot in *Shalako (By courtesy of EMI Film Distributors Ltd)*

14 The Lone Ranger. 'The glossy and glorified version of the saddle tramp'

mentally gentle gunman, although he dies forgotten in his bed.

The outlaw gunman can be as attractive as the man upholding the law—even more so, perhaps, as there is very often the added attraction of the lonely outcast. It is no accident that *Firecreek*'s outlaw leader is more sympathetic than the stalwart homesteader. His gun contributes to this as well as his horse. His gun symbolises his leadership as well as his power and, in this case, is a foil to his gentleness and the fact that his strength is reduced—for he is wounded—as well as continually reminding us of his deadliness. The wounded outlaw, wrapped in bandages, tended by a beautiful woman, his gun taken from his hip: there is an appealing piquancy in such a situation.

There are sometimes heroes who successfully combine the qualities of gunfighter and civilised living, without compromising their vitality by the latter. Some screen actors are particularly good at this: Gary Cooper is one. A number of Ernest Haycox's heroes manage it—in fact this achievement tends to be their trademark. Haycox is a novelist of some skill, and he presents with authority heroes who possess the possibly dubious combination of sophisticated, educated Easterner and skilled, courageous Westerner. Kern Shafter in *Bugles in the Afternoon* is a polite Southerner who belongs to the West by right of experience as a man of action. He enjoys a good fight but at heart he is a gentleman. He has all the tough qualities of the Western hero, but these don't destroy his sensitivity. Tom Gillette, the younger hero of *Free Grass*, is a native Westerner but educated in the East. Whatever else the East has taught him he has learnt not to underrate the man of the West who can ride and shoot and protect his own.

Why should it be necessary for the Western to lean to the East in order to prove the qualities of the West? The answer is clear. The gunman is not being extolled for his own sake, although for his own sake he may have attractions on the screen. He plays his significant role because he is necessary to the process of civilising the West—which does not mean making it a place fit for Eastern dudes, but a place for families, women and children, schools and churches, for the owning of property and the making of money. The gun destroys threats to this kind of stability. The gun protects.

[3]

Young Wild West and his two pals Cheyenne Charlie and Jim Dart ride into Border Bend. This is *Young Wild West's Whirlwind Riders* by An Old Scout, published in 1903. Their first task becomes clear when they see the town bully in action.

Look out, thar, ye pesky gimcracks! I'm goin' to begin shootin' right away! I'm a whistlin' streak when I git agoin', an' I feel one of my spells comin' on now. I'm goin' to trim ther eyebrows of some of you fellers with bullets. Look out, thar, now! Every time I shoot I expect to see a greaser jump nine feet in ther air! I'm Buster Bill, ther boss of Border Bend, an' when I git mad I spit out red hot coals. Ther fun is goin' to begin! Here she goes!'

Crack! Crack! Crack! [13]

Needless to say, Young Wild West, 'a specimen of the true boy of the Wild West' soon puts a stop to this. ' "Stop that!" thundered the handsome young fellow, his dark eyes flashing dangerously. "Hold up your hands, you cowardly coyote! Up with them, or off goes the top of your head." ' [14]

Young Wild West doesn't shoot off the top of the boss of Border Bend's head. He usually prefers to beat people up with his fists or shoot the guns out of their hands. The violence lies only in the words. However, the distance between the threat and its accomplishment is only a matter of degree. From the threat of Young Wild West, the boy scout hero, to Lee Van Cleef in *The Good, the Bad and the Ugly* shooting a man in the face through a pillow is not much more than a step.

It is hard to believe that the classic gunfight between two foes will ever cease to be a staple of the Western as long as the Western exists in a recognisable form. Even in *The Good, the Bad and the Ugly* Clint Eastwood is ultimately victorious in a stark three-cornered duel which owes much of its effect to its combination of conventionality and the range of possibilities the situation offers. It was really the screen that discovered the clean lines of what we now think of as the classic walk-down, the two men slowly approaching each other on the deserted main street and the sudden explosion of their guns. One cannot help but go back to *High Noon* for the perfect rendering, a profoundly satisfying climax to a spare, crystal clear film.

There is an unhappy contrast in *The Last Sunset*, a movie which hardly contains promise of the much better pictures Aldrich has made since. A lush Western, with Rock Hudson in his bad old days of spastic acting and Kirk Douglas trying desperately hard to do justice to what was apparently intended as a psychological portrait of a gun-fighter: it ends as *High Noon* ends. The two men, one in dramatic black the other in light grey, approach each other on foot. It is sunset, not noon this time, and the already harsh colour of the film is strained further by a garish red light. Kirk Douglas bites the dust and sheriff Rock Hudson stands with his smoking gun looking surprised. The camera looks down on the sprawling figure, the upright Texan, the deserted street. Two women rush to their lovers. The camera lingers on the touching scene.

A classic situation saturated to the point of total sogginess. But even second-rate screen gunfights are generally superior to what can be achieved in fiction, for so much depends on a total visual effect. Young Wild West's 'Crack! Crack! Crack!' will hardly do. The sound, too, is a part of the impact. If the shooting in the silent Westerns at times seems perfunctory it is partly due to the absence of sound. We see William S. Hart, grim-faced and tight-lipped, with both guns drawn—in *The Gunfighter* (1917), for instance, which he also directed—and suddenly there is a body on the ground without us being aware that a shot has been fired.

The shooting is equally perfunctory in the written Western of these early years, as it almost certainly was in reality: scruffy, disorganised, muddled street shootings, Wild Bill Hickok killing his best friend by mistake. The great build-up drawing the protagonists face to face is generally absent from real life confrontations. In Wister's *The Virginian* the hero has no illusions that Trampas (in the original novel Trampas is a villain: television has translated him) who has already shot a man in the back, is going to play the game according to the code. He comes out into main street with caution, making sure that no one can get him from behind. And it is not the Virginian who draws first—there is no chance that we can call this murder.

A wind seemed to blow his sleeve off his arm, and he replied to it, and saw Trampas pitch forward. He saw Trampas raise his arm from the ground and fall again, and lie there this time, still. A little smoke was rising from the pistol on the ground, and he looked at his own, and saw the smoke flowing upward out of it.[15]

It is described as if in a dream, the effect is to dull the violence. The Virginian has done his duty according to the code by which he lives, which would not let him rest until he had defended an insult against himself and killed a known murderer. The argument of the schoolteacher from Vermont, whom he is going to marry, has no place in Wyoming. 'There's something better than shedding blood in cold blood. Only think what it means. Only think of having to remember such a thing! Why, it's what they hang people for! It's murder!'[16] For the Virginian it is easier to have murder on his mind than the accusation of cowardice.

Ernest Haycox's picture of the classic duel is perhaps more honest —he is not so oversensitive about the good character of his hero as Wister is—but it almost certainly owes something to the screen, written at a time when twenty years of screen Westerns had evolved an easily recognisable mode. Here is the climactic fight in *Free Grass*.

Nothing was said between them; that time had come when there were no words to carry any meaning either would understand. They were, the both of them, thrown back on instinct, back to the stark and ancient promptings. So they closed the interval, and for all the emotion they displayed they were as men coming up to shake hands. San Saba's body swayed forward of his feet, and his little nut round head nodded. Gillette advanced erect, watching how the ex-foreman's eyes grew narrower at each pace. Time dissolved into space and, save for the sound of his own boots striking, he would never have known himself to be moving. Somewhere a spectator coughed, the sunlight grew dim, the spotted dog ran between them. And then all his range of vision was cut off and he saw only San Saba. San Saba had stopped. His arm rose slowly away from his belt; a bull whip snapped twice, sounding to Gillette strangely like guns exploding. The spotted dog raced back, barking, and men ran out into the street and made a circle round a San Saba who had disappeared. Gillette stood alone, wondering. His arm felt unusually heavy, and he looked down to find a gun swinging from his fist; the taste of powder smoke was in his throat.[17]

There is still the dream-like quality, as if to emphasise that heroism is ingrained, not calculated. The effect here is intensely visual, and it is this as much as the pattern of the fight that suggests a debt to the cinema. Tom Gillette stands alone and lonely, after his killing. The Virginian, having slain the villain, is surrounded and congratulated by the townspeople.

Quite a different kind of thing is J. T. Edson's description of a gun duel in *The Ysabel Kid* (1968). Here is a killing with no pretence that readers don't enjoy a picture of violent death.

Flame tore from the barrel of the Ysabel Kid's rifle. Giss felt the sudden shocking impact as lead struck him. He reared up and through the whirling pain haze saw the Kid get up, take out a bullet and push it towards the breechplate of his rifle. Then the Kid lifted his weapon again, his right eye sighted along the smooth blue barrel, and his finger squeezed the trigger lovingly. Even though Giss was staggering, the Ysabel Kid shot and hit. Giss rocked back on his heels, threw his rifle to one side and crumpled forward. He lay there on top of the Lookout Rock dead without ever finding out how he came to make the mistake which cost him his life.[18]

The mechanics of killing are here. Not only that—the killer, the hero, derives a certain satisfaction from what he does. He is revenging the death of his father and this, even if we can charitably believe that he does not normally get pleasure out of killing, adds something to the moment when he pulls the trigger. Gillette is also killing his father's murderer, but Haycox does not allow him to enjoy his revenge.

Just as it is a short step from the threat of violence to the acting out of violence in hideous detail, so there is not much to divide the necessity of killing from the joy of killing. If according to the code it is necessary for Gillette and the Ysabel Kid to kill their fathers' murderers the code is flexible enough to allow them some pleasure out of their revenge. If on the frontier death by violence is a fact of life it is as well to be skilled in death dealing, and only natural that one should come to take some pleasure in one's skill. The more the insistence on the gun's neutrality as a tool the more natural it is that the good man should enjoy using it skilfully. The charming Sundance Kid takes a quiet pride in his breathtaking ability with guns, though George Roy Hill's film does not allow us to think that he actually enjoys killing. Shooting is both an art and a way of life for him, and he takes it completely for granted. The film is clever here, and skilfully tricks the audience by depending on a well-schooled reaction to the Western hero and at the same time continually inviting a fresh reaction and a fresh enjoyment of Western material.

The staccato ballet of the full-scale street battle can rival single combat in tension, if in the hands of a good director. One of the best in this area is Howard Hawks. Two of the screens most memorable street gun fights occur in *Rio Bravo* and *El Dorado*. Hawks' street fights are never static, and this is an essential feature of their success. His moving gunmen, hunting for cover or hunting for prey amidst the bare apparatus of town living, characterise his fights. In *El Dorado* the night time battle is swept into the gaunt interior of a white washed church where the gloom and the empty echo add grimly to the total effect. One of the shot foe tumbles from the top of the tunnel-like bell tower. The most famous of all town fights is probably the one at the O.K. corral that took place in Tombstone in 1881. It has featured frequently on the screen, but as in reality it only lasted sixty seconds there is not much that can be done with the fight itself. Ford had a try at what he considered the authentic version in *My Darling Clementine* (1946) and Sturges has had two attempts with different emphases— *Gunfight at the O.K. Corral* (1957) and *Hour of the Gun* (1967), of which the former is much superior. Inevitably these movies are more concerned with the circumstances surrounding the fight than the fight itself, although they all attempt to set it up in detail 'the way it was'.

When the gun battle moves out into the country there are the added dimensions of horses and landscapes. The chase with its wildly inaccurate shooting tends to be confined to the B Westerns of the 1940s. Much more impressive are those elemental conflicts with the terrain itself contributing to the outcome, what we get so satisfyingly in Anthony Mann's Westerns. The weapons, the rifle shots, the rocks and the hatred compose the naked conflict at the end of *Winchester '73* The harshness and the taut deliberation of Mann's climax is quite different from the almost delicate treatment of the final duel in *Rough Night in Jericho* in which George Peppard and Dean Martin stalk each other through shimmering saplings and pale green foliage. With Indian skill they move amongst the trees, each with the knowledge that the other is his equal in this final test. As Dean Martin lies dying with a knife in his breast he recognises that he lost in a fair game. The death is satisfactory. The wounded hero pulls himself onto his horse and having killed a man and freed a town rides back to the comely widow who awaits him.

In the frontier context it is almost impossible to argue the gun away. We yet await the weaponless frontier hero: probably, he cannot exist. In the movie *Friendly Persuasion*, directed by William Wyler (1956), even a Quaker's principles are not sufficient to stand up to the challenge of the gun. The film, while poking gentle fun at Quaker beliefs, appears to extoll them. In fact, what it is saying is that non-violence does not and cannot make sense. If men have principles they must fight for them and die for them. Principles otherwise have no meaning. If men oppose slavery they must take up arms. If men want to protect their homes from marauding guerrilla bands they must take up arms. Wyler poses the dilemma with some honesty, yet the most revealing moment in the film is when Gary Cooper, as the head of a Quaker family, decides that he must fight and opens a cupboard in his bedroom fortuitously stocked with rifles and ammunition. If the weapons are there it is only too easy to use them. We realise that the law of the gun has been operating at the heart of the vigorously peaceful Quaker family, and the film itself does not seem to recognise this. Or rather, it is simply taken for granted: a Quaker family on a well-established, profitable farm needs to be able to shoot.

The gun culture is self-perpetuating even without the kind of justification that 'the good man with a gun' lends it. It has perpetuated itself into the 1970s without any difficulty. The father teaches the son to shoot. Guns breed guns. If the ritual words are self-defence the ritual feeling is that of manliness. Once again, if the gun culture is taken out of the context of the Old West its character changes. What is not always realised is that myth can only genuinely perpetuate itself in words and celluloid, not through reality. No amount of contemporary reenactment and imitation will bring the Old West back.

EIGHT

Vigilance and Violence

... kill or be killed, and Walt had done the only thing he could,
quickly, unthinkingly, as instinctively as an animal would.

Lewis Patten *Valley of Violent Men*

'I'm an American in an honest business, I reckon. And I'll fight
for it.'

Luke Short *Hurricane Range*

[1]

In Walter Van Tilburg Clark's justly classic story *The Oxbow Incident*
a posse of men ride out to seek justice for the killing of a cowboy
and the rustling of cattle. They are citizens, not lawmen, and they
hang three men. It is the mid-1880s. Events are witnessed through
the neutral eyes of Art, a young cowboy who, being wounded, is
hors de combat, and being a stranger, is uncommitted.

Much of the story's force lies in the way that Clark shows, through
a neutral non-heroic observer who only obliquely guides our sym-
pathies, that the entire action was wrong from the moment the posse
began to gather in the main street of Bridger's Wells, long before it was
discovered, too late, that the men were innocent and the 'dead' cowboy
only slightly wounded. Clark always keeps to the particular. He makes
no general comment on justice and the law. He controls the tone of
stunned incomprehension in the narrator so that it reflects on all the
participants: none of them really understand the implications of what
they have done ' "My God," ' says Gil, Art's friend. ' "I knew it didn't
feel right. I knew we should wait." ' [1] When they discover their mistake they are sick and angry, but they are all guilty. They all know
they could have stopped it.

The incident involves the entire community. Gil and Art do not
belong to the town, and they can ride out, glad to get away, hoping to
forget. Those who remain are all implicated. The sheriff who appears
on the scene too late is ready to collude. ' "I haven't recognised anybody here. We passed in a snowstorm and I was in a hurry." ' [2] Even
the judge is more concerned with 'the good name of the valley and of

the state' than with incontrovertible facts. The law is helpless in the face of the majority.

It is a community crime and Western individualism is unable to challenge it. In Clark's story frontier aggression is seen in its most sinister form, that of mob vengeance. Individualism is present only in terms of the mob leader and his dominance over the others. Independence is seen only in terms of freedom from formal law. Clark's story is restrained, detailed in its location in a Western environment, positive in its refusal to generalise, which strengthens its implications. It is, above all, a highly ominous story. It was filmed in 1942 by William Wellman without any loss to its point, although some feel that it is not Wellman's best Western.

This is what Clark himself said about the book.

The book was written in 1937 and '38 when the whole world was getting increasingly worried about Hitler and the Nazis, and emotionally it stemmed from my part of this worrying. A number of the reviewers commented on the parallel when the book came out in 1940, saw it as something approaching an allegory of the unscrupulous and brutal Nazi methods, and as a warning against the dangers of temporising and of hoping to oppose such a force with reason, argument and the democratic approach. They did not see however, or at least I don't remember that any of them mentioned it (and that *did* scare me), although it was certainly obvious, the whole substance and surface of the story, that it was a kind of American Nazism that I was talking about. I had the parallel in mind all right, but what I was most afraid of was not the German Nazis, or even the Bund, but that ever-present element in any society which can always be led to act the same way, to use authoritarian methods to oppose authoritarian methods.

What I wanted to say was, 'It can happen here. It has happened here, in minor but sufficiently indicative ways, a great many times.[3]

As Clark says so unequivocally the Oxbow incident was, in its way, typical. It illustrated not only an element in society but a feature of frontier life. Killing the killer, extra-legal action: and the only way in which the lynching could have been stopped would have been if someone had pulled a gun. The would-be killers stopped by threat of killing. The dilemma is presented with total clarity, and the only way out is to acknowledge, as Clark clearly intends, that vigilante lynching is wrong, under any circumstances, however patent the victim's guilt.

It is wrong because the logical implications of such action spread far beyond any localised issue. Themes of justice are the Western's most challenging. They tend to be the most ambiguous. Much of the myth's material relies on the fudging of this specific issue, and right and wrong are presented in appealing symbolic terms rather than in genuinely moral terms. Situation and realism can reinforce a positive identification of good and bad, and a particular, limited judgement is vital. But an overall moral judgement is generally avoided, has to be avoided. The conventional Western can mould the amoral into symbols of good and bad without much thought for the Olympian heights of moral judgement, and can evade the law while doing so.

The Oxbow Incident is so effective because through a carefully localised incident it operates right outside the Western context. Few Westerns even attempt to do this. This is part of their charm, but also a cause of dismissal. A fairly recent Western that does attempt a moral view that is not specifically tied down to the Western context is Richard Brooks' *The Professionals* (1966). The band of professional toughs and killers sent on a mission that has the appearance of respectability, to rescue the kidnapped wife of a railroad tycoon, we judge both within and beyond the Western environment. Their courage and skill in the face of frontier difficulties reveal their stature as people rather than as limited heroes. They perform their mission successfully, but when they discover that the luscious Claudia Cardinale was forced into marriage they return her to the Mexican bandit kidnapper, whom she loves. The professionals win both as toughs and as people and in the process avoid Western stereotyping.

It helps to illuminate the spurious realism of *The Virginian*. Wister's southern gentleman never has to face the consequences of his morality. The stern law of necessity requires him to kill his enemy on the day before his marriage to the fastidious school teacher. Earlier in the book the Virginian has lynched two rustlers, and this is Wister's weakest moment. He blandly sidesteps all the issues. His hero is presented as a man of courage who makes himself responsible for a distasteful but necessary job. The narrator, Wister himself more or less, sees his own Eastern sensibilities as a kind of cowardice. 'How could I tell them that I shrunk from any contact with what they were doing, although I knew that only so could justice be dealt in this country? Their wholesome frontier nerves knew nothing of such refinements.' [4]

Refinement equals inferiority: Wister's admission of it is his excuse for being involved in a dubious episode. The lynching is carried out, off-stage, and the Virginian is deeply troubled, but not so deeply that he feels he has actually done wrong. Stoically he bears the pain. Wister broods a little over the dark cottonwoods where the deed was done but he is not so indecorous as to let us witness the hanging. If we had seen what the Virginian did it would be hard for him to remain unsullied in our eyes. Wister, sliding over the essentials, withdraws not only the Virginian and himself but also his readers from responsibility.

It constitutes a serious flaw in Wister's novel, so much admired and enjoyed. And it demonstrates with simplicity the argument *for* fictional and screen violence: there are times when to push known violence out of sight is irresponsible. In general the Western presents violence in a context and within a convention that is acceptable, and does not find it necessary to justify violent action. The frontier context is sufficient justification. Wister, in trying to make the West palatable to the East, interferes with both the Western context and Eastern susceptibilities.

In Ted Post's film *Hang 'Em High* we see another aspect of Western justice presented without oversensitivity. One of the climactic scenes involves the legal hanging of six assorted murderers, rapists and cattle rustlers in Fort Grant (clearly based on Fort Smith, Arkansas, the famous Judge Parker's stamping ground) in front of thousands of hymn singing spectators. The sequence is based on fact: Parker's public executions were much like this. We see them also in Henry Hathaway's *True Grit*, in which the names are not changed. It is both a holiday occasion, with candy sellers doing a brisk trade in the streets, and a moment of great solemnity. The crescendo of prayer and song leads to the moment when the traps are sprung and the six men are expertly dead. The film has opened with a private and much speedier lynching.

It is impossible to state unequivocally that legality is always preferable. A blanket condemnation of vigilante action is difficult to justify. Vigilance committees have always been a dubious feature of American history, especially where their tendency has been to supplant the law rather than act where no law exists. But in the mining camps of California, and later on in Montana, where there was no law except for what the residents themselves organised, and where the quantities of gold and cash were a constant temptation, there was no alternative but to act without reference to legality. When in 1864 Henry Plummer and his gang were hanged by vigilantes it would have been hard to question the justice of what they did. The community rid itself of a disruptive force. The frontier was full of situations where it had to act for itself or perish, or become totally degraded by violence and corruption. Yet one historian of the frontier states categorically that at that time 'Montana was sufficiently settled ... for men to have recourse to law.'

But in *Death of a Gunfighter* the community acts for itself and kills the sheriff because, ironically, he is a symbol of frontier violence. We see him in action: when a hunted man takes a shot at him he shoots to kill. The citizens don't like it. Their town, they feel, has grown out of such rough justice. Frontier habits die hard. If the nearest lawman is several days ride away is that a justification of hanging? If a horse thief is caught red handed who will blame his captors for carrying out the traditional penalty of hanging there and then? If a rustler is caught with a branding iron or a stage robber with gold in his saddle bags, is it not simply frontier justice, hard but in its way merciful, sparing the torture of jail and trial, to execute these men on the spot? And if the band of hired detectives meet up with Butch Cassidy is it not better to shoot him down than to make an arrest and bring him back for trial? Either way, they will collect the bounty money.

It is because this summary justice becomes a habit rather than an exigency that we must regard it with suspicion. It is not just that innocent men may be despatched by the hasty decision of a posse of citizens: officially constituted law is not infallible and has undoubtedly sent innocent men to the grave. But there is a point at which the habit becomes a threat even to the most untamed community, rather than a protection, and a point at which it becomes, if it was not always, intrinsically self-destructive. It is a habit of independent action that turns very sour as soon as the law officially takes over from the individual. It leaves too many opportunities for questioning the efficiency and impartiality of the law.

The law had a hard struggle. It could be seen as challenging the basis of the frontier ethic, that frontier people could look after themselves, do things their own way without the interference of the envious East. Westerners fought their own battles, suffered, endured: many felt they had won the right of independent action. In the face of corrupt lawmen, frightened witnesses, slow courts, and pressures from the East the old West did not give up easily.

Wayne Gard, who has written extensively on frontier justice, says this about vigilante action.

In the early West, vigilance committees and people's courts, which were characteristic particularly of the California gold camps were spontaneous expressions of the American spirit of democracy. They showed that men in isolated communities could cope with a difficult social problem without waiting for formal action from the outside. Their activities contrasted sharply with the lynching bees of the South. The latter usually represented a deliberate flouting of statutory laws and of elected officials who ... were able and ready to handle the situation. The informal actions in the West, on the other hand, were not a mockery of the law, because there was no effective law. They were the only alternative to anarchy in places where statutory law did not prevail. They were the forerunners of the established courts.[6]

But informal action did not give way gracefully to formal law, and at this point it became very much akin to Southern vigilantism. As late as 1884 in Caldwell, Kansas a suspected arsonist was lynched in spite of the presence of mayor, sheriff and county attorney. In 1888 Theodore Roosevelt was relating, with a certain pride, how 'notorious bullies and murderers have been taken out and hung, while the bands of horse thieves have been regularly hunted down and destroyed in pitched fights by parties of armed cowboys.'.⁷ Just as the Southern lynchers justified themselves (when they bothered with justifications at all) by claiming that the authorities, cramped by legality, could not handle the situation, so some independent Westerners kicked against hamstrung formality.

When in the opening sequence of *Hang 'Em High* an innocent man is lynched (to be cut down in the nick of time) it is not through any particular malice but rather a near automatic acting out of vengeance, with which justice is so often confused. Here the very force which might in other circumstances have been a threat to anarchy has become an instrument of anarchy, because in this case law does exist. There is a court, a judge and a jail, and officers of the law.

Hang 'Em High illustrates alternatives of justice and vengeance—lynching, private revenge, killing inspired by fear of exposure and retribution and killing in self-defence, the operation of formal law and its corollary, public execution. It illustrates them without any obvious preference. If the public execution seems sickening, with the judge murmuring religious platitudes at his window, we can see just how and why the vast crowd is drawn into the emotional experience of official death. If Judge Fenton seems ruthless in his commitment to the death sentence he is sincere—and probably right—in his belief that it was the only way to bring some sort of order to a territory swarming with criminality. If Clint Eastwood as Marshal Cooper seems icily vicious in his man-hunting we can sympathise with his motives for revenge. And when finally revenge has brought him to a commitment to the law as represented by the Judge, in spite of the fact that he believes the gun to be a cleaner instrument of death than the noose and the celebration of public hanging sickens him, we have to accept that he has no choice. His motives of personal revenge are trapped by the law into working for the law.

On the frontier even formal justice has to be savage. The implications of Cooper's transformation into dedicated lawman are that the frontier can only be tamed if men are prepared to move beyond the personal and individual. There is a revealing paradox here. Clint Eastwood becomes ultimately a symbol of officialdom, Eastern civilisation, Fort Grant reaching its tentacles westwards into untamed territory. He makes the transition from far-riding do-gooder to policeman who must always act with reference to what he represents, but achieves this without losing any of his frontier qualities. Cooper is the law, but he never seems to be quite the law that Fenton is. The law roaming freely through anarchy can never be quite the same as the law contained by the four walls of a court room.

The real Judge Parker was as ruthless as any self-appointed vigilance committee. He sent out his marshals from Fort Smith to bring in by the cart load every variety of criminal. Parker was a dedicated man: in twenty one years he sentenced one hundred and sixty men to death, and seventy nine of them were duly hanged. He established, as no single man was able to do anywhere else in the West, the power of the Court. He was no man-hunter himself, and without the framework of the law which he represented he as an individual counted for nothing. But historically he was the West's most effective embodiment not only of formal law but of the individual as a weapon of justice. His dedication and his self-denial were absolute, and even if we can face the seventy nine hangings without flinching this fact alone is disturbing.

'This court is but the humble instrument to aid in the execution of that divine justice which has ever decided that he who takes what he cannot return—the life of another human being—shall lose his own,' Parker said.[8] His very humility gives him an authority which is less attractive than the authority of the gun. Simultaneously he is abdicating his responsibility as an individual—which the authentic Western hero can never do—and enlarging it. He reminds us of what the far-riding, quick shooting instrument of justice is not and confirms that men such as he can never be admitted into our gallery of Western heroes. Divine law is always a dangerous quantity to invoke: the Western hero does not need to call on anything less tangible than steel and horseflesh in support of his actions.

Formal law can be savage. It can also be fallible. Who is to question its morality? The independent just man can be a ruthless killer, but in the Western context it is up to him to demonstrate that he is right. One factor, amongst others, helps him: if he makes a mistake he has only himself to blame. If the law fails, an entire system is at fault. Yet the just man cannot escape the structure of the law that trails him. At the end of *Southwest to Sonora* Marlon Brando wins horse and girl. He acts in a moral and courageous fashion, retrieves stolen property, stands up for the poor and helpless, yet it is an intense and personal fight, crude and ruthless. The laborious complexities of civilised behaviour would have been ludicrous in the spare landscape and the struggling homestead. But all the same, has not Marlon Brando, riding his pretty Appaloosa, dogged, taciturn, struck a blow for the law's bureaucratic army which will soon follow the trail of his retributive ride? He has demonstrated that those who act against human life and property need not win. The law backs his instincts if not his authority.

[2]

In a situation when vigilance enacts violent punishment and formal justice repeats the pattern with the stamp of legality it is inevitable that the habit of violent retribution becomes ingrained. Officers of the law had a license to behave exactly as the murderers they hunted. (The situation is not confined to frontier America.) Personal vengeance, a staple theme of the Western, is virtually endorsed by a law that takes its own revenge on those who threaten its authority. Of course vigilantism and all that it implies did threaten the law's authority, and hence the ambivalence that has been woven into the violence of the Western myth. The extra-legal hero has established himself as a freely operating figure. Although he must not be seen to challenge the law directly, except where the law itself is corrupt, he does contain an implicit threat to the formal, the static and the conventional. Substantially, that is why he is so admired.

The hero is allowed to kill. The Western convention allows us to see him in action and defines these actions generally in a stylised and recognisable fashion. Other warrior heroes within other conventions are also allowed to kill. But the camera brings us closer to killing than we are ever likely to be in the normal course of life. The camera presents a literal intimacy. The Western convention operating at its best presents a moral intimacy: we are shown not only how a man dies but *why* he dies. It is the operation of this moral intimacy that very often distinguishes the good Western from the inferior. A certain kind of perfunctory righteous killing has characterised the second-rate Western for a long time. Matt Dillon, marshal of Dodge City in the television serial *Gunsmoke*, kills three men. Who are they, what are they—nothing but shapes in the dust. There is no death in any meaningful way because there was no life. The shapes only existed in order to be shot down by the marshal.

Convention plays strange tricks on the quality of our belief. On the stage we do not expect realism, nor would it help our understanding. If blood spurts we know it is not real. On the screen we are more likely to believe that it is; we are more likely to believe what our eyes see. And it is just this that makes the whole question of screen realism of such interest. Stylisation of language, acting, verse form, stage set, can all increase our perception of death, which is why the increasingly common claim of Westerns, that 'this is the way things really were' is irrelevant to the Western form. Without interpretation—even good documentaries must be interpretative—reality means little. Like all other forms a great deal of the Western's effect relies on stylisation and convention, and because of the intimacy of the camera the operation of these factors is crucial. A director like Anthony Mann is impressive because he makes both the intimacy and the conventions work.

In recent years the Western's much discussed realism has attempted to ask from the audience a new response to the portrayal of killing. But it has not destroyed the basic convention, which is that the Western is a type of heroic drama about men killing and being killed. No elaborate attempts to manufacture real killing can destroy the precept on which the Western has always relied: that in the Western killing is, to a greater or lesser degree, acceptable. Killing is a heroic way of life. Movies such as Arthur Penn's *Little Big Man*, greeted as an anti-heroic Western, continue to uphold this.

What is crucial is not the degree of bloody realism (although anything that is patently fudged or inconsistent is disastrous) but what we know and what we care about the protagonists. We care less about an anonymous redskin than we do about a noble, tortured hero. Of course, the Western has exploited this inevitable lack of caring to the full. The unknown, the insignificant, the shape the camera passes over, can die unnoticed. This hardly alters even when the camera focuses in mid-battle on a face we have never seen before and shows it dissolving in blood. In general, it is nasty to see human flesh decimated, in particular it means nothing.

The way we care depends on the moral impulse of the book or film concerned. Traditionally the moral impulse of the Western has relied on an easily recognisable confrontation between good and bad, with variations on this theme—the bad man with a heart of gold, the good man with a fatal weakness (drink perhaps) or a fatal ignorance. Acknowledging that life surrounds us with violence, and even the smallest child speedily grasps this, it provides some relief to find in the Western the legitimising of violence. Here is the good, who is allowed to kill with impunity, and here is the bad, who is punished. (The bad can be identified through his lawbreaking, his viciousness, his relish of killing, his lack of respect for women and so on.) The 'realistic' Western starts from this point. The hero is allowed to kill, though less often with impunity. Death is not necessarily less perfunctory, but it is messier. Crucially, it is still possible to distinguish the good from the bad, and as soon as a Western crops up in which this appears to be difficult, reviewers begin to murmur about the form's demise.

Yet the acknowledgement of the violence observed and experienced in daily life (and surely no one would deny this) can serve as an opening into areas of crude and facile violence which are much more questionable. Sam Peckinpah justifies the violence in his films by saying 'You can't really escape it anywhere.'[9] But the reality of violence in life does not automatically render it meaningful, acceptable or of any point whatsoever in art. The maker himself must do that.

Western writers and directors create and imitate violence: do they do this effectively and appropriately? Do they, especially in the case of a director like Peckinpah who appears to be attempting through violence some positive illustration, relate this violence in any meaningful way to the violence the audience lives with?

Peckinpah creates difficulties for he both relies on the conventions of the Western and attempts to undermine them. Without the long life of the traditional Western to support it—and to support us, the suffering audience—the finale of *The Wild Bunch* would be repulsively pointless. (Whether it is in fact anything other than that is arguable.) When, in *The Magnificent Seven*, we see the knife-thrower's weapon protruding from the breast of his victim we experience shock, but instantly accept this death as proper. The code is clear and accepted. It is a perfect illustration of the Western code and the acceptable death. It is violence brought within well defined limits and made understandable. Of course we know that violence is usually not brought within well defined limits and made understandable, but art is not life and realism not reality, and part of the purpose of even so unintellectual an art as the Western is to translate and interpret life's confusions.

Establishing violence within a convention is not necessarily related to our enjoyment of it, or to the assumptions made about our enjoyment. Our relish for blood on the page or the screen is often said to be akin to our relish for sex. Blood means thrills. It has probably had a more consistent place in art of all kinds than sex, and the Western has often deliberately angled its appeal in terms of blood.

Surrounded by a screaming horde of Indians soaked in the blood of the 7th. Cavalry, two men sworn to a lifelong hatred made a final accounting of their feud on the body-strewn grass of the Little Big Horn ...[10]

Now, he vowed, he would get himself a gun, and make others learn the meaning of fear. And he didn't care how many lives he had to take in order to teach his bloody lesson ...[11]

These are the blurbs of two Western novels. The contents are not half as blood soaked as these suggest, but the assumption is that the readers will be attracted by 'the body-strewn grass of the Little Big Horn' to read on. What is being promised here? Action, a word which has become a euphemism for violence: excitement, a vague word, inevitably these days suggestive of sex: most precisely killing. For hundreds of years there has been art and literature founded on the assumption that people like to see and read about death by violence—and that other people like to write about it and paint it and, now, recreate it and film it. Are those of us who are not homicidal maniacs continually repressing a passionate desire to decimate human flesh? Or is it simply that we gain a vicarious but insignificant thrill from seeing others act out the forbidden? Or have we perhaps been conned by the convention itself into believing that we enjoy it?

A significant feature of the Western is that it compresses degrees of violence. Anger may mean a punch in the nose or it may mean a bullet in the heart. The distance between death and a black eye is telescoped. The response to mild provocation is extreme and threats are not only made but carried out, unlike the real world where an intricate structure of confrontation by threat prevails without the serious intention of implementation, although there is always that possibility. There is an insidious attraction in the Western's straightforwardness: it is a part of its predictability. When the gunslinger threatens to drill you full of holes, he drills you full of holes.

When at the end of *The Wild Bunch* the four gunmen walk out to their death the movie is depending on the audience's acceptance of the logic of this enactment of all that the four men stand for. If the audience is allowed to see it as a totally negative gesture the entire movie is a failure. If the audience sees these men, in spite of their ruthlessness and irresponsibility, as anything but heroes then the bloodbath that follows is simply the worst kind of cheap and vicious indulgence. The parallel with the finale of Peckinpah's earlier Western *Ride the High Country* is illuminating. There the two heroes rise larger than life to the occasion acting out their roles as gunfighters according to their tradition and the demands of the situation. The moment is a splendid crystallisation of the Western's heroic convention. In the later movie there is a very similar shot of the four walking abreast, the camera looking up at them, heroes calmly balancing their weapons. A man's gotta do what he's gotta do. As in *Ride the High Country* it is a stylisation of the mainstream Western heroic code: the effect is immediately shattered by massacre which precipitately reverses the mode of the film, wrenches it around so that it is biting its own tail. It is impossible to care any longer about who dies or how (God forbid that we should ask why) or which piece of mutilated flesh belongs to whom.

Although most of us probably wince at the gruesome reconstruction in a book like Truman Capote's *In Cold Blood* we can witness violence on the screen or read about it in fiction without being moved in any way. The language of violence is cliché ridden and often no more expressive than the standard 'Wham' and 'Ug' of the comic strips. When, for instance, in the disappointingly flaccid book *The War Wagon* (the movie was so good) Clair Huffaker describes a fight, it is hard to have any reaction.

Instead of retreating, Taw lunged forward at an angle to meet him, shoving the scythe blade up at the contorted face above him. The tip of the blade ripped the breed's arm, and the sharp edge swept on up, slashing deep across the middle of his nose.

The victim is a half breed, face 'contorted', victim 'ripped' and 'slashed'. The description continues.

Iron Eyes' gasp was an agonised, almost whistling intake of air as he dropped to his knees and grabbed at his cut face. Switching the heavy handle of the scythe to use it as a club, Taw swung it in a mighty blow that caught the other man behind the ear, crunching savagely against the bone.[12]

This is instant predigested violence, an assortment of flavourless thuds and crunches which make little impression. All that is conveyed, and we find this in the more stilted Western movies too, is a sense of the complete lack of participation of the protagonists.

The Spoilers, directed by Rex Beach, 1914, provided the first screen version of an all out climactic punch-up between hero and villain. John Wayne claims to be the first really to hit the man he was fighting and certainly some of his fights do have a powerful sense of physical contact. It is this that makes the fist fight so much more brutal than the gunfight. A man can be killed by a bullet at a great distance. A knife can be thrown. But to damage a man with bare fists means intimate contact. The close quarter mutilation of Brando's gunhand in *One Eyed Jacks* (1961), directed by Brando, is infinitely more savage than shooting. So the fist fight, which in the early days of Young Wild West and other boy scout heroes was the accepted mode of conflict, is in some ways more vicious, more indicative of aggression and a love of fighting, than bullets. Fist fighting has often been extolled as a noble art: brain as well as brawn is necessary for success. And it is interesting to reflect that in these days of armchair annihilation, when thousands of faceless human beings can be killed without doing anything more energetic or skilled than pressing a button, there is something to be said for face to face brutality.

Within the Western convention the fist fight is definitely an inferior type of contest, but it appears regularly and no Western hero worth his salt would shun one. The bar-room brawl in particular, with its broken chairs, smashed glass, spilt whisky and bleeding lips, is a set piece. Unlike the gunfight there are no rules in this game, and the fist fight can vary from a fairly good natured brawl to a deadly contest. A variation can be introduced with the use of improvised weapons, chairs very often, bottles, pitchforks and other such implements felicitously to hand. On a more sophisticated level there is the snaking bull whip wielded by Slim Pickens in *Rough Night in Jericho*, sinister but not in the end effective, for in spite of it Pickens is battered to death.

The criterion for a good punch-up on the screen is not the quantity of action or damage, but the intensity with which it is enacted. John Wayne is always purposeful, although that embarrassing struggle between the two old fellows at the end of *Chisum* was a terrible nadir for the Wayne vigour to descend to. Clint Eastwood achieves a naked intensity in his fights, which heightens the brutality. Anthony Mann's taut direction gives his fights their particular distinction. There is no negligence in their presentation, nothing dispensable. There is an emotional necessity in the fighting, which transforms the Western's inevitable reliance on generalised material.

[3]

It is only fairly recently that Westerns have been so consistently denied to child audiences and this is as much because of the sex as because of the blood. No one has seriously questioned the conventionalisation of violence in the Western. Television Westerns are still mostly catering for younger audiences, which tends to mean not that there is no killing but that the dead are either anonymous or patently evil, and they die swiftly often in the dark or the shadows. Whether this is more desirable than obvious brutality is debatable. Even the so-called adult series such as *The Virginian* or *The High Chaparral* (it is surely significant that *The Virginian* has been shown earlier and earlier as its life is prolonged with every kind of artificial aid) have little in them to offend. Even the nastier sorts of death on the television screen cannot compare with larger than life Panavision.

The Western is unique in the way it has established a convention, rising directly from frontier experience, that simultaneously subverts long standing moral and social codes and affirms a prototype of the American, and ultimately universal, hero. The Western allows 'moral' killing outside the law and even provides exemplars of extra-legal killing with a moral. Heroes, of course, have always killed. It is only comparatively recently that literature's heroes have striven on the battlefields of love rather than of war. But war has always been a proper occupation for a gentleman, and to kill in the name of king or country or faith or union is perfectly acceptable in the traditions of art. The Western hero, however, kills in the name of something more ambiguous, often himself (personal revenge), sometimes progress (social revenge). If he kills for a community it is generally because he is a gunman and has a reputation as well as human lives to defend. In *The Magnificent Seven* some of the seven eventually feel involved in the village they are defending, but their initial motives were the wish for money and action. They were gunmen at a time when the need for their guns was growing less and less.

On one level we can think of the mythic West as a gigantic battlefield where every man had to prove himself as a warrior. Until recently every age has developed a means of making war acceptable. Society has clothed the soldier in codes and uniforms, glorified him, glamourised him and stylised his actions. The gruesome horrors of the battlefield are controlled for general consumption by the spit and polish and the parades. In a similar fashion the gruesome horrors of violence in the West have been controlled, defined and limited by legend's evolution of the cowboy as a heroic type. Not only does this mean that we can accept and enjoy violence, it encourages us to view history through the lens of legend, and justify violence. As John Ford says, not the way it was, but the way it ought to have been.

America launched dramatically on a course of violent history and violence continued to be the logic of its existence, its development and its expansion. As historians have pointed out, Americans are fascinated by their violent history, 'The remarkably tenacious appeal of the Leatherstocking saga and the wild western surely reflect an abiding romantic fascination with our violence-prone frontier origins.' [13]

Joe B. Frantz in an essay on 'The Frontier Tradition: An Invitation to Violence' describes an incident in which, in 1872, three mounted men robbed the gate takings at the Kansas City Fair. During the incident a small girl was shot in the leg. This was what a reporter of the *Kansas City Times* had to say of the incident: '... so diabolically daring and so utterly in contempt of fear that we are bound to admire it and revere its perpetrators.... It was as though three bandits had come to us from storied Odenwald, with the halo of medieval chivalry upon their garments and shown us how things were done that poets sing of. Nowhere else in the United States or in the civilised world, probably, could this thing have been done.' [14]

With such encouragement to adulate the lawlessness of its own present the frontier was hardly likely to be restrained. 'Nowhere else in the civilised world...': the frontier implicitly prided itself on fusing two contradictions, on bringing civilisation rapidly and upholding the anarchic individualism of a lawless world. The totally unrealistic elevation of outlaws to heroes went side by side with the fact that the response to violence was more violence. This has always been the inherent contradiction of the law but in the West it was much more pronounced. The vigilante tradition encouraged (and still does encourage) the individual to act out retribution for himself, and communities to make their own law.

To murderers, confidence men, thieves.
The citizens of Las Vegas are tired of robbery, murder, and other crimes that have made this town a byword in every civilised community. They have resolved to put a stop to crime even if in obtaining that end they have to forget the law, and resort to a speedier justice than it will afford. All such characters are, therefore, notified that they must either leave this town or conform themselves to the requirement of law, or they will be summarily dealt with. The flow of blood MUST and SHALL be stopped in this community, and good citizens of both the old and new towns have determined to stop it if they have to HANG by the strong arm of FORCE every violator of law in this country.

Vigilantes.[15]

This was New Mexico 1880. (The parochial concern is much in evidence. As long as the 'murderers, confidence men and thieves' left town, presumably to operate somewhere else, the citizens of Las Vegas would be satisfied. They were concerned with the good name of their own town, not with bringing an end to frontier lawlessness.) Instead of the admiration of daring law breakers, heroes in the old tradition, there is a kind of self-admiration amongst the vigilantes who will adopt the violent ways of heroes to counteract the violent way of desperadoes. The two responses are not entirely different. 'Perhaps the most important result of vigilantism has not been its social-stabilising effect but the subtle way in which it persistently undermined our respect for the law by its repeated insistence that there are times when we may choose to obey the law or not.'[16]

Not only does America, and the West in particular, have a violent heritage, it admires this heritage. The individual still believes he must be allowed to defend himself with lethal weapons. He still believes he has a right to subvert the law. The Western code, nourished, fostered, exploited and enlarged by fiction and the film, can only encourage this belief. There is always the possibility that movies such as *The Wild Bunch* and *Bonnie and Clyde* will encourage an admiration of violence, not so much in making us want to imitate the actions portrayed but in their reinforcement of America's violent tradition. When Sam Peckinpah talks about his own attitude to violence there is a hint of self-admiration. 'It has a marvellous ending. Everybody dies. But they always do in my pictures.'[17]

The admiration of the desperado is not a curious phenomenon. Many societies have traditionally admired their bandits, seen often as legitimate rebels against an oppressive social order. The natural corollary of our admiration for the man who faces death is an admiration of the man who inflicts death, for almost always facing death means accepting the possibility of killing. But this kind of admiration is tempered by the fact that violence in the Western has usually been domesticated, housetrained even. The gun can fit into the role of husband and father, even Quaker, as easily as the role of outlaw, sheriff, gambler or cattleman. It goes with the clothes, the horse, the landscape, the false-fronted saloons. And with the near-homeliness of the gun goes the near-homeliness of violence. The gun becomes homely because the Western convention exists to prevent us pondering the implications of what we see.

We enjoy the ritualised gun duel, the clash of Sioux and cavalry, the wide screen epic charge and the flickering black and white chase. They all have their own kind of viable stylisation. We see these things often in symbolic terms, the clash of good and evil, of progress and barbarism. The victims are bad men who deserve to die or good men who die in a good cause. The way in which they die reflects their desserts. In *Hondo* the good Indian dies cleanly and the bad Indian bloodily. In *The Searchers* the deaths of the white family are savage and shocking, thus indicating the extent of their martyrdom and the savageness of the white heroes' opponents.

Part of the attempt to split the Western convention, a genuine attempt in many cases to inject an old form with new meaning, has been a growing preoccupation with how people die and how people kill, with the look of death. It is the mutilation of human flesh and the agony that we are shown. There have been attempts to make us understand not only the viciousness but the horrifying naturalness of the killer. It is this that is worrying in a film like Arthur Penn's *Bonnie and Clyde*. It is not that in *Bonnie and Clyde* we see a celebration of killing, but that we see how easy it is to kill. Given that people carry weapons there is no surprise in the fact that they are used. From the moment that Clyde produces his pistol there is an alarming logic in the killings, a logic that we tend to accept unthinkingly even while we are shocked.

In the case of directors who are concerned with telling us something about human violence, as both Peckinpah and Arthur Penn are, it is arguable that the more visual the emphasis on the results of violence, the less the focus on killing as a human impulse and violence as reality. When at the end of Don Siegel's *Two Mules for Sister Sara* there is the standard Mexican massacre with a close-up of a face being sliced by a sabre the whole thing is meaningless in both human and cinematic terms. It is not simply that the sequence is distasteful —it is pointless. The violence is gratuitous because it fails artistically. As a contrast, *Bonnie and Clyde* is a very carefully controlled film and it is precisely the exhilaration of killing that is deliberately communicated. The audience needs to know this. It is an essential part of our vision of the two killers, attractive, romantic, even heroic, and beautiful symbols of the subversive spirit. It tells us something vital about the terrifying people they are and the terrifying society that destroys them.

Bonnie caressing Clyde's pistol in the early part of the film does not necessarily reveal Bonnie as a psychological killer. Practically anyone who handles a weapon for the first time feels some kind of thrill. It does reveal Bonnie's understandable anticipation of a bit of excitement, with a sexual suggestion as much in evidence as a violent one. Penn's images of violence, the face shot through the car window, the wounded Bonnie and Clyde in the back of the car, the death of Buck and the final slow motion jerking into death of Bonnie and Clyde themselves, are very precise, carefully woven into the texture of the film, climactic yet restrained. They are highly stylised, as is the whole film with its memorable counterbalancing of pace. If we condemn the film, which after all shows with dazzling clarity the horrors and hopelessness of a life of desperate crime, we are in a sense condemning our own reactions to images of violence.

There is a scene towards the end of the British film *Accident*, directed by Joseph Losey (1967) not unsimilar to the finale of *Bonnie and Clyde*, although the violence is of a different kind. Two young people, one of them dead, lie trapped in a crashed car. The long hair and white coat of the girl lie spread over the seat. The body of the young man is caved in at an unnatural angle. This is violence as shocking as anything Peckinpah can offer us and infinitely more pointed. For most of us this is the violence of every day, a car crash on a quiet country road. However distant we may be from Mexican massacres the car and its vulnerability is with us all the time. The frontier tradition does not have a monopoly of violence, and a picture of the frontier 'as it really was' does not necessarily become more real because people die.

When Lee Van Cleef kills with such cool satisfaction in *The Good, the Bad and the Ugly* we have a moment of particular viciousness which tells us not that killing is easy but that the killer is evil. When in Leone's latest movie *Once Upon a Time in the West*, Fonda shoots a small boy it is an equally vicious moment but it has a ghastly logic. Leone shows little concern for the Western's traditional code. He makes Westerns without unequivocal heroes. 'The Good' is only a marginal improvement on 'the Bad' and 'the Ugly' and has nothing like the romanticism of *Bonnie and Clyde*—or of *The Wild Bunch*. Leone's version of the West is total anarchy with scarcely any room for heroism. It is grotesque (the macabre coach full of open-eyed Confederate corpses), there are no laws, no rules, no sustaining feeling for the past and no vision of progress. Only the individual counts, and the individual, in order to survive, is forced to be more ingenious, more unscrupulous, more violent than any other situation has demanded. Yet 'the Good' is not the same as 'the Bad' and our response to the movie depends on the difference. Perhaps only a non-American can make Westerns that move with commercial success right out of the traditional framework.

In the early days violent action depended much more on the style of acting than on elaborate effects. The early cowboy heroes, Broncho Billy, Hart, Harry Carey had to impress as men of action without the help of bloody wounds, yells and gunfire, and they tended to rely on their faces and their gestures to communicate toughness. As sound and colour moved in visually the cowboy hero became smoother and smoother (Wayne carries on from the earlier tradition in this respect) from Tom Mix through to Rock Hudson. If in the thirties and forties the Western hesitated to go to town on blood it made up for this lack by presenting a circus of trick riding, roping and stunting of all kinds. But most of the spare effect of silent black and white was lost.

Anthony Mann recaptured some of this spareness. Ford moved right away from it. Boetticher's Westerns, *Ride Lonesome* (1957) and *Comanche Station* (1960) for instance, have a certain leanness reminiscent of the earlier style, helped by Randolph Scott who physically was not at all like the softer heroes of the period. Boetticher tends to avoid towns and isolate his characters, and his heroes fairly consistently avoid involvement with women. But in Boetticher the violence is casual, the heroes and villains continually facing a gamble on life and death which is accepted philosophically. There is not the sense of strained conflict within the protagonists that Mann achieves.

An important stream in the Western tradition has tended to narrow the area of violence to a face to face personal contest. Death can happen all over the screen but what really counts is the hero's final test against a specific enemy. In such Westerns heroism is a very individual thing. It has more to do with the man than with the environment. Amongst recent Westerns we find this in *The Stalking Moon*. The contest between the ex-scout and the Apache chief is intensely personal. It has little to do with what the West expects and a great deal to do with a particular situation and particular people. We have seen the results of the Apache's violent killing but the violence in the film is condensed into that final long sequence (possibly too long, although the tension does not slacken) in which Gregory Peck's commitment to killing his enemy becomes desperately total.

Personal conflict of this kind, which goes beyond the confines of convention, is in some ways more shocking than wholesale slaughter. Do our four heroes of *The Wild Bunch* think in the midst of massacre, are they conscious of their actions, or do they fight blindly hardly aware that they are killing and will themselves die? *The Stalking*

Moon's hero must think, must strain his senses to their uttermost, with the express purpose of killing.

Yet personal conflict often does not *seem* as violent as slaughter on a large scale. The traditional walk-down and its variations contain the violence: and these are real contests while battles on a larger scale hardly can be. Something that Leone and Mann both do is to show us the violence of the personal killing. The significance of the personal conflict, whether it is conducted with guns, knives or fists, is that a man kills knowing his antagonist, looking him in the eyes, sometimes becoming intimately aware of him physically. There is nothing to soften the knowledge the killer has of the killed except the cushioning of convention. What we see is the acting out of a ritual. What we must also see is that the ritual contains the perception of death by the protagonists. We do not need to see real death, but we must see that they do. Of course in hundreds of Westerns this never happens.

[4]

Any discussion of the reality of violence on the screen is bound to be misleading. As far as historical authenticity is concerned, in general the frontier was probably more violent than the Western represents, though not necessarily with the particular forms of violence that the Western tends to emphasise. To say that the conventional walk-down and the villain dying with his hands clutched to a neat bullet hole is not 'real' is as pointless as remarking that the whole of cinema is artificial. The whole of recent realism is bedevilled by the assumption that one form of stylisation is *per se* more realistic than another, or that simply to break up stylisation is automatically more realistic.

There is an added difficulty in the discussion of cinema realism owing to the fact that no other medium but the camera can show us, directly, what is being described. We may be seeing actors who pass their non-working life in lounge suits, but we see them moving on real earth, with real dust on their boots and all the accoutrements proper to the Western heroes. Nothing can compete with the immediacy of the visual impact, and this essential difference between the camera arts and any other art form often interferes with our response to cinematic realism. It is in the nature of the camera to show us the way it is. We ask from the artist who works with a camera, whether movie director or still photographer, much more than this. Realism is about creating an *illusion* of reality, and this is where consistent stylisation comes in.

Many of the best Westerns have been, in their different ways, highly and carefully stylised: *High Noon, Shane, Hombre* and *Butch Cassidy* for instance. We judge them for their style. If there is a legitimate criticism of *The Wild Bunch* that is based on more than a distasteful reaction it is that the style collapses. It wobbles dangerously in Peckinpah's earlier *Major Dundee* (1965). Realism can never be a substitute for style—in fact, it can't exist without style. If Leone has to be admired in spite of possible distaste it is because he does have a consistent and coherent style, not just, as Clint Eastwood put it, 'an interesting approach to violence.' [18]

The Wild Bunch opens with a sequence which must be amongst the very best the Western has ever produced. The unhurried but measured riding into town of the Wild Bunch (no relation to Butch Cassidy's outfit) followed by the ambush and gunfight are superbly controlled. There is confusion but the camera is not confused. And within the confusion there emerge sharply and dramatically points that are going to be of the highest importance in the development of the film. We don't know who these men are, we can barely distinguish one from the other in their stolen uniforms, but the character of the group emerges. They are cool, deliberate professionals, ignoring unnecessary details, eliminating whatever appears to be hindering them including, during their escape, a wounded member of the gang. It does not matter to them that townspeople become involved, that there are children on the streets, or that people are dying around them. They simply carry on with their job, and it is precisely this, their experience and courage, which identifies them as heroes at the same time as exposing their ruthlessness. On the roof their attackers are hysterically trying to kill, rivalling each other for the blood money there will be on every corpse. At the very beginning, out of a brutal gunfight that takes place in the middle of a populous town, a moral distinction is made.

The moral distinction is of the greatest significance. The pursuers, officially on the side of the law, are abhorrent. The pursued, killers and lawbreakers, are heroic. The first thirty minutes tell us everything. They need no exposition, yet having brilliantly made his point Peckinpah, carries on to weaken it rather than strengthen and support it. The episode in the Mexican village is a drastic lapse in mood and style which interferes with the remainder of the film as well as presenting a distressingly sentimental picture of Mexican oppression.

The Wild Bunch, the four men who survive, finally march out to certain death in a gesture of solidarity with their captured Mexican comrade Angel. Angel has his throat slit and the massacre commences. What follows is a sequence of carnage that only the camera could make such a mess of—the camera's immediacy can be dangerous: it is highly sensitive to lack of control. As the camera quivers and jumps individuals (individuals?) are decimated by machine gun bullets, slit by sabres, ripped apart by powerful guns at close range. The four heroes die of multiple wounds, none of them instantly, having slaughtered what seems like three quarters of the Mexican army. Just as in *Butch Cassidy* it takes an entire regiment of Bolivians to despatch two gringo gangsters so in *The Wild Bunch* our white American heroes decimate the ranks of the Mexicans before finally expiring.

This itself is distasteful and unfortunately a common feature of recent Westerns. The expendable Mexican has taken the place of the expendable Indian. But it is neither the gruesome detail nor the slaughtered Mexicans that ruin this climactic sequence, but the fact that it is artistically out of control. The economic intensity of the earlier part of the film is totally lost, precision melts away. Full as he is of ingenious ideas for achieving certain effects of savaged flesh one wonders if Peckinpah remembered that he was making a film. He seems to have lost himself as well as his actors in the carnage.

The last few quiet moments of the film with their obvious symbolism —the vultures circling above the heads of the manic bounty hunters who at last arrive on the scene—reassert control but cannot restore the balance. The delicate process of illusion has been shattered to no effect and Peckinpah, who appeared to have an implicit understanding of this art in *Ride the High Country*, is floundering. 'Peckinpah insists on getting the details of his movie violence right. He was positively lyrical about the nature of gunshot wounds when he was making "The Wild Bunch", and defends the bloodier aspects of the film as a kind of catharsis for the audience.'[19] The next step, presumably, is actually to slaughter several hundred Mexicans in order to get the details right: it's the only way to be sure about the gunshot wounds.

As the Greek tragedians so well understood, violence itself is no part of catharsis: identification, however, is vital. The cowboy is backed by so much solid tradition that even the vicious hero can establish a consistent, purposeful identity by which his actions can be measured. In *Two Mules for Sister Sara*, in which the gratuitous slaughter is certainly cheap violence, the sequence though bad is not artistically so disastrous as in *The Wild Bunch* because throughout a positive identification of the hero is maintained. Siegel offers us comedy as a channel for identification—our hero casually tossing off sticks of dynamite and finally arriving at 'the best whore house in town' with his trunk of gold triuphantl yborne on a wheelbarrow—and the slaughter is almost irrelevant background. It makes the violence even more gratuitous, but prevents the movie from collapse.

For some years the Western has been straining against its traditions, and this restlessness emerges most forcefully in the handling of violence. It would be too neat to say that the Western has gone from one extreme to another, from bang, bang you're dead to wholesale carnage. But clearly a large part of present 'realism' is reaction. Meanwhile, the consistent character of the traditional Western hero has fed an entire genre of influential writing, the thriller, and the way violence in that field has developed in recent years is of some interest, Chandler's Philip Marlowe has all the qualities of the classic frontier hero, a loner, skilled in action, but only killing when the circumstances are extreme and the victim clearly evil. In *The Big Sleep* the victim has already fired six times before Marlowe responds.

He whirled at me. Perhaps it would have been nice to allow him another shot or two, just like a gentleman of the old school. But his gun was up and I couldn't wait any longer. Not long enough to be a gentleman of the old school. I shot him four times, the Colt straining against my ribs. The gun jumped out of his hand as if it had been kicked. He reached both his hands for his stomach. I could hear them smack hard against his body. He fell like that, straight forward, holding himself together with his broad hands. He fell face down in the wet gravel. And after that there wasn't a sound from him.[20]

This is intimate killing, a climax carefully worked up with deceptive casualness, a climax of violence in a climate of violence that lurks just beneath the sunshiny surface of California. It is roughly contemporaneous with Ford's *Stagecoach*. The inheritors of Chandler have not reversed the essential identification on which the whole persona of Marlowe depends. Detailed violence does not necessarily destroy this; but the character and the moral stance of the killer are of the essence.

So that in, for instance the much-praised *The French Connection*, directed by William Friedkin and surely overrated, the hero who has virtually no personality and certainly no moral stance, is almost a non-person. And he is surrounded by so much silliness—crudely type-cast 'Frogs', extraordinary failures of common sense on the part of the pursuers and pursued—that the movie has very little substance apart from its melodrama. It is a wild Eastern without the benefits of the West, with spasms of Leone-type irrational violence thrown in.

A writer who is beyond any trends and to whom we can go for examples of a way in which violence of an extreme and sometimes grotesque kind can be described is the incomparable Chester Himes. Without any doubt he is one contemporary writer, perhaps the only one, who can translate violence into language. He, too, has drawn on the Western tradition, and his writing acknowledges it. His two tough cops, Coffin Ed and Grave Digger, have their flaws, and they are significant ones, but they have a solid, positive identity, meaningful in terms of the community within which they work and the actions that their job entails.

Coffin Ed was hanging head downward from the roof, only his head and shoulders visible below the top edge of the kitchen window. He had been hanging there for twenty minutes waiting for Sheik to come into view. He took careful aim at a spot just above Sheik's left ear.

Some sixth sense caused Sheik to jerk his head at the exact instant Coffin Ed fired.

A third eye, small and black and sightless, appeared suddenly in the exact centre of Sheik's forehead between his two startled yellow cat's eyes.

The high-powered bullet had cut only a small round hole in the window glass, but the sound of the shot shattered the whole pane and blasted a shower of glass into the room.[21]

This is not Himes being 'lyrical about the nature of gunshot wounds'. He is simply describing meticulously the effect of the shot, describing it in intensely visual terms, but without any gratuitous overtones. He has established the identity of the killer in the very beginning of the book, and the identity of the victim. This is no spontaneous deed perpetrated on an anonymous victim. At the same time as making it clear that the killing is horrible we know exactly why Coffin Ed killed and we know also, for Himes is writing about this all the time, that Harlem's violence cannot be soothed away by a cool hand.

Coffin Ed and Grave Digger are our action heroes, wives and families at home, risking their lives constantly, coming into contact with murder and crime at their most vicious extremes, likeable, respected, understandable men. Himes' writing is precise, stark, apparently detached yet informed by a moral viewpoint. Writers and film makers who dabble in violence could learn a great deal from him.

NINE

Gold and Locomotives

Once more on Hanktowns hills we delve,
On Murderer's Bar we mine,
At Nigger's Tent and Boston Jim's
You Bet, Red Dog, Port Wine.

                                        Anon.

[1]

It was the chance discovery at Sutter's Mill on the Sacramento that brought the first gold rush, the famous one of 1849. 1858 saw the Pike's Peak gold rush—gold had been found in Colorado. In 1860 an ex-California miner found gold in Idaho. Rapidly the search spread into Montana and those famous cities sprang up—Bannack, Virginia City, Alder Gulch, Helena—that were to become bywords of the frontier.

Throughout the second half of the nineteenth century there was a virtually continuous hunt for precious metal. In the late 1850s both gold and silver were discovered in Nevada and the renowned Comstock Lode began to yield up its millions. In the '70s silver and lead were discovered in Colorado, gold in the Black Hills, silver in Arizona— through which Tombstone and Wyatt Earp became famous. There was hardly a state which did not have its mineral hunters, even if no substantial strike was made. Rumours of lost mines and fabulous mystery strikes kept up the excitement. In 1896 the Klondike gold rush started it all afresh, providing material for films like Mann's *The Far Country* and Hathaway's *North to Alaska* (1960).

Bonanza mining, even just the hope of bonanza mining, could transform an area in a matter of hours. Those who followed the gold rushes were not necessarily men who planned to dig in the ground or pan the streams for metal: they were often shop keepers, merchants, freighters, saloon keepers, tarts, entertainers, hangers-on of all kinds who hoped to benefit from a rich flow of gold dust and nuggets. Those who made money and kept it were not usually those who brought the metal out of the ground. Later it became almost impossible for an individual working on his own to amass a fortune. Mining rapidly became highly organised. The wide-open free for all of the early California or Montana days could not last. Complicated machinery was needed, monopolies moved in, and those who sold out to the big firms and moved on were much better off than the miners who remained and worked for wages that bore little relation to the sky-high prices.

The overnight transformation from open country to mining camp begs for comic treatment, and it is not surprising that it is movies like *Paint Your Wagon* (1969) directed by Joshua Logan, and Burt Kennedy's *Support your Local Sheriff* (1968) that utilise this situation. In both the initial discovery of gold is made in a newly dug grave. Although the handling is comic what we see in *Paint Your Wagon* the creation of an instant mining camp, happened repeatedly. Ramshackle towns with saloons the most important feature sprang up out of nothing, muddy streets because of the constant traffic, improvisation everywhere, prices soaring, and a largely unshaven, unwashed population, and 'lice as large as chili beans fighting with the fleas'. No Name City, the hell-thiest spot in the West, population drunk, is not too far from the real thing.

But in one significant area No Name City softens the reality. Mining camps were lawless, and with a great deal of precious metal and money in their vicinity they invited crime of a less friendly nature than that perpetrated by Lee Marvin and Clint Eastwood. Henry Plummer was the most notorious of the outlaws who preyed on the mining camps, and he was hanged by vigilantes in 1864. But it was not so much individual action against individual bandits that characterised the mining towns as the sheer chaos and confusion that reigned in them in the early days, and the intensity of the violence that lingered long after some kind of formal law had been established. The rough squalour that typified the camps suggested the kind of life that was lived in them. In 1884 a journalist described the town of Murray, Idaho.

It is composed of a hideous half-mile-long street of huts, shanties, and tents, with three or four cross-streets that run against the steep slopes after a few rods of progress.... A more unattractive place than Murray I have seldom seen. The trees have been cleared away, leaving a bare gulch into which the sun pours for sixteen hours a day with a fervour which seems to be designed by nature to make up for the coolness of the short July nights, when fires are needed. Stumps and half-charred logs encumbered the streets, and serve as seats for the inhabitants.... Every second building is a drinking saloon.... The town was full of men out of employment and out of money, who hung about the saloons and cursed the camp in all styles of profanity known to miners' vocabulary. Nevertheless, gold was being shipped out every day by Wells, Fargo and Co.'s express, and new discoveries were constantly reported.[1]

Mining camps were in high country and very often hemmed in by mountain slopes. If there is a distinct tone of disapproval in this journalist's account Luke Short's fictional description of Piute, Colorado puts things a little differently, although in their essentials Piute and Murray could be the same town.

Piute was a hell's broth of a town that left Cole stunned at first sight. Entering it, the stage driver had literally to fight and curse his way through the traffic of the big main street. It was jammed with big ore wagons on their way from the mines scattered on the mountain slopes above the town to the reduction mills on the flats a ways below the town. The sidewalks overflowed with miners of all nationalities: and buckboards, spring wagons, carriages and saddle horses jammed the tie rails of the four long blocks of the main street. There was a carnival air here, for Piute was a boom camp on the upswing, and all the foot-loose trash and hangers-on were here from all over the West to provide it with the inevitable swindling and the drinking and rioting that gold and silver attracted.[2]

It is this collection of varied, bustling humanity that really charac-terises the mining camps. In contrast with the roughness of most of the miners were the genuine luxuries that were often available, ship-ped at enormous expense and with great effort from the East. Most of the Denver saloons were serving champagne by 1860. The flimsy board houses often contained elegant furnishings, pianos, pictures, and the best brandy and claret. There was so much money and so little to spend it on that a large proportion went on shipping in such tangible symbols of elegance and civilisation. And if you had no taste for a piano you could always get rid of your gold dust at one or other of the well equipped gambling establishments. Gambling was a way of life in the mining camps.

There were some efforts to present the mining towns in a less rough and gaily uncivilised light. To one vistor Leadville, Colorado 'was like some thriving provincial town. The men would not have looked out of place in the street, say, of Reading, while the women, in their quiet and somewhat old-fashioned style of dressing, reminded me very curiously of rural England.'[3] A pamphlet on the mining town of Kingston, New Mexico, published in 1883, took some pains to show that things were properly under control.

Its society is characteristic of the frontier, but contains a greater number of refined and educated people than one would expect to find so far from the comforts and conveniences to which they have been accustomed in eastern homes. ... The rough house is often furnished in far better style than its exterior betokens, and probably there is as much real enjoyment and family contentment amid such surroundings as in the brown stone or marble palaces of the great cities.

However, it does add that there is a certain lack of amenities.

As to churches, this has not seemed to be a specially inviting field for missionaries. No church buildings have been erected, nor have any societies been organised.... Although it is by no means unpopular to take a drink of beer or whiskey, and temperance societies would not secure a large membership in the camp, there is but little drinking to excess, and no more drunkenness on the streets than is usual elsewhere.[4]

If the last sentence is somewhat equivocal we can hardly blame the writer for trying to suggest that Kingston would be a pleasant spot for ordinary family life. In a predominantly male society, which included of course the kind of female who earned her bread from this situation, the idea of the family could become positively messianic in its influence. 'Annals of mining camps are filled with tales of grizzled prospectors who paid a dollar a head to look at a woman's bonnet, or to touch a little girl's skirt, or to dance about a post on which a lady's hat was enshrined,'[5] Ray Allen Billington remarks. The miners were not necessarily deprived of sex, but they were deprived of comforting symbols of conventional life.

Life in the mining camps was very often a hand to mouth existence. Just keeping alive, assuming you avoided the bullets, could be an expensive business. Basic foodstuffs, flour, coffee, sugar, were catastrophically expensive, as the mining camps were in full swing long before effective systems of bulk transport were in operation. The inhabitants were at the mercy of the freighters. The Montana camps were partly dependent on the Bozeman Trail, that led northwest from the Platte, but it was a tough route at the best of times and continually threatened by Indians. The canny Mormons quickly saw an opportunity of doing good business and supplied the Montana and Idaho camps with goods from Salt Lake City. These included such choice items as chickens, eggs and vegetables—but at a price. In *The Hanging Tree* (Delmer Daves, 1959) the cynical doctor (Gary Cooper) keeps the shatteringly high prices from the young blind girl (Maria Schell) who is a newcomer and does not know her mining camps. If enough people could and would pay these prices it mattered little to the storekeeper or the freighter if there were some who could not.

The camps were notoriously wide open to crime, perfunctory violence (one thousand homicides in San Francisco, gateway to the California gold camps, between 1849 and 1856) cheating, swindling, dishonest gambling dens, petty theft, racial intolerance, corruption, opium smoking—the list could be even longer. In Peckinpah's *Ride the High Country* the picture of the mining camp is gothic in its excess, its contrasts, and the sheer power of drunken viciousness amongst its inhabitants. Such a place, we feel, can only destroy itself. The mean-eyed, lustful Billy Hammond (an unusual part for James

Drury who is now synonymous with the Virginian) becomes a creature of total evil, as does the enormously crude prostitute leering over the wedded couple, drunken Billy and innocent, white-clad Elsa. This is surely one of the Western's most gruesome whores, oozing flesh, strident, central to the camp's profound corruption.

This emphasis on integral corruption, as if to imply that the search for gold is itself decadent and demoralising, is not a usual emphasis. What is much more common is the portrayal of the civilising process brought to bear on the initial confusion by the camp's denizens themselves, or by some good influence who rides in and clears up the mess, as Cole Armin does in Luke Short's *Western Freight*. The vigilance committees came first, citizens who banded together to apprehend and punish criminals. The real Helena hanging tree was much in use. The vigilantes were often highly organised, but they do not usually appear in the Western in this form. Summary justice certainly does, in all its varied forms; frequently we are shown the mob in action, frequently the sheriff holding off a band of irate citizens determined on a hanging without waiting for the judge.

The sheriff came late to the mining camps, in spite of the fact that transport, the appurtenances of civilised life and statehood for the mining territories often came relatively early. Tombstone had Wyatt Earp but most mining towns were more famous for their outlaws than their peacemakers. Many camps did not survive long enough for a civilising process to make itself felt. For those that did survive the real trouble often did not begin until the place was fairly mature. Later in the century labour troubles were to become practically synonymous with the railroads on the one hand and the mines on the other. William Cox in *Black Silver* is describing the labour unrest which as early as the sixties resulted from big companies taking over the workings of the Comstock Lode. Cox sets his story in 1866, a time when everyone was worried that the Comstock riches were coming to an end. There were many men out of work. He describes the formation of a union (the Comstock was controlled by the Bank of California) that established a minimum wage of $4 a day for men working below ground on an eight hour shift. This was twice as much as in some parts of the West, but it did not help the men who had come thousands of miles, perhaps brought their families, only to find that the work ran out. The Comstock was to revive in the seventies but during this troubled period it was building up a legacy of conflict between miners and owners, as were most of the mines in the West.

In 1872 the *Arizona Miner* described an incident in which three hundred Idaho miners protested against a foreman called Jewell.

The men held a meeting and notified him to leave, but the acting superintendent of the mine backed Jewell and sent up from the town forty armed men and howitzers to keep the peace. Then the miners from four neighbouring mines got together and agreed not to fight and not to go to work as long as Jewell remained at the mine. Jewell vacated the premises.[6]

This was a victory for the miners, but more often than not the armed men and the howitzers had the final say. The mine owners brought in Pinkerton men as strike breakers—that optimistic cowboy, Charlie Siringo, became one in his latter years—and thus reinforced in the popular mind the association between Pinkerton and the mining and railroad monopolies.

Although the mining camp is frequently a Western venue labour troubles do not often appear. Troubles with unscrupulous bosses do, and on these the hero can apply his liberating techniques just as he would on a ranch boss, but specifically the struggle between labour and capital, so present a force in the developing West, is not a feature of the legendary frontier. Gold, silver, lead, copper and the railroads spontaneously combusted labour troubles everywhere. The itinerant industrial organiser came to be as typical a figure as the drifting cowboy. In 1884 the Knights of Labour had a brief moment of victory when they won a Union Pacific strike, and even cowboys were at times attracted by such an organisation. John Clay describes with indignation a strike of cowhands on the ranch he was managing, but the story ended to his satisfaction with the loyal help of haymakers in getting the cattle to market.

Racial troubles on a violent scale were also characteristic. There were always the Indians as legitimate targets for itching trigger fingers, but there were plenty of other racial minorities too which became a focus of antagonism. In California there was widespread discrimination against Mexicans. In a Sacramento mining camp a Mexican girl was hanged on very little evidence other than that she was Mexican. The Chinese who worked extensively on the railroads and in the mines in many parts of the West, were a continual object of hatred. In 1885 in Rock Springs, Wyoming, a group of Chinese workers were massacred in a spontaneous outburst of white violence. As late as 1903 the *Jerome Mining News* described the following incident.

A mob of twelve to fifteen men invaded Chinatown yesterday afternoon and at the point of guns compelled a number of Chinamen to leave town at once. Several who did not comply at once were badly beaten and dragged to the outskirts of town and told to take the road to Sodaville .... Ping Ling, a seventy-three year old man, the proprietor of a wash-house, was one of the victims.... His body was mutilated and found three miles west of town. Chinese were also robbed of several hundred dollars. Eighteen men, mostly cooks and waiters, have been arrested and are now in jail. Among them is the president of a labour union.[7]

The precipitous birth and disordered growth of the mining camps seemed even more conducive to brutality than the free-ranging anarchy of the wide open spaces. In such disorder the traditional frontiersman cannot operate. As the mining camps acquired the character of company towns the labour hero took over from the Western hero. The ringing clarion call that had urged men West and reflected all the excitement and idealism of every gold rush soon became no more than a muffled echo.

HO! FOR THE GOLD AND SILVER MINES
OF NEW MEXICO

> Fortune hunters, capitalists, poor men,
> Sickly folks, all whose hearts are bowed down;
> And ye who would live long, be rich, healthy,
> and happy; come to our sunny clime and see
> For Yourselves.[8]

But independently of the mining camps gold exerted its influence. Many Westerners knew something about precious metal, how to recognise it and value it, how to identify and assess quartz that might mean silver. The figure of the lone prospector which the Western has done so much to perpetuate, usually an old man with a grey beard and a flow of tobacco juice and profanity, is not very accurate, as most prospecting was organised and carried out on a large scale. But there was always the dream that an individual might discover some secret source of wealth.

This dream did bring some strange people West, and has provided a theme for many Westerns. The hero prospecting in the mountains, surrounded by potential hazards, bent on a search that necessarily takes him away from humanity is the ultimate in potent loneliness. The hunt for a lost mine or hidden treasure is often a way of bringing an unlikely Easterner to the frontier, as in T. V. Olsen's *Savage Sierra* (1962) or Louis L'Amour's *Mustang Man* (1966), and teaching them something about a wild country. The lust for gold can also make men mad. In Olsen's book Charbonneau, a rival gold hunter, proposes to kill two men and two women to get the gold. When one of the men, an Easterner, expresses his horror the frontier hero replies:

'A transplanted Southerner, once a gentleman.... A frontier man now ... seems like everything would go against it. In his right mind, it would. And he'd take our word not to tell anyone about the gold. But he's lost his right mind, Jim. Look at him.'[9]

In *Mustang Man* a brother and sister from the East are crazed by gold lust. They are prepared to murder in order to track down the lost mine they are hunting. This kind of gold drama is quite different from the drama of the mining camps, although sheer greed plays a large part in both. Greed can grow into madness; it can also stimulate delightful ingenuity. We can only admire the intricate plans in *The War Wagon* (1967) directed by Burt Kennedy and in *Sam Whiskey* to acquire massive quantities of gold. It is the idea of pulling off such a coup that charms us. Both these are comic Westerns with somewhat ludicrous plots but in neither is gold lust out of place. Great riches inspire great deeds. The tantalising vision of wealth brings out the best from men of courage, intelligence but dubious reputation. An essential part of the comedy is that, in the end, none of them are any better off than they were at the beginning. Very few of those involved with the precious metals of the West were.

[2]

Gold certainly helped to spur the railroads westward. In the 1850s the first trans-Mississippi railroads had been constructed, but, with the interruption of the Civil War it was 1864, after many years of discussion and proposal, before charters were granted for the Northern Pacific and Union Pacific Railroads. The railroad rapidly became a part of the Western legend and a folk symbol throughout the United States. It is no accident that the first Western movie ever was *The Great Train Robbery*, made in 1903, for the railroad was recognised throughout the West as representing both tyranny and the powerful surge of progress. The laying of track across the continent was itself a much celebrated enterprise (although most of the men who did it were despised Irishmen and Chinese) and the meeting point of East and West at Promontory Point in Utah was a splendid symbol of national triumph. Union Pacific and Central Pacific met in 1869 and the laying of the last rail has been reenacted countless times as the riveting of a continent. Although what it really represented was the personal victory of Collis Huntington, the hardware merchant from Sacramento, and his prodigious colleagues.

The surging of the railroads into the Western states is most often seen as a triumph of American progress and individual endeavour. The railroad had its heroes, from the political lobbyists to Buffalo Bill, and there is no dearth of material for the Western that makes the railroad its centre. Problems of land grants and finance were only the first hurdles. There was deserts and mountains, rivers and canyons, Indians and outlaws, and rival outfits. Even where the train supplants the horse, as it does virtually in Haskin's *Denver and Rio Grande* (1952), the locomotive is a dramatic substitute. And it is a machine that has a certain satisfying affinity with the Western landscape, dwarfed like men by its grandeur, vulnerable in spite of its steel, yet gallant. The locomotive rolling on its steel rails through vast areas of empty space has a challenging appeal which has in some Westerns been beautifully utilised. The opening sequence of Burt Kennedy's *Young Billy Young* (1970) is a notable example.

Yet before the railroads there had been the stagecoaches, the freighters, the mule trains and the Pony Express, short lived but legendary. The first overland mail service was started in 1848 with a run from Independence to Salt Lake City. In 1849 it went on to Santa Fe and in 1851 it crossed the sierras to San Francisco. It was the gold camps more than anything that lured transport westward. The first transcontinent stage line was in operation in 1858, St. Louis to San Francisco, run by the enterprising John Butterfield with those famous Concord coaches which are universally recognisable. It cost $200 to travel to the West Coast by stage and a three week cruelly uncomfortable journey was guaranteed. By 1866 the big man in stage lines was Ben Holladay who at that time controlled 3000 miles of stage line. He had taken over the company of Russell, Majors and Waddell which at one time dominated Western freighting. Holladay's Overland Stage Company commanded government mail subsidies worth a million dollars a year.

To travel any significant distance by stage was likely to mean several days of suffering.

Two days and two nights on a stage climbing from desert country in the high reaches was a great breaker of conventions. The tedium, the jolting, the noise, the lurching, the dust and the heat could make passengers forget disparity in wealth and opinions and level them into one suffering mass of humanity.[10]

Or, as a song of the time put it more succinctly:

> The ladies are compelled to sit
> With dresses in tobacco spit;
> The gentlemen don't seem to care,
> But talk on politics and swear.[11]

Travelling long distances by train was not much more comfortable. The seats were hard. Dust filtered in through the windows, the sun beat down. Travel by both stage and rail was subject to certain hazards. Although the Indians had expended most of their efforts on preventing the rails being laid they did attack trains as well as the much more vulnerable stagecoaches, and on occasions had some success. Both were victims of outlaw gangs. Lifting a stage of its cargo of bullion or a train of a strongbox of wages is a staple episode on the screen. The great gangs, the James brothers, the Daltons, the Wild Bunch, considered the railroads as prime targets, and in the eyes of many they were legitimate targets, especially after the initial railroad euphoria was past. Railroad companies were seen as tools of injustice and to rob them was often considered praiseworthy reprisal.

If the construction of the railroads was seen as romantic and nation-building, spurred by idealism and individual courage, the nature of the railroad towns was little different from that of the mining camps. They catered for a hard working, hard drinking male population initially, although of course later many of the railroad towns were to become thriving and respectable cities. They certainly sprang up as quickly as the mining camps.

We passed through Ellesworth, a wonderful place, having seven or eight stores, two hotels, fifty houses of other kinds, occupied by nearly a thousand persons, and yet just one month old. Six weeks ago the wild buffalo was roaming over its site, and the Indians scalped a foolish soldier whom they caught sleeping where the new school-house now stands. The day of the Indian and the buffalo have passed for ever; never again will the one graze, or the other utter a war whoop on this spot.[12]

The Iron Horse shows the instant collapse, removal and re-erection of railroad camps, the saloon being the essential, to keep pace with the end of steel. The population kept pace also, both the railroad workers, and those many hangers-on who reaped their profits from the mass of labourers.

The Government supported the railroads, were generous with land grants, but not everyone in the West shared this enthusiasm. The Indians' attacks on the construction camps and the locomotives themselves did temporary damage. Cecil B. de Mille's *Union Pacific* (1939), epic railroad drama on a lavish scale, shows that well-known incident of a successful Indian attack on a freight train after which the Indians amused themselves by trailing bolts of cloth after their galloping ponies. But it was not only the Indians who objected. Individual ranchers, blind to the advantages the railroad could bring them, frequently refused right of way to the oncoming steel rails. They did not want to lose the land and they did not want messy, noisy machines ruining the range.

Most of the battles the railroads won, in one fashion or another. Personal influence, bribery, threats helped to solve some of the problems—and provided rich material for the Western. The situation was in constant flux, and reveals the dual nature of the railroad's image. It could be seen, as Frank Norris was to see it so uncompromisingly in *The Octopus*, as a giant machine of oppression run by unscrupulous, self-interested business men. Or it could be seen as the front line of expansion, piloted by courageous and far-sighted individuals with the interests of the nation at heart. The genuine idealism that did exist in the early days was dwindling in the 1870s. The optimism which had been so hopeful that the railroads would bring development and prosperity to Western communities, ranchers and farmers began to turn sour. The railroad didn't go near many of the towns that needed it. In many cases the service was poor and unreliable. Men had made money, sometimes through corruption, out of the construction of the railroads, and the running of them efficiently was a secondary consideration. But the power of the railroads did not dwindle and there was nothing to put a brake on the rates they charged. It was the railroads above all that stirred the growing unrest in the last quarter of the century amongst the farmers and settlers.

Rivalry between individual companies did not help matters. Those who got in the way suffered more than the companies themselves. Corruption at the higher levels only made those who could have benefited from the railroads more helpless. Company rivalry is another theme that the Western often handles. It is the basis of *Denver and Rio Grande*, a less than balanced movie about the real battle between the Atchison, Topeka and Santa Fe and the Denver and Rio Grande railroad companies in their race to take a share of the Nevada gold field profits. In the film William Palmer, head man of Denver and Rio Grande, appears as a noble and dedicated patriarch and the Santa Fe men as a gang of ruffians. In fact there was not much to choose between them. Although there was a certain amount of mutual interference and the construction crews of the two companies did take to arms the final settlement was worked out by the courts.

The real joy of the railroad Western lies in the beauty and power of the locomotive itself. Even in an inferior Western it is a pleasure to watch the steel rails carrying the smoking engine over rough country, and in Westerns where the railroad is incidental the locomotive becomes a symbol of Western power and Western progress. The railroad becomes a part of the bustling Western town's activity; it can make all the difference between a one horse dump and a thriving metropolis. It suggests distance, speed, communication, expansion. A town on the railroad line was on the map.

The railroad suggests also, traditionally in American folklore, loneliness. Not only the loneliness of the hobo riding the rods, who in the twentieth century was to travel the West as constantly and as thoroughly as the drifting cowboy in the nineteenth, but simply the loneliness of the traveller, destined for some unknown place, suggested by the whistle blow and the locomotive's stabbing headlight in the dark. Ernest Haycox's *Riders West* begins with the arrival of the heroine in a small town thousands of miles from her native habitat.

She stood there in the darkness, with her luggage around her, ridden by a loneliness she could not help. The rest of the deposited passengers had gone off, and she was quite alone, smothered in the shadows. Small impressions came to her—the smell of sage and wood-smoke, the clatter of a telegraph key. Along the station wall was a sign that read: 'See Townsite Jackson.' But her mind was on that fast-fading red-and-green glow of the train; and as the lights grew dimmer and dimmer, so did her courage.[13]

In *High Noon* the railroad is ominous, for it is the noon train that brings the threat to the community. The empty rails stretching into the distance and the little station set apart from the town in the dust and the glaring light become a focus of tension. The train itself becomes associated with violence. The association is natural, even without *High Noon*. The power that means progress can also mean destruction. Locomotives bring gunmen, carry troops, or the fifty hired guns to Johnson County. They are also the objects of attack and destruction, attract danger as well as carry it. Men fight modern machines with modern weapons: the locomotive can mean exploding metal and ripped up track and can become on the frontier just as vulnerable as a man. But equally it can be a totally convincing symbol of aggression with a determined personality of its own.

The locomotive becomes involved with outlaws and revolutions, the latter in Mexico where trains were vital as troop and supply carriers. In *100 Rifles* (1968, Tom Gries) government activity is focused on the train, and a train is the object of the Yacquis Indians' attack. In *Viva Zapata!*, a much earlier movie, supply trains are attacked. In *The Professionals* the four heroes make their getaway by train, and they have been hired by a railroad magnate. In *The Wild Bunch* it is the railroad's money the outlaws are after and in *Two Mules for Sister Sara* Clint Eastwood and Shirley MacLaine blow up a trestle just as a troop-carrying train is half way across it. All these films are set, wholly or partially, in Mexico.

We become familiar with the techniques of destruction: the obstructed line, the little parcels of dynamite. They are a part of the locomotive's suggestiveness. In *Butch Cassidy and the Sundance Kid*, the train becomes a concrete threat when we see the Pinkerton men jumping their horses surrealistically out of the box car. It is a stunning moment, the mood changing from the comic to the sinister, and yet lingering to pick up the last fragments of comedy, the outlaws snatching at the scattered money, before concentrating on the intensity of the chase. Stunning in spite of the fact that it was not an original sequence. George Marshall had used it in *When the Daltons Rode* in 1940, with the horses leaping magnificently down from the train and the raised bank. And there is a very similar sequence in *The Wild Bunch* when a bunch of raw troopers clumsily jump or drag their mounts from the train to set off in pursuit of Pike Bishop and his gang. It is done yet again in *Young Billy Young*.

The railroads had the money and hired the detectives. Pinkerton men were employed to hunt down habitual train robbers. In both *The Wild Bunch* and *Butch Cassidy* it is the railroads who finance the hunt and offer rewards. In the popular mind this became part of its tyranny, and because of this helped to boost a number of dubious Western lawbreakers into the realms of legend. The locomotive itself retained its lonely, dogged character, with fist fights on the box cars and gunfights on the footplates to encourage its affinity with the Western hero.

Both the mines and the railroads were readily absorbed into the frontier myth. Both were partly responsible for the frontier's disappearance, which perhaps just adds to their poignancy. The locomotive's whistle mingles with the coyote's call and the whirring of the stamp mills with the wind in the trees. Neither caused the Westerner to lose his identity; both gave more scope for heroic activity. If the hero got the gold he soon spent it on whisky, cards and women. It was the more dubious gains from property and business that were to hasten the frontier's end.

TEN

Women in the West

A woman on the prairie is an unwanted thing. Nothing but a burden and a tie-down, keeping the ones she loves from doing what they want to do.

Alan Le May *The Siege at Dancing Bird*

There were no wallflowers on the range.

Emerson Hough 'Society in the Cow Town'

[1]

She looks like one of the English poor women of our childhood—lean, clean, toothless, and speaks like one of them, in a piping, discontented voice, which seems to convey a personal reproach. All her waking hours are spent in a sun-bonnet. She is never idle for one minute, is severe and hard, and despises everything but work.[1]

We cannot recognise this as the Western screen heroine. This is a woman in Colorado described by Isabella Bird, herself a most proper but delightfully unconventional traveller in the West. 'She' is typical, unlovely, hard-working, characterised by her sunbonnet, a strictly utilitarian piece of apparel, worn from sunrise to sunset, day in, day out, limp, sweat-soaked, layered with dust, as necessary, and in its way as symbolic, as the cowboy's wide brimmed hat. More than anything else the sunbonnet represented a combination of drudgery and respectability. The heroine of the Western does not wear a sunbonnet. Nor does the dance hall girl. The woman who did was a woman who worked in the sun, washing clothes at the pump, trudging beside a covered wagon.

The sunbonnet suggests also a married woman, or a woman whose vision is encompassed by the idea of marriage, not a girl on the make, coming West with a good nose for a boom town, nor the pretty rancher's daughter whom the hero will probably win. The sunbonnet suggests a mate for the dirt farmer, not for the range rider. The heroine of the Western must, generally, have either more or less than the sunbonnet represents.

Women were not a plentiful commodity in most parts of the frontier. It was often easier to import pianos and champagne than to bring out suitable mates for frontiersmen. The motives that took women West were limited. They might go as wives, daughters or nieces. They might go as adventuresses—the only equivalent of the heroic man who sets forth to open up new territories is a woman of dubious reputation. The only respectable job that could take a woman West was school-teaching, and for that smaller communities would tend to rely on local talent. Or they might go, occasionally, as 'mail order' brides, lonely wives for lonely ranchers brought together through correspondence.

History has institutionalised the frontier woman, and she is trapped in a narrow image. It is an image that interweaves decency and endurance—look at the tight lips and scraped hair of the women in any old photograph of a frontier family—and an aggression that echoes that of the men. The legend has done nothing to free women from this narrowness: the conventional Western can only offer a romanticised alternative. Occasionaly the courage, determination, independence and incredible capacity for endurance is allowed to contribute richly to the Western, but not as a rule.

Some argue that the Western could profitably dispense with women altogether. Frederick Woods wrote in 1959, 'Time after time, one can detach the females without endangering the structure of the main plot. The West is a man's world, and the women are relegated to mere decoration ... most often they are prizes only, to be gathered in by the handsome hero when the gunsmoke has drifted away.' [2] Yet the woman as a prize only echoes long established narrative conventions. The Western incorporates a treatment that has long existed. To the extent that the Western often imports its characterisation of women from another convention Frederick Woods is right. To argue that the Western cannot legitimately use women characters, and cannot do so without retaining the romantic conventions that much of its audience will look for, is misleading. It consigns to oblivion the women who were there.

The ordinary pioneer woman is elusive on the screen. The glimpses that we do catch are most often of a hatchet-faced caricature. She is sometimes comic. She is sometimes helpless. She is almost always peripheral. She is the lean housekeeper in *The Oxbow Incident* spitting her sour aggression at the range hands. Transformed, her origins unacknowledged, she is Lola Albright in McLaglen's *The Way West* (1967) in unconvincing middle age, charmingly tousled and dirt-smudged, crossing the plains and mountains bare headed. More genuinely, and very rare, she is Eva Maria Saint in *The Stalking Moon*, yet even here, though we see a raw, bewildered woman, the screen star is too attractive to be entirely honest to the original book's portrayal. In the book T. V. Olsen emphasises throughout the physical and mental damage that ten years of Apache life have done to a woman who was once a pretty, over-protected girl. There is an appropriateness in this scarred woman finding a home with a rough-living scout who has in his way been equally damaged by his years of killing and bare survival.

It is a little easier to track down something reminiscent of reality in print. The pioneer heroine appears in her most noble and solid form in Willa Cather's novels of Nebraska life; in them we can see how the demands of the frontier linger on long after the frontier itself has ostensibly passed. It was not only a hard life on the frontier for a woman accustomed to any kind of comfort or even a minimal relief from hardship, it was often bitterly resented. The celebrated woman of courage is difficult to square with the embittered helpmeet who has long ago relinquished the possibilities of choice in her own life. 'Virgin land usually spelt to a woman isolation, disease and hopelessness,' writes Andrew Sinclair, historian of woman's emancipation in America.[3] Walter Prescott Webb wrote that the Great Plains 'repelled the women as they attracted the men. There was too much of the unknown, too few of the things they loved.'[4] This is perhaps meant to suggest that for women the trivialities of civilisation were more precious than for men, but perhaps a more useful emphasis is on the fact that women had limited opportunities and experience to deal with the unknown. While the men rode out to meet it the women stayed at home trapped in a gruelling round of tasks that were necessary in order to convince themselves that decency could be preserved. In *The Siege at Dancing Bird* Alan Le May provides us with a striking picture.

Matthilda Zachary would have hated and feared the prairie if no Indian had ever ridden it. The galling month-long winds; the dust that sifted forever from the walls and roof of the hole in the ground where they lived; the spreading stains of mud that leaked through with every rain; the few poor things they had to do with, so the endless toil showed no return; the cruelly harsh home-boiled soap, which made cracked, hurting hands the price of keeping clean—all this Matthilda could have forgiven. But she could not forgive what seemed to her the prairie's vast malignance, as boundless as its emptiness, and as mighty as its storms.[5]

Although there is a young, attractive and less bitter woman in the novel, it is Matthilda Zachary that the novel is about. Le May has shown in a number of his novels that he has strong grasp of the quality of life on the frontier, and much of this is presented through a sympathetic portrayal of women. Matthilda does not survive, but she fights, in spite of the fact that she hates what she is fighting for.

There must have been many like her. Even Miss Bird's pioneer, soured and grim as she was, had courage, though it may seem to us now to be perverse and negative.

The tragedy of the frontier woman was that she so rarely did share all that we celebrate in the frontier man. She acquired some extra-domestic skills, riding and shooting, but had not the scope to employ them in a positive way. Yet the type of heroine that gives most pleasure in the Western is precisely the hard riding, tough girl who helps herself to a share of the frontier's freedom. (Just as there can scarcely be a single reader of Scott's novels who does not find the adventurous Di Vernon the most attractive of his heroines.) It is a positive claim that can be made for the Western, that its climate of anarchy *can* grant women a greater than conventional licence in their actions. It is all the more pity that so often it does not.

In the Western context one might look for heroines who are in fact heroic. They are rare. Where they do occur they are generally comic or caricatured, like the numerous Calamity Janes. Most of these are glamorous, jolly, gun-toting females without the remotest suggestion of the original. Calamity Jane was in fact a repulsive character, though an interesting example of what could happen to a woman on the frontier. She was crude, frequently drunk, and unparticular about whom she shared her bed with. Most of her heroic exploits were, as far as can be judged, fabrications, and her romantic link with Wild Bill Hickok seems to be a myth.

A more authentic female tough with a greater heroic potential, though scarcely more attractive than Calamity Jane, was Belle Starr. She was leader of an outlaw gang, probably the mother of Cole Younger's child. She was no glamour girl. Photographs show her, in a long velvet dress and riding sidesaddle, looking grim, prim and stone faced. She operated in Indian Territory, and was killed more or less in action in 1889. She has since featured in a number of movies, all of which have emphasised femininity at the expense of what might be seen as heroics.

The nearest we can get to a genuinely glamorous female outlaw is Etta Place, who, in her photographs, is beautiful and, as we know from *Butch Cassidy*, was a close associate of Harry Longbaugh, alias the Sundance Kid. Etta Place is a truly fascinating woman, in many ways both more mysterious and more appealing in history than the solidity Katharine Ross gave her in the film suggests. Although there is some doubt as to whether she was a schoolteacher or the inmate of a Fort Worth brothel it is well established that she could ride and shoot and that she accompanied Butch Cassidy and the Sundance Kid on a number of their exploits. She had both elegance and courage, and Butch Cassidy's verdict—'She was the best housekeeper in the

Pampas but she was a whore at heart' [6]—adds a further dimension to our picture of her.

Etta was an outlaw of dubious morality. It is generally true that the women who achieved any kind of success comparable to that of men were not the respectable citizens, the wives and daughters whose presence helped to transform the frontier town to a civilised community on something like an Eastern pattern. The only women who were able to make use of the flexibility of an untamed society were those who risked their reputations—or had no reputations to risk. The woman who made money and owned property and had the kind of power money and property grant was most often a brothel or saloon owner. And there were not many such women. The fate of those who started out in such professions was generally less enviable.

In George Roy Hill's movie Etta Place says she will follow Butch and the Kid because they represent the only excitement that ever came into her life. It was a romantic, heroic dream come true. Etta is genuinely absorbed into the myth, on more or less the same terms as the heroes. It is a distinctive feature of the film. She is wholly untypical of what the Western generally supplies, but contains perhaps a promise for the future. How many young girls, trapped in the isolation of the prairies and the mountains, must have longed for the frontier legend to appear on their door-step? Most women in the West were victims of the consequences of the fight against the wild, victims of drudgery and loneliness, their own and that of the men around them. Those who survived into respectability felt that their endurance gave them a natural superiority over the fallen. It was an echo of the heroic Western male, the character that John Wayne plays repeatedly, who considers that he has won his right to be right. While the heroes killed to confirm their status the women could only confirm theirs by giving no quarter to those who had no pretensions to achieving it.

[2]

The cowboy's respect for womankind is a powerful feature of the legend. It was said that a woman could travel the length and breadth of the Western territories in greater safety than she could walk the streets of New York. In the 1870s Isabella Bird calmly travelled alone for hundreds of miles in the Rockies, sometimes with the company of one or two men. Never did she tremble for her safety. She was a good rider and quite handy with a gun, and she even developed what she considered a practical form of dress for her rugged life: she called it 'The American Lady's Mountain Dress' and it consisted of 'a half-fitted jacket, a skirt reaching to the ankles, and full Turkish trousers

gathered into frills which fall over the boots—a thoroughly service-
able and feminine costume for mountaineering and other rugged travelling in any part of the world.' [7] She rode astride, unthinkable for a
well brought up woman, although she sometimes switched to sidesaddle in populated areas.

For hundreds of miles and many months she was unmolested. We
may be sceptical about Western, clearly derived from Southern,
courtesy, but there is nothing to suggest that any of the West's heroes,
good or bad, behaved reprehensibly to a decent woman. But the
Western has nursed a sense of threat, a murky shadow, a hint of a
fate worse than death, usually administered—or rather, *nearly* administered—by a whisky breathing desperado in need of a shave. Rape,
the dread word, has hovered just behind the print of page after page
of Westerns since they began. It is in part carrying on the tradition
of the rescue of the maiden in distress by the gallant knight. As in a
medieval landscape populated with dragons and sorcerers and wicked
barons the Western terrain could contain special hazards for the vulnerable female. In many cases these are deliberately exploited to make
the most of that most enduring aspect of femininity, sexual helpless-
ness. Every aggressive phrase, every lowering look, every degree of
rough handling, can be made to suggest the possibility of rape.

In the Western less trustful women, or more experienced, carry a
lady-like derringer which a gloved hand can produce from the front
of a dress if the need arises. According to Hamlin Garland such a
precaution would have been unnecessary. He wrote, in *The Moccasin
Ranch* (1909):

Formalities counted for little, and yet with all this freedom of inter-
course, this close companionship, no one pointed the finger of gossip
towards any woman. The girls in their one-room huts received calls
from the bachelor neighbours with the confidence that comes from
purity of purpose, both felt and understood.[8]

This is in the halcyon days of the early settlement, and the enterprise is regarded both romantically and from a sternly conventional
viewpoint: it is the women who might have been the victims of
gossip. This transplantation of a very limited social attitude does
not read well in a Western context.

It does not always happen that respectability breeds respect, and it
is here that the Western does manipulate the more open society of the
frontier. There *are* circumstances under which a decent woman might
be molested without reflection on her character. It is tempting to make
the most of female frailty in a situation that would seem to demand
more toughness than we would expect from an Eastern young lady.
And it is tempting to provide an opportunity for the hero to exhibit

his gallantry. An impeccable attitude to women, whether or not he becomes romantically involved, has always, with occasional exceptions, been an important facet of the hero's character.

It is, for instance, easier in a Western context to allow a hero to behave with courtesy towards a prostitute. The first Western writer to allow his hero to treat a tart like a lady was Bret Harte in his famous story *The Outcasts of Poker Flats*. John Oakhurst the gambler is the only man to treat the prostitutes evicted by the town's moral citizens with any decency or kindness. The situation reappears with distinction in *Stagecoach* (which is to say Ernest Haycox's story *Stage to Lordsburg*, on which the movie is based) where the Ringo Kid behaves with quiet gallantry towards the sad and nervous prostitute who has been run out of town by upright ladies.

At one time it was felt that the Western hero didn't have much to do with women.

... the Western hero stands apart from all other male 'leads' of the screen. Romance is barred from his life. Always impeccably good-mannered and gallant towards women in an aloof, impersonal way, he never becomes emotionally involved—and certainly, for all the rough stuff to which he treats the villain, would never behave with the famous James Mason brutality.[9]

But this has never been quite true. A strain of romance has run right through the Western, certainly from *The Virginian* on, although the hero who rides off into the sunset to pursue his lonely way is possibly the most significant type of Western hero. In most cases the fact that the hero will be romantically involved is established from the outset. It certainly is in Zane Grey's stories, in which women feature prominently. They are often quite tough heroines, but always beguilingly feminine, and frequently in real danger with the hero suitably arriving at the eleventh hour to perform his rescue.

Grey dwells salaciously on the virgin innocence of hero and heroine, and we find lingering descriptions of narrow escapes from fates worse than death. In *To the Last Man* Grey reaches great heights in this vein. In a heavily breathing scene witnessed by the hero the villain rips off the heroine's blouse. As Grey puts it, 'the unleashed passion of the man required violence'.[10] The hero tries hard to avert his eyes from the girl's nakedness, but as he must also be poised to save her (he is wounded, which gives Grey an opportunity to prolong the scene) this proves difficult. The scene is a stew of lust, blood and nudity with Grey holding the reins of propriety with practised ease. He is a master at this: it is allowable for the girl's breasts to be bared if the ostensible motive is to appall us through the eyes of the hero, and not to titillate. He renders the conclusion of *Riders of the Purple Sage* acceptable, by taking the edge off its impropriety—unmarried hero and heroine are trapped in a sealed valley, perhaps for ever. He deftly blurs the issue in a haze of romance lit by a glow of purity, purity all the more powerful, not to say astonishing, for the burgeoning sexuality of both throughout the book.

Ellen, the heroine of *To the Last Man*, escapes. In 1921 this was obligatory: it also makes the element of exploitation more apparent. The heroine of *Hang 'Em High* (1969) is the victim of rape, and lives, respected, in a bustling frontier community. She is a competent woman, aloof, certainly not helpless. Her fascination (she is played by Inger Stevens) is due precisely to the fact that she is not a pathetic female ruined by rape, and her unconventionality makes a good partner for Clint Eastwood's Marshal Cooper. It is of interest that the Western context is flexible enough to make both this situation and its opposite equally convincing. In *Duel at Diablo* the young woman who returns to her community after a period of captivity by Apaches is treated like dirt. It is known that she was forced to marry an Apache and the town feels that a woman who has submitted to an Indian might as well submit to the whole town.

The film, encased as it is in a thoroughly conventional plot, becomes interesting through that part of the plot that concerns the heroine's escape from her white husband, who can barely tolerate her, in her attempt to recover her half Apache baby. It shares some of the characteristics of *The Stalking Moon*. Both films make the point that if a woman is forced to choose between death and an Apache husband she is likely to choose the latter, and she is likely also to love her child even if she has little affection for the father. And as in *The Stalking Moon* a loner hero is drawn to a woman who is as unfit for a conventional life as himself.

In a novel by Will Cook, *Two Rode Together*, a white woman rescued from the Comanches has some feeling for her Indian husband and expresses her grief in traditional Indian fashion when he is killed by the white men who rescue her. Significantly when she is safely returned to the fort no one will dance with her at a ball given in honour of her deliverance. She is soiled goods. It is a sad little episode not, in the novel, central to the theme. What is of interest is that we have, though not as heroine this time, a woman forced into an isolated independence in much the same way as is a particular kind of Western hero.

The numb, inarticulate Sara Carver in *The Stalking Moon*, without relations or friends, an embarrassment to the army, unacceptable in normal white society, is like these other women an outcast, and it is by being an outcast that she achieves something close to the status of the loner hero. But neither she, the victim, nor the more active Etta

Place, are typical Western heroines of the last ten years. The mode remains, as a rule, traditional. We have slightly less glamorous prostitutes, and rather more glamorous gunslingers, a sprinkling of more realistic victims, but very, very few Western makers who have made convincing use of women's life in the West, either in terms of conveying something like the reality of their existence or of dramatising their mythic potential.

So the frontier woman has neither enjoyed the expansion of the myth nor a genuine attempt to present her difficulties. There is a great deal of potential and so far we have only had hints of the possibilities. Yet it would be misleading to underestimate the significance of the women who do appear. If many Western heroines are superfluous many of the women in secondary roles are of some importance: they are, in their way, essential to the myth. The myth cannot survive with only the support of the characterless, unsmudged heroine.

We are used to seeing the dance hall girl or the town tart as a brash, gay, sometimes witty woman with nerves of steel. She is of course a necessary foil to the young innocent whom the hero may win. She is also an important gesture towards the West's wildness and to a situation which everyone accepts but few care to elaborate. Sometimes she is a pretty little plaything, like the big-eyed lisping blonde in *Rough Night in Jericho*; sometimes a more sombre woman, suggestive of depths of character and passion. She can be anything from a floosie to a woman of power, and there is, not surprisingly, a much greater range of character amongst the fallen than amongst the virtuous.

The inmates of the Fort Grant brothel in *Hang 'Em High* are under the strict control of a regal and matronly woman who looks after her girls with some affection. The establishment has some elegance. But if here the relationship between drifter and brothel is all ease and relaxation it does ignore some problematic issues. The more comfortable, clean and acceptable such an establishment is the more ambiguous is the situation of those who work in it. Are they well-groomed, decent young women or are they victims of exploitation to be pitied and saved, or are they irredeemable sluts regarded with suspicion and bitterness by the community's respectable females? There was always the possibility that their own husbands and sons were customers.

In the Western we get most versions of the woman of ill repute, but least frequently do we get the girl who is really down and out. The life of a prostitute could be as grim, lonely and loveless as that of the most remote settler's daughter. They shared the same lack of choice in what they did with their lives. Girls came West lured by hopes of financial gain, like anybody else, and pushed by a grim understanding of the lack of opportunities in the East. Once West there was little a single girl could do. The dance hall, the saloon and the brothel were usually the only alternative sources of employment. A woman in the West was above all a commodity. If it was not her entertainment value that was bought and sold it was her domestic value. It was of course a situation not confined to the West, but the bareness of Western society emphasised it. It was, for so many women, their last hope.

As we have seen, women were one of the diversions a town had to offer men on the move. A girl's function in the dance hall or saloon was to look decorative and get the men to spend money. They were at the mercy of the proprietor on the one hand, the customers on the other. If they were not exactly prostitutes they were assumed to be of easy virtue. The Western has presented distinct types of the woman of not necessarily irreclaimable but certainly dubious morality. They are often of European origin—'Frenchie' appears in more than one Western. There are many Irish girls. 'Frenchie' is usually tough, resilient, influential, the Irish girl often worn out and bitter. The mainstream Western frequently presents the buxom blonde with a heart of gold, occasionally a fallen angel struggling to abandon a life she hates. Towns in the south-west always seem to be densely populated with sultry flesh at easy rates. In *The Wild Bunch* it is certainly not to Peckinpah's credit that he makes use of that opprobious cliché that all Mexican girls are tarts. Mexican women, like the men, are expendable.

There are a few memorable exceptions. *Ride the High Country*'s massive whore is probably the nearest the screen has got to what John Coleman called 'a gen-yew-ine clapped-up tart'[11] and she is superb. The climate of the film is such that we can readily imagine this queen of revelry spreading disease and Billy, a young resident of the mining camp who has clearly made use of its amenities, passing it on to his newly-wed wife. The self-hating, dignified Irish girl in *Killer on a Horse* is memorable for a different reason. She communicates a drastic loneliness, a depth of private suffering. But in recent years the brothel and the prostitute have become vehicles for comedy and light relief with no suggestion of misery or disease or desperation. Comedy that turns on sex always has immense potential, but the jollity and the wholesomeness that forms the dominant image leaves out a great deal.

William Cox's novel *The Duke* indicates a little of what most Westerns ignore. There are two women in this story who are important characters, one a twenty year old girl from New England who has come West for lack of opportunity back home, the other an older, experienced, toughened woman. The younger has a job in a bar; she serves drinks and wanders amongst 'the Saturday night gamblers, smiling at one and all'.[12] The older woman is a waitress, but is obviously not what she seems. She has behind her a mysterious, embittering past, has survived an overdose of laudanum, and before the book finishes contemplates another. The barrenness and cheapness of her life pushes her to desperation, yet she is not weak, but a positive and sympathetic character. The book ends, of course, happily for her, united with a man who understands the kind of life she has led. She is romanticised, she is beautiful, cultivated, educated, but she does suggest quite powerfully the vulnerability of a woman alone on the frontier.

Laudanum provided a not uncommon solution to misery, opium too. Neither were difficult to come by. Both were standard nineteenth century palliatives. There was not much in life for the ageing prostitute unless she was one of the few who rose to the heights of proprietorship, and the young were just as likely to succumb to depression and self-disgust. Andy Adams, writing from experience, describes the Dew-Drop-In Dance Hall in Ogallala.

Here might be seen the frailty of women in every grade and condition. From girls in their teens, launching out on a life of shame, to the adventuress who had once had youth and beauty in her favour, but it was now discarded and ready for the final dose of opium and the coroner's verdict—all were there in tinsel and paint, practising a careless exposure of their charms.[13]

Occasionally in the Western we do come across a whisky-sodden, worn-out woman, but the effects of liquor are usually represented in girlish giggles. It is curious that the descent of the innocent girl into the depths of prostitution, a much worked plot in fiction, has not found its way into the Western.

In 1893 a Colorado newspaper recorded a suicide attempt by a girl called Rose Vastine. The glib tone of the report does not disguise the underlying tragedy.

Rose Vastine, known about the camp as 'Timberline', became weary of the trials and tribulations of this wicked world and decided to take a trip over the range, and to this end brought into play a forty-one calibre pistol. With the muzzle at her lily white breast and her index finger on the trigger she waited not to contemplate the sad result. A slight contraction of the muscles caused the gun to empty its contents into Rose, the ball passing through the upper portion of her left lung.[14]

The wound was not fatal, but Rose's action, if not typical, was symptomatic.

The nature of her usual occupation meant that the drifting female made little impression on the communities that sustained her. Influence came from success, money and staying put. Those who did not reach the top had nothing to contribute—or were prevented from contributing—to the process of development. Her respectable sister could do little more than attempt to impose a well-understood old order.

There must have been times when she could have cried bitterly as she saw the few obvious pleasures monopolised by the young and the immoral. Understandable is the difficulty of choice when her husband died and her only possible occupations were boardinghouse keeper or prostitute. Every fibre of her being called for a new and better social order where the usual social values were respected and where children could be reared without contamination from a crude and lawless society.[15]

Almost every woman in the West felt threatened. The hold onto a conventional, protected life was so tenuous, the reversals could be so drastic, and any attempt to undertake an unprotected, unconventional life so demanding. In such a society the women, like the men, most often had to make a choice between feeding on the crudity and lawlessness and condemning out of hand anything that did not conform to a limited and unforgiving attitude.

Yet there were women who made a good thing out of their immoral trade, had no doubts about its value, and took a certain pride in handling things properly. There were standards in prostitution just as in any other form of business. Elliot Paul describes in his autobiographical *A Ghost Town on the Yellowstone* two establishments in Glendive at the turn of the century.

The principal madams in the Glendive stockade were both smart women and fine troupers, but not at all alike. Jack Little, short, squat and stocky, had a hoarse whisky baritone voice. She wore black silk stockings and a short, stiff ballet skirt that left quite an area of flesh tones uncovered, and was the 'hail-fellow-well-met type'. Mona Mason, on the other hand, had been a Southern society belle before, as she put it, she 'got on to herse'f'. Jack, in a tough land, wanted her cat-house to be the toughest spot, and attended to the bouncing herself, if anybody got unruly enough to warrant being thrown out. Jack's theory was that 'men don't shoot women unless they love 'em'. Mona was a soft-spoken, polite and languorous woman, who seemed to have no bones, and never raised her voice. She thought that, since Montana was doing so well by her, she could bring some Southern grace and hospitality into Montana, and she did. She could not get many Southern sporting girls, that far away from home, and the few she got from Dixie could not stand the Montana climate. So she trained the Middle-Western hookers who drifted West from Chicago, Omaha, Kansas City and St. Paul not to shout or drink beer from bottles, and no matter how many times they had to leave the dance hall or the parlour in the course of a night, they were required to put their corsets back on and hook them properly before they appeared again.[16]

As with the hero, fashions in heroines change. In the early days the helpless maiden was popular, and alongside these—they are regular denizens of W. S. Hart's pictures—are toughies in the shape of blatant bar-room girls. Zane Grey's books introduced some more active heroines, although as we have seen in a crisis they were suitably helpless. Ernest Haycox wrote about interesting women, though they suffered in translation to the screen. It was more than anything fashions in the cinema that forced the Western to be merely decorative. The Gene Autry era produced the heroine it deserved, a rigorously permanent-waved cowgirl in fringes and boots. The successor to this, reflecting a more general trend, was the woman who emphasised the positive good of domesticity, the woman who waited loyally for her man to return, prayed that he would give up his gun. We see women tending and feeding their men.

But almost from the start the most attractive kind of Western female is the girl who wears jeans and rides a horse and, to some extent at least, responds to an adventurous, demanding man's world by doing a man's work. There is something particularly appealing in a woman, with of course her femininity never in question, in masculine garb tackling masculine difficulties. The fact that this is usually manipulated in such a way as to enlarge the hero does not destroy the fact that in a context where a woman is allowed to enter a man's world there is much more scope for female action.

Emerson Hough's Taisey, young ranch owner in his novel *North of 36* (filmed two years later by Irvin Willat) dresses like a man and accompanies the herd she owns on the trail drive. Of course without the help of a dedicated man she would never win through, but although ultimately she is dependent she is able to make something of both her freedom and her responsibility. One of the nicest of tomboy heroines is Mariette Hartley's role in *Ride the High Country*. We respond to her partly because she does seem to be a genuine product of rough isolation. She shares the life of a demanding father and has to act as ranch hand, cook and cleaner. With cropped red hair and freckles and shapeless grubby trousers her transformation to a bride wearing her mother's wedding dress in a raucous mining camp has a wistful quality of reality.

There have been some long haired, wild riding female hellions. The girl in *El Dorado* has been brought up by a father amongst brothers (so often the wives have not survived) and is as instinctive and skillful as an animal who has to fight for existence. She is won by James Caan as the enigmatic knife-thrower and it seems a suitably eccentric match. These tough frontier women have been appearing quite frequently in the television serials, again reflecting trends elsewhere, in *The Virginian* for instance, a much needed contrast to the wholesome Betsy. There was a splendid though sad version of a Calamity Jane in *The High Chaparral* who shoots, holds her whisky and cusses with the best of the men. She runs her own freighting company, drives the wagons herself, completely untramelled by civilised life. Yet even here the emphasis is on the waif-like quality of this young, tough woman fending for herself, and she is not regarded as a suitable mate for the hero: he may be a degree uncouth but he belongs to a well-established, successful ranching family.

The particular appeal of the girl dressed as a boy, of the highlighting of femininity through masculine actions, is a vein the Western is likely to continue exploiting. What is to be hoped is that much more will be made of the immense potential for heroines that lies in the anarchy of the Western situation. For now, the tomboy remains an eccentric. What still dominates the Western is a changing image of the chocolate box heroine, who was so firmly established in the forties and reigned triumphant throughout the fifties. Raquel Welch with a rifle in her hand is really little more than an up-dated version of chocolate box. Her function is inevitably primarily decorative.

The chocolate box heroine has become more versatile, but her versatility has not made her more interesting. Although the stetsoned cowgirl never wholly emerged from the B Western there is now a more sophisticated heroine recognisable as being of a similar species. We find her most frequently in the television series. She does as well as a hostess in an evening gown as she does on a horse, and she can converse with State Governors as easily as with cowpunchers. She has the confidence that arises from a secure status. She is an all-purpose horse-opera heroine and she is generally very, very dull.

This all-purpose heroine is a fusion of what have been traditionally in the Western two general types: the decorative heroine, who is associated with civilisation, domesticity, the schoolhouse and the church, and the spunky heroine, who is not averse to riding the range and encountering man-sized dangers but who is almost always sufficiently tamed to provide a suitable mate for the hero. A lack of conformity to these types provides a clue to the more interesting Western movies and the more readable Western books. The fusion suggests that taste has outgrown the negative heroine, but it does not suggest that Westerns are in general responding to this. Traditional versions are being stretched to provide opportunities for more screen sex, but the new realism only seems able to cope with women in the West on these terms. Of course there are exceptions, some of which have been noted, but it is worth repeating that the Western has not incorporated women significantly and creatively into the myth although the potential is there.

Allied with the traditional division between chocolate box and spunky, and allied more closely with the rigid separation of decent and fallen, is a conventional pattern of dark and fair. Often enough to be of some significance the respectable heroines are blonde and ladies of dubious morals are brunette. The classic oppositions of *High Noon* provide an excellent example of this dark/fair pattern. The Quaker wife is fair, the woman with whom the hero has clearly been involved in the past is dark. The Quaker wife becomes a symbol not so much of love and purity as of lawfulness and civilisation, again a traditional role for the woman in the Western. The woman in Will's past is a reminder of passion and recklessness. With some irony the fact that Will's wife, once more a Quaker armed, takes unto herself a gun helps the balance in favour of the blonde. A touch of spunk is needed to match her with the hero. In terms of this pattern the redhead provides a useful compromise. A significant number of the Western's spunky but respectable heroines have red hair. It suggests spirit without vice, virtue without insipidness.

A majority of Westerns have the idea of marriage present at some point. What in fact is the Western's ideal of a wife? The wife, whether existing or intended, has a role of the greatest importance to play in the Western, for without her the note of romance, of reconciliation, of promise for the future on which so many Westerns end would not be possible. A few end with regret and parting or death and are sometimes equally romantic. But this does not change the predominant emphasis, which remains squarely on the fate of hero and heroine. The powerful, traditional belief that hope lies in a repetition of a conventional, sanctioned cycle, however extraordinary and anarchic the context, communicates itself in the Western as it does elsewhere.

Sometimes the ending is more than just a clinch, but a positive if highly romantic statement about the hero's new life. 'This was what he had to live for. And as he drew her closer, feeling the giving in her, he knew that all the uncertainty and the emptiness of his tomorrows was gone.'[17] This is taken from the last page of a Western by a highly prolific writer. The suggestiveness is pervasive but vague. The hero, a drifter, a fighter, can never, whatever his courage and physical achievements, fulfil himself without a woman. This is what it was all for. No more loneliness, no more emptiness. A life of mutual comfort and companionship. A standard theme of countless songs, novels and poems, and of course, which we all recognise, an undermining of most of what makes the action hero what he is. Because the Western heroine is repeatedly characterised as a civilising influence her effect on the independent hero can only be destructive.

The hero who rides off womanless on the final page retains his integrity. He has not been enticed by visions of domestic bliss, or if he admits their attractions he dismisses them. Every hero who continues on his lonely way protects something vital about himself. Yet the solitary exit does not occur as frequently as might be supposed. The fact that *Shane* embodies so much that is best about the Western almost makes us believe that its ending is typical. Shane is certainly so powerful that he carries the myth onwards and we see in him the preservation of the lonely freedom that countless lesser heroes, brought to a halt by the fair sex, lose. And Shane's attraction is enhanced by the fact that he knows he is leaving behind him a woman who loves him, and he knows he is right to do so.

For those who relinquish that particular brand of independence it is not just any woman who can fill the emptiness of those tomorrows. Time after time the Western hero unites himself with vacancy and thus does graver damage to the Western's total effect. It is a symptom of the failure to recognise that more positive heroines can only enhance the value of the myth. In the Western context, with hardship a part of everyday life, it is particularly crass to present marriage as a passport to ease and happiness, especially when it is so often to a woman who is ignorant, or at least not convincingly knowledgeable, of frontier life.

We look for wives who will not negate the heroes, and sometimes we can find them. At the end of Louis L'Amour's *Heller With a Gun* the hero significantly gets the tough, Denver-bred youngster who is ready to ride after him rather than the more proper and superficially more attractive young woman from the East. This is a favourite contrast of L'Amour's. In *Last Stand at Papago Wells* the sophisticated Jennifer has to learn from the rough and ready Junie before she can qualify as mate for the hero, whose initial remark is 'You look nice but you don't mean anything.'[18] In the course of an Indian attack Jennifer acquires some meaning. Yet there has to be more to the perfect mate than toughness. If a woman has to pass certain frontier tests she will not do to share the life of the Westerner if she cannot also make a home, a home that will be a refuge from the wild, and this has all the traditional connotations. L'Amour ends another of his books like this:

But he was remembering a long meadow fresh with new-cut hay, a house where smoke would soon again rise from the chimney, and where shadows would gather in the darkness under the trees, quiet shadows. And beside him a woman held in her arms a sleeping child . . . a woman who would be there with him, in the house before that hearth.[19]

A quiet vision consistent with the deep current of sentimentalism that runs through the Western as through all other forms of popular literature. But no soft moment can disguise the real content of such a vision. We are back to the harsh experience of Matthilda Zachary, dimmed and blurred. The Indians have been defeated, but that vision cannot be sustained without heart-breaking toil. No hero can soften the reality, though there is quite a chance that the idyllic picture will soften the hero. We can find a corrective, unexpectedly, in one of the later books of Eugene Cunningham, *The Trail from the River* (1939). His hero says:

You have read a book about the big handsome cowboy marrying the lovely school-ma'am. What you and the other fool-cowboys didn't read, though, was the book for grown-ups about the married life they had, people as different as day and night penned up in the same house year after year, one of 'em eating with a knife and the other eating with a fork! [20]

The big handsome cowboy is clearly the Virginian. Wister's Eastern school teacher gave the Western heroine a discordant start. The screen now trails behind the novel in giving us interesting and convincing heroines. Not only for the sake of the Western hero, who now seems more inclined to die than to marry, which is one way of preserving his independence, but even more for the sake of the unfulfilled potential of women in myth since the time of classical Greece, a test of the Western's ability to grant women a positive contribution to the myth would be a welcome experiment.

ELEVEN

Saddle Tramp

I always wanted to see what was on the other side of the hill. Sometimes on long distances me and a companion would move with a covered wagon and a chuckbox but oftentimes I'd just go alone with my horse. Longest trip I ever did do by horse was 1,000 miles and when I was sixteen I rode 600 miles from Throckmorton to Dumas, with a bedroll and cooking for myself on cowchip fires.

Orb Gosset, as quoted by Kenneth Allsop
Hard Travellin'

When the work ran out the drifting cowboy had to move on, maybe just to a neighbouring ranch, maybe a thousand miles. Movement, too, was part of the cowboy's personality. He rarely settled down. Even marriage did not necessarily mean a fixed abode. In 1952 John Leakey, a cowman all his life, was still drifting, back and forth from Texas to Montana, in a pick-up with the back converted into the semblance of a covered wagon. He was nearly eighty. Kenneth Allsop's Orb Gossett was seventy-nine and settled down when he had to give up riding two years before. 'I cried when I sold my saddle. I'd had that saddle for twenty-five years and when I sold it I figured "I'm through now". So I don't ride no more.'[1]

In Eugene Rhodes's story *The Bird in the Bush* (1917) Andrew Jackson Bates considers it time to settle down. But even before circumstances force him to ride away and abandon his ranch we sense his restlessness. 'You'll always be wondering what is on the other side of the hill, and you'll always be wondering what is on the other side of the world, and wanting to see', says the girl who refuses his proposal of marriage.[2] When he suddenly becomes disillusioned with his dream farm it is certain that it won't be long before he gets on his horse and moves on.

All of a sudden, I felt tired out and old and blue and bald and all-alonesome; and I couldn't get seein' things any more. I couldn't see myself makin' 'cequias and settin' out fruit-trees; I just knowed that

soil wouldn't grow alfalfa; my cows would climb out over them pin-
nacles; I couldn't think of no decent brand for 'em, and I couldn't
think of no name for my cussed lake; and as for rip-rappin' that dam
when the water got low, it made me fair sick to think of it.[3]

The cowboy does not often have any strong belief that things will be
better over the next hill. He may have a private dream of an ideal
spot where he will settle down and raise cows and kids. 'I like to have
a few cows and some fruit trees. A little place. Somewhere with good
water, and a house I build myself. I helped build two, three houses an'
I figure I can build me a good one,' says the young Lonnie Foreman
in Last Stand at Papago Wells.[4] But this kind of thing tends to be a
wistful hope, insistent in time of danger or hardship rather than a
feasible reality. And the young men who did settle down in the 1880s
or '90s, when the dust of frontier strife was beginning to settle, were
often the old men who moved on in the 1930s, when depression and
the Dust Bowl disaster undermined their livelihood.

The dominant image of the saddle tramp is of a tough, self-reliant,
easy-going character, who spends his money, when he has any, on
gambling, hard liquor and women, when he can get them, and philosophically accepts the fact that most of the time he is broke.

I thought I was tough and I didn't wear a slicker, one of them over-
coats that throws off the rain. I just toughed it out, sleeping in wet
bedding or riding all night. You don't get no strays now because every-
wheres is fenced in but then we'd have to ride fifty miles bringing in
the strays. The steers were wilder then—they weren't fed and they
lived wild. A rabbit or lightning would make them stampede and it
took days to round them up again, and you could get skinned real bad
if you got in the way of a stampede.[5]

He can look after himself, wears a gun, tends his horses. His comforts
and his solaces are relative to his hard life. The saddle tramp is not
always a cowboy: he can be gunman, horse breaker, outlaw or army
scout. But he travels on horseback, often alone, usually a stranger, and
these are the things that make up his character.

In Will Penny, with its quiet, lyrical moments, Charlton Heston
plays an illiterate, middle-aged cowboy. The job is over, the cattle
safely loaded into box cars. Will Penny rides north. Winter approaches
and there is not much work on the ranches. Will Penny rides into a
desolate town, a huddle of rickety structures on the dusty prairie,
gets his whisky and his woman, both of which he handles with a tired
acceptance of his needs, rides on. The camera strays with casual
affection over some of the details of the cowboy's life, revealing without any fuss moments of calm and stunning beauty.

The film emphasises with some delicacy (the effects are due almost
entirely to Lucien Ballard's camera and Heston's portrayal) the general

situation of the saddle tramp and the particular character of Will Penny. Charlton Heston, so splendidly both mighty and wistful in his heroism, has a restrained dignity. Will Penny is nearly fifty, getting old for the kind of work he has to do. He is alone, but he does have friends, and between them there exists an immensely important bond of loyalty. The code is a strict one: decency, courage, loyalty, not just for their own sake but because they are the things that make life bearable. What is there in life for an ageing cowboy, who has known only cattle and the West, who when it comes to employment is likely to be rejected in favour of a younger man, who has no home, no wife, no family?

It is not quite pathos that emerges from the movie, but a sad, admirable strength that works quite independently of a plot that demands heroics. There are crudities and foreseeable conventionalities in the action, but beneath there is struck a note of sensitivity that is quite alien to the conventional Western. The result is a film of unusual character. The drifter has moved out of stereotype. He is neither the community liberator nor the mean 'heavy'. He moves on, but not into the sunset with a roseate glow around him. He moves away from the chance of happiness and towards the inevitable deterioration of his life. His life is insignificant, yet he is of heroic stature. And Heston is much more convincing in such a character, the average saddle tramp, the common man, as hero, than Marlon Brando who attempts something similar in *Southwest to Sonora*.

Brando's gringo, returning with his only possession, a valuable horse, to the Mexican family with whom he grew up and who live, significantly, on the United States side of the border, is shabby and unshaven when we first see him. Brando tries to play him as 'an ordinary man', of not much consequence, despised by his enemies, but latent within him heroic qualities which emerge when the need arises. But there is a self-consciousness in the portrayal, a deliberately anti-heroic posture, which, even as he is suggesting the smell and the dirt seems to be insisting that given the right moment he will slip easily into heroism. We guess at once that this is no run-of-the-mill drifter, and when we see him later in black Mexican gear (Brando's usual Western outfit) we know.

Heston slips gracefully and with restraint into a role that utilises characteristics that are almost always present in his acting. Even as the magnificent El Cid in Anthony Mann's epic movie there was something touching, almost humble, almost shy, in Heston's portrayal of perhaps the most splendid of Europe's heroes. As the illiterate cowpuncher his acting has a quiet vibrancy which communicates a great deal of what is most attractive in the legendary Westerner.

In one guise or another the saddle tramp rides through most Westerns and has always done so. In the stories of Eugene Rhodes, who surely did more for the Western than ever Wister did, with his independent line and rich core of humour, most of the characters tend to be on the drift, or at the most temporary denizens of any one community. Their wandering past and uncertain future hang about them as part of their everyday equipment. If they are permanent residents, like Emil James the sheriff who features in a number of Rhodes' stories, very often the job they do takes them far afield. For the drifter it becomes a habit to resist certain kinds of temptation. He may succumb to a pretty girl, but when the time comes for him to move on he will leave her with feelings no more drastic than a pleasant regret. A great deal of American and European folk culture hinges on just this. The handsome stranger, who loves with passion but will never settle down, moves in and out of song and story, often leaving a baby behind him for remembrance.

The romantic possibilities of the wayfaring stranger are enormous. As each new Western hero emerges on the screen the challenge of mystery comes with him. The hint of temporariness, of an unhappy past, family brutally killed, a wife lost to the Indians, a faithless lover, an unnecessary killing, and an unknown future makes the most of the air of mystery which the satifactory Western hero carries with him. Shane, with past troubles on his mind. Sergio Leone's 'man with no name', without a past, without a future, tantalisingly independent. To be on the move gives the most stove-up of cow punchers something extra, something that the stationary man just does not have. Places he has known, mountains and valleys he has seen, rivers he had crossed, deserts he has survived: all these are woven into the tapestry of the drifter's experience and personality. The saddle tramps reinforced both the reality and the legend of the moving American.

In the Western he is, first of all, an object of curiosity. It is not just who he is that is important, but where he has been and what he has done. He may be a challenge, he may be a threat, or may be just a broke cowpoke looking for a job. When he first appears we look for hints of the function he is to have.

They appeared at the top of a small hill a good hour before sundown, a cold and blowing end to a hard day of riding that had never really warmed up, with the wind springing suddenly and causing each to pull hard on his hat. Three of them, their horses blending in with the brown grass of a Colorado November.[6]

Here is a description by a writer conscious of the cinema who presents his characters as the camera would. Gradually we form a reaction, first identifying the most important of the three men, then identifying the kind of man he is.

With a nod of his head, the one in the middle, the straight-backed, hard-faced man who rode his horse as if he were part of the animal, with his mouth and eyes tight and right hand trailing at his butt in a menacing and slightly arrogant readiness, proceeded down the side of the hill, and the others followed, carefully, but with no sign of hesitation as their horses slipped on the frozen ground, and then rode quickly, but not fast, to the trail.[7]

We have part of the characterisation already, 'menacing', 'arrogant', an alert gunfighter obviously. A few pages later we get a closer look at him.

A shade over six feet, a sheep fleece jacket, Cheyenne chaps, he looked mean and there was a hardness about him. A well-kept blue steel .44 Frontier Colt hung low on the gunfighter's right leg and was tied down over whipcord trousers.... The gun was bright and clean with what looked like an eight-inch barrel; the holster was the opposite, old and scratched.[8]

It is a portrait of a hardened gunslinger, and that is exactly what the man is. But he is also our hero, and if we had not yet guessed the fact is confirmed very quickly.

It was the gunfighter's eyes.... They were black and they looked straight at you; but they were *soft* eyes. It just didn't fit the hardness of the face.[9]

Now we can identify him completely: a tough man with a good heart.

These descriptions are taken from the early pages of Richard Jessup's novel *Chuka* (1961). All that he uses in his portrait of Chuka is conventional material. Not only is the man of granite with a heart of gold a standard Western figure, the details too are familiar—the gun, the right hand, the way he rides his horse. Our stranger, appearing suddenly on the crest of a hill in time honoured fashion, our range bum, is recognised as the action packed hero of the great outdoors.

On the screen we look for these things with nothing to guide us but our experience of the Western. If we are seeing one of our familiar heroes—John Wayne, Richard Widmark, Randolph Scott, say —we don't have to look for these details. We take them as read. But when the Western maker starts to take them as read then he has descended into the regions of stereotype, relying on the convention itself to provide what he does not. One of the reasons that John Wayne's screen heroes never fail (until recently) is that he never assumes that we all know who and what the Western hero is. He shows us everything. Each time we start afresh, while at the same time joyously identifying the Wayne we know and love.

The screen hero has made it easier for us to identify the hero in print. The writer has a visual frame of reference and descriptions often seem to be angled for the camera. The saddle tramp has reality in terms of screen personalities. Hart in his frequently ambivalent gun-fighting roles opened up the possibilities of the hard man with a conscience, where the toughness mattered most. It was what Wister was not able to do with the Virginian, for the rifts of sentiment, which Wister must have thought necessary to make him palatable for the East, are too wide. Even Zane Grey, who probably did more than anyone to fashion the Western hero who can kill and love, tends to lean so far into romance of a particularly unrealistic nature that the toughness seems a temporary quality which will be given up in favour of living happily ever after as soon as civilisation comes to the wild West.

Hart's steely loneliness has a striking quality which his contemporaries Buck Jones and Tom Mix lack. Mix was the forerunner of that glossy and glorified version of the saddle tramp that became institutionalised in the late thirties and forties when Gene Autry, Roy Rogers, the Lone Ranger, Hopalong Cassidy (very different from Mulford's original) and many others emerged in movies, comics and, for some, the television series. Here was the range bum with the dirt and sweat well and truly rubbed off and in clothes that would not have survived many hours riding in desert or brush country. He has a loyal horse, and very often a loyal sidekick, in the case of the Lone Ranger a tame Indian. He rides into a tricky situation, strums his guitar with one leg hooked over the saddle horn (often involving parted lovers or small boys), and suitably brings to justice the mean villain, whose meanness is possibly indicated by the fact that he is cruel to his horse and doesn't shave. Often the hero is a known and loved *deus ex machina*, applied to in time of trouble, often appearing unasked. At other times he is a mysterious stranger (the Lone Ranger) opportunely on the scene who will vanish when all is set right.

The gentle-voiced Shane is a splendid distillation of all this and an appropriate finale to the era. But Schaefer's story owes nothing to the slick singing cowboy. In the long run we have to look back to Hart and Zane Grey for the cool, composed, good hearted gunman. The forties attempt to make the cowboy over in its own image could have been disastrous for the Western myth. In the hands of directors like Ford, Howard Hawks and Anthony Mann, with Fritz Lang's three Westerns contributing and the remarkable movies *The Oxbow Incident* and Arthur Penn's *The Left-Handed Gun* (1948) as striking reminders, the Western maintained its balance and the durability of the myth. Anthony Mann's saddle tramp heroes, James Stewart almost without exception, have done as much as Shane to preserve that particular strain of Western character. The James Stewart hero is a lean Westerner whose relaxed, unruffled exterior, aided by

Stewart's superbly laconic croak, belies his guts and determination. This hero is a committed, single-minded man with no frills. The West he rides in is uneasy and threatening. Mann's wandering men are a product of this uneasiness.

The man from Laramie, or the hero of *Winchester '73*, are average men in the saddle with just that little extra needed to stamp them as exceptional. It is possible to identify them as the real Westerners, not the glossy exotics who ease the lives of more ordinary mortals, but men of the West capable of acting as real men of the West ought to act. If Mann's Westerns are often labelled 'realistic' it is because the distance between hero and common man is not so great, and yet we are not denied the satisfaction of seeing a man of more than ordinary courage and skill in action.

But the Western is populated with a vast array of anonymous faces, an enormous, restless population of drifters and outcasts, who provide the action with common men, cannon fodder, cowardice and reckless courage all of which helps us to measure the hero. The hero cannot exist without the unheroic. Every frontiersman had not that combination of courtesy and skill with which the myth supplies us.

... if you wish to be ridden over, stamped upon, get a cowboy to do it, and more especially the brand we employed in those days in the Sweetwater region. They were the real simon-pure, devil-may-care, roistering, gambling, immoral, revolver-heeled, brazen, light-fingered lot, and yet a dash of bravado among them that was attractive to the stranger. They had no respect for a man and little for a woman.[10]

This was the raw material of the Western hero. These were the men who provide those usually badly shaven, sullen faces that pattern the dusty town and the glowing landscape. They are the men who populate, for instance, the stories of Eugene Rhodes, one of the few Western writers who succeeded, or even tried, in making something attractive out of men whom he never attempts to present as anything but commonplace.

His 'heroes' tend to be grizzled or balding, shrewd, experienced, but nothing out of the ordinary. They know the country and they know their job. Or they are sometimes young and illogically optimistic, like Charlie Ellis.

Charlie Ellis did not know where he was; he did not know where he was going; he was not even cheered by any hope of damnation. His worldly goods were the clothes he wore, the six-shooter on his thigh, the horse between his legs, and his saddle, bridle and spurs. He had no money; no friends closer than five hundred miles. Therefore, he whistled and sang; he sat jauntily; his wide hat took on the cant joyous; he cocked a bright eye appreciatively at a pleasant world—a lonesome world just now, but great fun.[11]

This is in fact the opening of one of Rhodes' most sombre stories, in which Charlie, no more distinguished than the above description suggests, survives by keeping his presence of mind, not by any spectacularly heroic action. He is a saddle tramp with a certain amount of common sense, and the story that Rhodes builds out of this is one of his best. Charlie is in fact no more than one of the faces that in the average Western lurk in the middle distance. But he shares with the wanderers of more obviously heroic stature the fact that his moving on is not only a part of his personality but contributes to the very best of his qualities. The man continually on the move is a man always alert, never complacent, not materially ambitious (except perhaps in a dream of the future), not anchored by the responsibilities of property or family. He is necessarily independent, fast moving and flexible. And if he were not to a certain extent easy going, tolerant and uncomplaining he was creating unnecessary difficulties for himself. Above all, his own restlessness is a force he cannot resist.

Young as he might be called, he had worked stock all the way from the Panhandle to Powder River, and westward through the Beaverhead country to the Divide, and beyond. He had never been able to take root. Sooner or later, wherever he might be, the old nagging question always returned to him: 'Is this all there is?' And when that happened, all too frequently for his own good, nothing seemed possible to him but to move on.[12]

Often the restlessness is associated with the search for a 'good' woman, tough, strong, reliable and sympathetic, with the suggestion as the story ends that the restless drifter *will* settle down, make a home, have children and be absorbed into the static population of the West. In fact what we see when we are shown the settled homesteader is something that has lost all the romance of the lonely wanderer. When John Wayne as Ethan in *The Searchers*, in battered Confederate uniform, rides up after long absence and enters the settled home of his brother and greets his brother's wife and children he is instantly the focus of romance, heroism and action in the film. However strong is the appeal of family and the happy home the lonely, tired traveller dominates the sequence. The children cluster round him, his brother's wife is in love with him, his brother does not seem to be anything like the man he is. Joe cannot match Shane. The man with wife and home has become, almost, a Samson shorn of his hair.

Even in the less conventional Westerns there are usually only two alternative solutions to this difficulty. Either the travelling man mounts his horse and rides off, or he embraces the girl and the story is forced to stop short of emphasising too strongly his loss of status. Sometimes there is a kind of compromise: he rides off knowing that his faithful lover will be waiting for him. We do not actually see him abandon his independence. This can involve a final fling before he hangs up his gun. Chuka, in the last pages of the book, swears that he has just one more debt to pay off and then no more shooting. A decent home, kids ... these will supplant the gun. But on foot and weaponless, who and what is he?

Whatever he is he is less than he was with horse and gun and hundreds of miles behind and in front of him. Something that undermines many television horse operas is that they are so often based on static situations. The hero is pinned to an unchanging environment. He may be allowed to revolve around it at some distance, but the centre does not shift, and the centre is reinforced by a permanent hierarchy of characters, as in *Gunsmoke*. In *The Virginian* series Shiloh ranch, the Judge, his house and library, exude a sense of permanent property, fixed, the hub of an empire, and every cowboy on the ranch goes about his business on a long leading string. Such a situation, whatever the appeal of a particular hero, can never have the depth or the sparkle of the man who is not so firmly tied to the static. Property owning is even more dangerous to the heroic ethic than a wife, for the saddle tramp is, by powerful associations, against property as well as against marriage.

Westerns have tried to impose both marriage and property on the hero. The Western has to have its women (although it can do without them—the lack of women in *The Good, the Bad and the Ugly* doesn't damage Clint Eastwood's appeal) and it usually has to have a 'good' woman—particularly the written Western. The screen can afford to be more ambiguous. If there are good women about there has to be marriage, or at least the suggestion of marriage. And marriage in its turn suggests the owning of property—also, sometimes, vice versa. Commitment to a woman will almost inevitably mean commitment to values that go quite contrary to all that the saddle tramp's life implies. The Western has always, at least since Wister's time, been in danger of slipping into a version of romance rather than a version of the outdoor action story, and women will rise up to challenge the freedom of the saddle tramp in the most unlikely places. Young Wild West is so much a boy that manly lusts one would hardly expect to trouble him, though he does have a shadowy female waiting for him at home. However, once Zane Grey's version takes over from the boy scout themes the hero's virility is seen to be an intrinsic part of his strength, and at once a problem arises. What becomes of the bar girls the prostitutes that even Zane Grey's upright heroes would naturally have recourse to, in spite of their frequent shyness when faced with decent females? They are discreetly hidden away or at the most there is a veiled reference to a poor fallen woman. It is interesting how rarely Grey describes action in a town in any detail. Even a shot of whisky in a saloon was rather a daring undertaking for these great men. In fact, Grey's Westerns, for all his lush treatment of romance, retain a broad stream of the boy scout, which makes a striking contrast with his contemporary Eugene Rhodes. Rhodes manages to banish the boy scout image and, to a large extent, women.

One of Shane's splendours will always be that he rides off leaving behind him a woman who loves him, having fought for property he himself does not own. The way he has acted has stemmed from his own personality, his skill and his conscience. He is absolutely without ulterior motive and he gains nothing for himself. He has nothing to gain, and nothing to lose, apart from his life, that is. His actions implicate nothing, represent nothing, but his own being as a hero. That is the beauty of the frontier saddle tramp, even of the hundreds who have no claim to heroic status. When the Westerner makes his lightning decisions and leaps to action, his only consideration needs to be a question of his own life or death. His freedom reduces him to the bare essentials: on this foundation his conscience and his feelings can operate. But when the episode is over the superstructure crumbles, adds, perhaps, to the strength of the foundations, but does not interfere with whatever it will be necessary to build next.

It is as if every time the lonely horseman moves on he begins again from scratch. Each time he meets a new situation, or rides into a new environment, he has to re-establish his identity. He has to test himself against new factors. He can never be quiescent, and it is this that makes the saddle tramp a romantic and a mythic figure. His mystery is fresh each time he appears. He is the incarnation of the poor man who turns out to be a god, the begger who turns out to be a king. Very often his function is precisely the same as that of these standard characters of myth. He tests a community, a household, or even an individual, and saves it if it is worthy. In doing so he establishes his own identity, exposes his real persona, confirms himself in relation to the situation and the people he has acted for. Having done so he is free to travel on.

He carries with him a glowing aura, splendidly composed of the very names of the places he has known. The names of rivers, mountain ranges, passes and badlands, deserts and water holes he has experienced inevitably romanticise him and sustain him—and are a part of the intrinsic romanticism of the West. It is one of the most magnificent things the West has to offer. Any man, however weak, or cowardly, or even evil he may be, however simply insignificant, is given something by the resonance of names, and this if all else fails will give the saddle tramp an everlasting superiority.

TWELVE

Who are These Guys?

'If the facts conflict with the legend, print the legend.'
  Edmond O'Brien in *The Man Who Shot Liberty Valance*

He laughs at death and scoffs at life;
He feels unwell unless in some strife.
He fights with a pistol, a rifle, or knife,
This reckless, rollicking cowboy.

'The Cowboy'

[1]

The screen's Butch Cassidy and the Sundance Kid are magnificently absorbed into legend in spite of the film's assurances that most of the events portrayed really happened. In such a film myth defies reality. The true facts of the Hole in the Wall gang are not important; what is, is the way the facts have lent themselves to absorption by an existing myth. Butch and his friends pulled off some daring crimes. Etta Place did exist and she was beautiful. But Butch and Etta have been invented many times and did not need to exist in order to make George Roy Hill's film possible. All he needed was the myth itself and something like one hundred years of interpretation.

In *True Grit*, Hathaway's satisfactory old fashioned film, Wayne gets away with self-parody because he himself has been absorbed into the myth. In any movie he makes he can kill, abuse, smash men's faces, and because he long ago established himself as the Western hero we simply accept this. When Wayne himself says, 'I don't act ... I react. Whatever part I'm playing ... I always have to be John Wayne just living through the experience' he confirms this.[1] Wayne has been such a success because he has become the Western hero. When in *True Grit* he charges, reins in his teeth, weapons firing in all directions, into the midst of a group of outlaws and emerges triumphant and unscathed it may seem incredible but it is certainly true to the Wayne image: if it is not what he could have done it is what he would have liked to do. The sudden transition in this sequence from a level of reality to dreams of glory is comic: the audience laughs. But it is only doing what countless Westerns have done before, and revealing once more that the myth is a lot tougher than the toughest realism.

It did look briefly as if Butch and Rooster were going to be the Western's last romantic heroes. The Eastwood persona is establishing itself as the latest in a long succession of hero types, and many Continental Westerns have tried to reproduce him. But one of Peckinpah's most recent Westerns, *The Ballad of Cable Hogue* (1970), can reassure us that the romantic Western hero is not dead. Cable Hogue becomes through Peckinpah's direction the epitome of all that is softest in Hollywood's soft centre. Wrapped in the sentiment of the stars and stripes and a whore with a heart of gold Cable Hogue, down and out, killer, materialist, becomes a highly romanticised good man—but neither Jason Robards' forthright acting nor the Western myth itself can rescue him from the woolly oblivion to which the paceless direction sends him.

Peckinpah has tried to fashion a hero from unconventional material, the West's last good man, loved by a whore, killed by an automobile. He has abandoned the hero's conventional props—he is not a dead shot or a superb rider. He trundles around on a beast barely recognisable as a horse. But to replace the props that the myth provides, well seasoned by time and constant use, Peckinpah uses such sloppy substitutes that the film almost disintegrates. In spite of some splendid visual moments, in spite of actors like L. Q. Jones and Strother Martin, a grotesque Laurel and Hardy pair out of the Peckinpah stable, the film is barely able to struggle to its sentimental conclusion.

If *Butch Cassidy* and *True Grit* are not less romantic they at least have the solidity of the myth to sustain them. *Cable Hogue* contains, undermining its modernity, a reminder of Gene Autry's cowboy code, produced in the 1940s to encourage American boyhood.

1. A cowboy never takes unfair advantage—even of an enemy.
2. A cowboy never betrays a trust.
3. A cowboy always tells the truth.
4. A cowboy is kind to small children, to old folks and to animals.
5. A cowboy is free from racial and religious prejudices.
6. A cowboy is helpful and when anyone is in trouble he lends a hand.
7. A cowboy is a good worker.
8. A cowboy is clean about his person and in thought, word and deed.
9. A cowboy respects womanhood, his parents and the laws of his country.
10. A cowboy is a patriot.[2]

In fact a surprising number of these child-sized ten commandments had long since been incorporated into the myth but their presence, except in child-sized Westerns, is generally less overt than in *Cable Hogue*.

The strength of the Western is that traditionally it has been able to combine the essence of Gene Autry's code with the excitement of human brutality. This is not something new. Legend from time immemorial has been based on just such a fusion. If the Greek heroes are not much concerned with being polite to each other they are always testing themselves against a demanding and ennobling code. The roundtable knights also, and here courtesy and honour are of intrinsic value. Robin Hood and the great legendary bandits have obviously found their way into the Western, and in their case the fundamental decency, the protection of women and the poor, is central. The Western hero belongs solidly with all of these, and in spite of the many different forms in which he has appeared and in spite of changes he will continue to do so. Cable Hogue would be nothing if we did not see him in this light. Eastwood's brutality would be unacceptable if he did not adhere to enough of the legend's basics.

In the following description we get an idea of just how the Eastwood hero does conform to what the legend demands. This is from Boetticher's original scenario for *Two Mules for Sister Sara*.

It's rock country and bleached-white spires burst jaggedly up through the desert sand in a wavering line opposite the setting sun, from south to north, where they grow in stature and seeming dignity to eventually jut their way into becoming a part of the Sierra Madre. As we scan the terrain we discover an almost imperceptible movement mostly hidden in the long evening shadows tight against the rocks. Zooming closer we recognize the figure as a lone rider astride his horse; followed by a pack-pony, loose, who trots to keep up with the long-legged animal before him. The saddle horse is a blood red roan; a thoroughbred.... The man is tall and lean, dressed in the colours of the desert and the rocks. The tans, and the browns, and the grays of his tight-fitting outfit are only broken up by the black and yellow beaded Indian moccasins which he wears instead of boots. The plain leather holster of his Colt revolver is thong-tied down just above his right knee, and his long gun, a Winchester, swings slightly with the movement of his animal, in a dirty canvas scabbard attached to the saddle just behind his left leg. A new leather case containing U.S. binoculars hangs from the saddle's pommel. And now we get our first real look at the man himself. It is impossible to determine his age. He could be thirty, or maybe even forty, but we'll never be sure because the wrinkles around his eyes and at the corner of his tight lips could have come into being from the desert sun. He wears his sweat-stained hat low down over his eyes to shade them from the fading light, but there is a sparkle of all-consuming awareness in those eyes that makes you feel certain that not even a lizard mor'n half a mile away could skitter across the sand without his knowing which way it was headed. Unpleasantly there is an aura of meanness about the man. Watching him you smell the sticky odour of hate that seemingly envelops everything around him except his horse. But in spite of the meanness that you feel, or the suspicion that his deep-rooted loathing includes even the sand and the rocks, you are suddenly overwhelmingly aware that the man is all-over, downright, beautiful. Even the slight movement of his body as he swings his head and shoulders around to check his pack-pony is cat-like and deadly ...[3]

There is enough here to indicate that this is a hero of the sixties and not of any previous decade of the Western. But there is even more that places him firmly in the tradition of a certain kind of hero. First, he is alone, and not only alone, but alone in the desert, a potentially dangerous environment. The Western hero as a lonely man in an inhospitable environment. His horse is a thoroughbred, the man himself is 'tall and lean' and wears a 'tight-fitting outfit'—the classic garb, whether in silk or denim, of the Western hero for decades. He carries a Colt and a Winchester, the West's classic weapons.

In his appearance there is the suggestion of mystery. It is impossible to guess his age. Whatever it is he clearly has vast experience behind him. The 'all-consuming awareness'—an essential in the Western hero. He may be mean, but not to his horse. He may hate, but the man is beautiful. Why? Because he is lonely, independent, self-reliant, expert, moves like an animal, and is deadly. It could be Shane, or the Virginian, or the glamorised version of a Western outlaw. The fact that this is our updated hero, mean, vicious and self-seeking, does not interfere with the hard core of the image.

The hero has changed to the extent of banishing all that is unnecessary to the image. In this case the tethers of domesticity, to a civilised life have gone. 'It was a little late when our friends got back to the ranch, but as a warm supper awaited them, they did not mind the delay.'[4] This is vintage 1904. A suggestion of homely domesticity, of young lads returning to the parental kitchen after a day's outing, pervades many of the dime novels of the period. It is there in Wister (1902). The hanging in the cottonwoods and the shoot-out with Trampas never quite dispel the essentially civilised flavour of the whole proceedings. Ned Buntline's Buffalo Bill was essentially a gentleman. There were of course ruffians and bullies, but they were rarely anything worse than ruffians and bullies.

The movies helped to bring the hero and the villain closer together although the means of distinguishing them have never disappeared. When one saw both hero and villain on the screen carrying the same weapons, dressed roughly in the same way, riding similar horses, facing the challenge of the same terrain, one could see them as products of the same environment. This element of the romance of the West survived a temporary return to the boy scout hero. From Hart onwards there was always the question, who is the stranger, good man or bad? Richard Schickel describes the W. S. Hart persona like this:

... Hart's major creation was his screen character—the good-bad man who rides out of nowhere, sets things to rights, and moves on to an unknown future.... This ambiguous character, the staple of westerns (and of other action drama as well), has had a limitless appeal for American audiences, representing as he does a sureness about his individuality, his masculinity, that needs no explanation, no external motivation. He acts not so much to defend abstract concepts of justice and morality as to defend his self-image against the intrusive world.[5]

The early heroes rarely suggested the consuming loneliness that is Hart's and which all the most powerful Western heroes have since shared. Comradeship and loyalty are values that have emerged in the early Westerns. They become less important later on. Boetticher's Randolph Scott hero, Anthony Mann's heroes, Wayne in most of his roles, Eastwood all fit into this description of Hart. Even Cable Hogue. But the Western hero has not held to this consistently and we can see him frequently as the herald of a new way of life, the man who tames the country's wildness and makes it a fit place for women and children to take up their abode. This is the hero that began to develop in the thirties and became a staple of the B Westerns. The smoothed down heroes were themselves smoothing the way for the weak and helpless. The very fact that series Westerns became so popular suggests that the appeal of the mysterious stranger was being neglected. The audience always knew who the hero was.

It was by establishing recognisable identities that these heroes became household words. They had public personalities that went beyond the fictional screen image and stepped into the average child's tangible world. Rocky Lane might indeed come riding down a town's main street. During this phase, developing through the thirties and at its height in the forties (Gene Autry's first starring role was in 1935, Roy Rogers' in 1938) this type of Western did lose an important feature. If the audience could now accept the do-gooding hero as the tamer of the wild and guardian of a community this was at the expense of the lonely, independent Westerner, the man who was simultaneously at one with his environment and in conflict with it. Such heroes still did appear, but many of them had a strong leaning towards community building and often the suggestion, perhaps not intended, that the hero was succumbing to the blandishments of civilisation rather than upholding the virtues of the frontier.

Ford is one of the few directors who has been able to preserve this paradox and make it work. His films tend to balance the essential actions of the independent hero and the solid drive of the community. Often he makes grand, forward looking sense out of their fusion. *The Iron Horse* is a perfect example. The hero, heavy with the sense of early loss and injustice, atunes his personal revenge with the forging of the railroad that his father originally helped to survey. The railroad's achievement means something special and personal to the hero, but he is also working for the nation's progress. Ford never loses sight of the dramatic value of this kind of hero. It is significant that he says of *Liberty Valance* that Doniphon is the true Westerner. He is the unsung hero who acts in loneliness and bitterness, and without him the progress that the lawyer represents would have been impossible. Ford's cavalry Westerns have the same kind of involvement with the balance, and possibilities for friction, between the individual and the community. The lonely individual is the officer on whom all responsibility lies and the community his men and what they are fighting for. In *Fort Apache* (1948) the colonel is responsible for the unnecessary deaths of his men, but just as Ford sees the independent hero as vital to the frontier community's survival he feels that an officer's authority should never be questioned even when he is patently wrong. This is part of the loneliness of the officer's position, and is the basis of a favourite character of Ford's, the man who must be hard and apparently unfeeling if he is to do his job at all.

Ford makes his position quite clear on this. The leader, the man superior through experience, understanding and innate ability—not everyone can be a Western hero—is essential to the community and the nation and must be recognised as such. This leads straight to the often expressed political opinions of John Wayne, and we know that Ford and Wayne are very close. Ford says, 'In Vietnam today, probably a lot of guys don't agree with their leader, but they still go ahead and do the job'[6] and Wayne acts out the leader who must be obeyed. All of Ford's heroes have this innate superiority which often emerges in spite of rather than because of the situation they are in.

Ford maintains that heroes are essential, not only in a particular sense as saviours, tamers and sometimes martyrs, but in general. A nation needs heroes. 'We've had a lot of people who were supposed to be great heroes, and you know damn well they weren't. But it's good for the country to have heroes to look up to.'[7] The ordinary man needs an example. He needs to believe that men can be almost superhuman. The country needs to believe that in the frontier territories a man had to be almost superhuman in order to survive.

If the psychological and political dangers of this kind of encouragement to hero worship are fairly obvious it does make a great deal of sense in the American context, and culturally it was almost inevitable. Most cultures have had heroes rooted, however remotely, in the past.

White America had no folk heroes with origins dim in the mists of antiquity and so had no choice but to create them out of the recent past. And the past itself offered plenty of opportunity for the emergence of such heroes. This Ford recognises, and in his films he exalts the opportunities as much as the heroes. Many lesser directors assume the existence of such heroes, and their products are the weaker for the assumption.

If America was more enthusiastic than middle aged Europe in the process of creating heroes out of a history that was still unfolding she was not unique. Europe's heroes were not all mythic figures from the distant past. The popular imagination was busy absorbing Napoleon (hero and arch-villain), Garibaldi and Dick Turpin as fast as America her Paul Revere and Jesse James. But what Europe did not produce, at least on such a large scale, was a whole breed of heroes, who were heroes not so much because of what they did, but because of where and when they lived. The American imagination was ready to transform the whole of life West of the Mississippi between the 1840s and 1880s into a legend, and in a sense has been doing this ever since. It is not only legend that has taken over from history. Culture too has done this, and helped to ensure that the Western myth will survive in spite of history, in spite of progress, and in spite of movies debunking the Western hero.

The problem for those who attempt to destroy this hero is that the popular hero is in many of his guises a rebel, and remains so in resistance to efforts to formalise and domesticate him. America's great national heroes—Washington is the pre-eminent example—are rebels. They are men who do not conform, who think and act independently. The West gave scope to men like this. Men who found the institutions of the East constricting tended to go West, just as men who found Europe too slow-moving, tied to archaic social and political structures, tended to make hopefully for America. Official America has tried to make heroes of some of her institutionalisers but the American people show an inclination to adopt men like Jesse James and Clyde Barrow, or men who exemplified the road from rags to riches, for both kinds of hero were challenging the existing structure of society.

Many Western heroes are rebels in spite of their directors or their authors. Any man who is independent and self-reliant is by inclination non-conformist and anti-social. He does not need society though society may need him. Robert Mitchum as the mountain man in *The Way West* is a lonely, ageing man, losing his sight, but it is he who gets the wagons through and he who will not reap the benefits of his success. Although the movie is carelessly undisciplined it is one of Mitchum's finest Western roles; with dry restraint he conveys the character of a man who is profoundly a-social, who knows that by guiding wagon trains into unpopulated territory the lonely West which has given him his strength will gradually fill up with people. It is the mountain man's loneliness that lingers in spite of the pressure of a nation-building movie.

Mitchum is a voluntary outcast, and from voluntary outcast to forced outcast is a short step. In *The Magnificent Seven* it is virtually impossible for the gunmen, already aware that they are fast becoming anachronistic, to do anything but try to carry on in the old way. They are casting themselves beyond the law, beyond the pale of a growing society whose progress inevitably brings materialism as well as stability. Stability is anathema to the real Western hero. And again the rejection of stability emphasises the potential danger to society that the Western hero contains. He cannot be appealed to on the grounds of normal citizenship. In a country where the whole idea of citizenship plays such an important role there is adulation of a hero who by definition rejects much that is a part of the citizen's role. As soon as the hero identifies himself entirely with a community his nature changes.

The man who needs neither family nor community nor the support of law and government is bound to threaten, if only indirectly, all of these. When we understand the implications of the Western hero's independence we can understand also why the Western has tried to domesticate its heroes. The archetypal Western hero is indeed too dangerous to be absorbed into daily life. It was almost inevitable that he should be refined, and that he should emerge even now in various domestic guises. The television series has taken over the process of enclosing the Westerner, of forcing on him the role of developer and defender of property. He becomes firmly tied to the ideal of the solid citizen.

Some Westerns are concerned with showing the death of the independent hero as the necessary casualty of progress. *Ride the High Country, Death of a Gunfighter, Lonely Are the Brave* are all about the obsolescent hero. Yet, although we have seen him outmoded in the Western environment, he still lives. Novels and films with contemporary settings still tap the resources of the independent hero. Hemingway's heroes obviously owe a great deal to the frontier heroic tradition. They tend to be independent men of action, intellectualised (the hero of *For Whom the Bell Tolls* is a college teacher) versions of the Westerner. Gary Cooper in the film of the book, suitably released during the Second World War, plays himself as a man of the frontier. He rides and shoots in Civil War torn Spain just as he does in frontier America. Even the terrain is similar. When Hemingway dwells on the lonely pleasures of the wilderness he is going right back to the mountain man, or even further to the Leatherstockings of the New York frontier. His heroes are self-reliant in the grand tradition, a-social, cut off from whatever family or community ties they might have. By implication they are rebellious; without doubt they are non-conformist.

Hemingway revitalised this strain of the American heroic tradition, but it was strong enough to live without him. It has lived in the Westerns themselves, which owe little to Hemingway, and in all those books and movies, some of which owe a great deal to Hemingway but owe even more to a tradition that flourished long before him, in which heroism still means independent action. In the crime novel, the thriller, to a lesser extent the war novel, the hero still often flourishes as our well known Westerner. Movies in the sixties with fresh zest present heroes fighting in a contemporary jungle of corruption and crime, forging the identity of a man skilled in weapons, lonely, resourceful, without social backing, with only his own personality and actions to make sense of his existence. They too are rebels against the system, against any kind of combination of power whose salutary effect is oppressive.

When the independent hero is translated into contemporary society he can be, and generally is, much less responsible than the frontier hero. His environment does not make demands on him; in some respects he is able to act even more independently than the Westerner. In, for instance, *The Thomas Crown Affair*, the hero's sole purpose is to test himself as a lone man against a formidable complex of social institutions. Hemingway's heroes test themselves in similar fashion. They tend to be neurotically involved with testing their identities as individuals. The true Westerner tests himself because the circumstances demand it. He does not hunt out suitably demanding circumstances.

To remain independent amidst the multiple turmoil of modern urban society is bound to differ crucially from frontier independence. Frontier loneliness is a necessity. Urban independence almost has to mean selfishness and brutality. Even urban heroes who borrow the frontier code, as Himes's Coffin Ed and Grave Digger do, find that it translates into something considerably uglier in the context of modern city violence. The code works best when it is stripped of an essentially sentimental morality and becomes a bare issue of survival. In the city issues of survival are too complex for the code to function.

The code only works where the antagonists have no choice, or where the choice is between courage and obvious cowardice, or the obvious shirking of responsibility. In a situation where we can be convinced that non-action will expose a community to danger then killing must be done. Alternatives of action have much less meaning in the city, where a single quarrel can have multiple repercussions, or a single thoughtless gesture cause disaster. In the spare Western context this kind of thing is much less likely to happen. Only on the untamed frontier is a situation where the threat is real and one man's courage can resist it likely to arise. At the end of *For Whom the Bell Tolls* the hero dies over his machine gun while his fellow revolutionaries escape. In a Western context such a martyrdom would be entirely convincing. In the context of ruthless and tragic modern war such a death in grand heroic style only appears contrived. (Other twentieth century writers might well have taken pains to demonstrate that the old heroic style is meaningless, which only helps to reinforce the impression that Hemingway is much reliant on a traditional and romantic notion of heroism.)

Hemingway and writers influenced by him have tried to modernise the Western heroic myth. Meanwhile, the trend now seems to involve attempts to replace the myth with a more realistic version of the West. Now we have Westerns based on books like Thomas Berger's *Little Big Man* and Charles Portis's *True Grit*, books which do not claim to be Westerns but simply use the Western environment. But in doing this they cannot escape entirely Western codes and conventions. Berger's hero is nothing more splendid than an engaging character with a highly developed instinct for survival, yet he is in his grimly comic manner as splendidly unrealistic as the most exalted of legendary heroes. It is this, the fusion of a comically incredible hero with authentic history and realistic detail that gives the book its particular distinction, but it maintains its roots firmly, as the film highlights, in the traditional Western mode.

True Grit is a very different kind of book, a modest work beautifully executed. It is much more remarkable as a book than the highly traditional Western Henry Hathaway made from it. It should have emerged as a unique product, a Western in which the heroine is of considerably more significance than the hero. Instead John Wayne inevitably dominates the film and supported by Hathaway's enjoyable mainstream direction romps home simultaneously parodying and exalting the traditional Wayne Westerner. The book, written in the words of an elderly spinster looking back on her teenaged adventures, carves its own individual route through the Western context.

Marshal Rooster Cogburn was at one time a lawbreaker, and the legality of the Western hero is frequently equivocal. There are few hard distinctions between independent, outcast and outlaw, and much of the Western's romance derives from this. By being beyond the law the Westerner can be an outlaw without actually challenging the law. The revolutionary potential and the threat to organised society is again apparent. The Robin Hood figure, the man who robs the rich to support the poor, the man who rights his own wrongs, is far too dangerous to be allowed solid reality. He must be confined to myth. His role must be defined in such a way that no one will take it entirely seriously. And so the trappings of the Western remain largely unrealistic. Billy the Kid is still a romantic and loyal young man. Even in Penn's *The Left-Handed Gun* where Billy is explained rather than exposed the legend is upheld. If the bad man is seen as successful in terms of history rather than as romantic in terms of legend, then his dangerous potential has been fully realised.

The legend, while inflating the hero, also tames him. The artificial domestication of the hero is largely unnecessary. The legend itself confines the hero, and on the whole it is the directors who recognise this, who do not attempt to release the hero from the legend, who make the best Westerns. The legend makes it acceptable for small boys to rig themselves out in Western gear and weaponry and re-enact the fatalities of the frontier. The legend does not mean the prevention of realism or the falsification of historical fact, but it does involve the recognition that the potency of myth is far greater than that of fact.

The tendency of fact to translate itself into myth bears witness enough to this. Myth adheres to every war, every battle, every contest between nations, many contests between individuals and societies. Part of the explanation for the widespread contemporary repugnance for war is that modern warfare prevents myth from performing its usual function. Myth has always helped to make the grim and ghastly more palatable. In the case of the frontier, legend was being consciously invoked while history was being made. Men indeed became 'living legends', or at least were a part of a world in which it was possible to believe in living legends. The process of putting the legend into words and pictures was going on long before the events that fashioned the legends had played themselves out. The backlash of this process has been that sometimes the West finds it hard to accept that the events have played themselves out.

Ultimately our judgement of the Western hero must be a moral judgement, a moral judgement that depends not on a rigid, institutionalised code but on an individual assessment of individual situations. Leatherstocking sums it up.

'I do not seek blood without a cause, and my bullet is well leathered and carefully driven down for the time of need. I love no Mingo, as is just, seeing how much I have consorted with the Delawares, who are their mutual and nat'ral enemies; but I pull no trigger on one of the miscreants unless it be plain that his death will lead to some good end. The deer never leaped that fell by my hand wantonly. By living much alone with God in the wilderness, a man gets to feel the justice of such opinions.'[8]

Significantly it is no external code that brings Leatherstocking to these opinions but a feeling of their rightness that living alone in the wild has brought him. For all Leatherstocking's simplicity and simple-mindedness, and the fact that Cooper can never bring himself to make him quite the all out hero that the later Westerner becomes, many a Western hero would instinctively echo him here. Wilderness and lone-liness give to the traditional Western hero an implicit sense of justice.

The Western hero has been debased repeatedly, but he still survives. He survives all attempts to update him, he survives bedroom farce raciness, he survives grotesque violence. Clint Eastwood, regardless of his conquest of whores, Mexicans and murderers is still the lonely man of action who is kind to children and ladies. If Rooster Cogburn rides the faithful Blackie to death he does it to save the life of a young girl. If Peckinpah's Pike Bishop blasts umpteen Mexicans to smither-- eens he does it in the name of loyalty and comradeship. Unshaven, smelly, sweat-stained, but still the cousins, if no closer kin, of those well-bathed decent fellows who rode their apparently polished and manicured quadrupeds across the screens of thirty years ago.

THIRTEEN

There Must *be a Lone Ranger*

The only film, as a type, that has any real authority is our much-scorned Western. At least there, if you have banality of plot, you have some of the stone and gravel and grassland of America thrown in as incidentals.

Eric Knight 'Synthetic America'

[1]

For myself, personally, I always thought he was the greatest and best man I ever knew. Some said Sieber was no fit company for man or beast. That was because he would go for days at a time and never speak to anyone. No one knew where he came from originally. A few people in Arizona had known him in California, but before that he was a blank. I don't think anyone ever did ask him where he was born or raised, for he was not the kind of man that one cared to ask such a question. His face always looked stern, and perhaps savage, to one who did not know him, but to me he was always good and kind and never, unless in the heat of battle, did he speak loud or cross. He was spoken of by the Indians as the 'man of iron', and of iron he must have been. He was shot in Indian battles twenty-eight times with bullets and arrows, and the twenty-ninth time he was crippled for life.[1]

Al Sieber, army scout in Apache country, origins unknown, described by Tom Horn. Sieber could be the prototype of the Western hero of the 1960s. He is a basic man, a man totally in control of himself who puts the emotional and the intellectual to shame. Only a man like him, it is suggested in Western after Western, can cope with a life stripped down to the bare necessities. Throughout the existence of the Western hero, even at his softest and most cultured, there has been an undercurrent of scorn for those who are men of feelings and thoughts rather than of deeds.

It was men like Sieber whom Teddy Roosevelt (the rugged politician who rode the range on his Montana ranch and organised the Rough Riders out of men of the West who, he was convinced, would make the toughest soldiers) acknowledged as models of American manhood. America had had her backwoods boys and victorious generals at the top of government: here was something like the real frontiersman. Hot on the heels of Roosevelt came Owen Wister, pen poised to make the Westerner fit for Eastern consumption. The crudities of the popular version, consumed voraciously for many years before Wister went West, were smoothed away.

Wister has been celebrated as the man who really started it all. As we have seen he responded to the West, publicly at least, as the last territory of romance. He polished up the men like Sieber, glossed the roughness with humour, gave his Wyoming cowhands a boyishness and charm. Any unwholesome elements were legitimately purged; Wister renders articulate the assumption that the further West you are the more American you are. The West not only denotes superiority, it suggests a finer breed of American-ness, and the essential features of this are all those qualities we identify with the ideal Westerner.

John Wayne's father advised him, 'don't go around looking for trouble. But if you ever get in a fight, make sure you win it.' [2] This demonstrates one of the essential features of the Western ethic, and it demonstrates also the continuity that has brought the Western ethic alive into the present day. Wayne was brought up to believe that the West was and is the real America and the Western ethic a viable code. He acts out in real life the legend he portrays on the screen; or perhaps it is the other way round, that he enacts on the screen a reality in which he believes. 'There's a lot of yella bastards in the country who would like to call patriotism old-fashioned,' he says. [3] In the days of the Western frontier Americans were fighting their country's enemies on American soil—Indians, Mexicans, Spaniards. The Texans carving out their territory, fending off Mexican marauders, were establishing themselves by right of arms. Any settler who fought for his quarter-section felt that his struggle strengthened the quality of his ownership. The logic that Wayne pursues is that fighting for your country makes it more yours than it was before—and more yours than the pacifist's. The myth of aggressive patriotism is bound to be self-enhancing. The stronger the patriotism the more necessary it is to prove it, and once patriotism is established as an unequivocally good and powerful quality it has to be fed. Wars threatened or real are necessary nourishment, and this fact has to be built into American patriotic culture which for two hundred years has been very much concerned with sustaining the good American and the goodness of America.

In 1960 Wayne made *The Alamo*, his first venture as a director and not very successful, 'to remind people not only in America but everywhere that there were once men and women who had the guts to stand up for the things they believed.' [4] But we don't need Wayne to tell us that the Western is, or can be, very much about patriotism and the American-ness of America. Who is Cable Hogue but the good American in yet another costume of the ordinary guy—neither Cain nor Abel?

It is the virtues of strength that Wayne embodies, virtues echoed and reflected in a hundred lesser cowboy actors, but in Wayne emerging preeminent. It is strength that gives Wayne the licence for dry comedy, that allows him to be passive but successful in romance; above all sheer physical strength that gives him his cool, confident superiority, the superiority of the big man. 'In spite of the fact that Rooster Cogburn would shoot a fella between the eyes he'd judge that fella before he did it. He was merely tryin' to make the area in which he was marshal livable for the most number of people.' [5] The breathtaking confidence, and the casual ignoring of the limitations of an individual's authority, are Wayne's trademark. If *Red River* marked the turning point in Wayne's middle aged career he was a success because he believed that the man he played was right, in spite of the fact that the movie itself doesn't quite go along with that.

In the West strength was necessary for survival. In Wayne strength is a moral quality that grants a licence for action. Weakness and cowardice are contemptible. In the Western if you can't or won't fight for yourself you either die (and deserve to die) or shelter behind someone who will fight for you. Women and children legitimately and properly shelter behind a strong man, but no man who calls himself a man, i.e. an American, would do such a thing. Even the true American woman is no sissy when the times require aggressive action from her.

Wayne claims that he was responsible for overthrowing the boy scout image of the screen cowboy. 'When I came in the western man never lost his white hat and always rode the white horse and waited for the man to get up again in the fight. Following my dad's advice, if a guy hit me with a vase I'd hit him with a chair. That's the way we played it. I changed the saintly Boy Scout of the original cowboy hero into a more normal kind of fella.' [6] Wayne's early career in Westerns coincided with the white hatted *deus ex machina* and they loped along side by side for quite a while before *Red River* punctuated the B picture fade out. But in fiction the boy scout had for some time been much less secure. Zane Grey's heroes did have a touch of the saint about them, but they were tough men too. Rhodes wrote about men who were far too normal and profane to win any scout badges. Max Brand's easy going half humorous heroes are polite but their fights are to the death. Haycox's heroes may be gentlemen, but they are also grown up.

The writers of the twenties and thirties were rather more robust than the movies into which much of their material was transformed, perhaps because they themselves had been nourished by earlier screen heroes who were less polite. Haycox's heroes enjoy a fight for its own sake. They are matched up against villains who are as tough and canny products of the frontier as they are themselves. Wayne was not creating so much as embodying something that had been there all the time. Whether he can act is not really important. He can certainly project, and Wayne playing Wayne doesn't need to do anything more.

No one can successfully imitate Wayne on the screen and although he will remain for most of us the archetypal Westerner closely associated with John Ford's movies he is not only archetype. He is the most logical embodiment of the all-American qualities the Western inevitably celebrates but he does not represent the only valid interpretation of the West, even though on the screen and to some extent in fiction it has been the most accepted one. *The Magnificent Seven* was hailed in 1961, by many who are not Western enthusiasts, as something new and real from the West. The fact that it is a direct reworking of Kurasawa's *The Seven Samurai* is hardly relevant to its character as a Western, for it failed to utilise so much that is subtly distinctive in the original. Here were gunmen who were vulnerable, who exposed their loneliness and the weakness of their trade. Here were men with nothing to lose but nothing to gain either. Here was a movie that appeared to be saying that the Western hero was all very well, but there was an awful lot that he wasn't. But in fact it was a movie upholding the finest of screen Western values. The men are killers, but what killers! The coward who dies in the act of saving another's life, the lover of children who dies protecting a child, the black-clad professional gun whose nobility shines through his ruthlessness, all supported and enhanced by Elmer Bernstein's superb musical score which seems to do more to carry the film to its conclusion than the direction.

But not only this. In some respects the film can be seen as the purest justification of the more dubious aspects of American foreign policy. The gallant Americans, the men with the courage, the weapons and the skill, ride over the border and defend a threatened Mexican village. The Hitlerian overtones in Eli Wallach's portrayal of the bandit chief are obvious. American democracy overthrows dictatorship, and the community is eternally grateful. The theme is not unique to this particular film. Who, over and over again, rides in to save the villagers, aid the oppressed in their fight for freedom, rescue the girl, supply money, arms, technical skill to the scruffy bands who fight dictatorship but the American hero? Jim Brown in *100 Rifles* may be black, but he is a lot more American than Yaquis Joe.

Jim Brown is a boy scout too. Whatever Wayne says, the boy scout image adheres naturally to the doer of good deeds, unless like Eastwood he tries hard to dispel it or like Lee Marvin his very aspect makes the idea laughable. Wayne's actions however tough are rarely selfish enough (ego-building is something else) to convince us that he is no boy scout. There is always the suggestion that he is striking a blow for right, sometimes for the right. In *Red River* the nation-building element in the foundation of a cattle kingdom is evident and if the Wayne hero appears to be a self-centred man he is in fact doing what he feels is the best for cows, for Texas and for America. Wayne the Westerner is always to some extent a public man. It is the more interesting personal heroes, like Mann's who successfully avoid being white washed with the boy scout brush. Mann's heroes do of course do good here and there, but their motives tend to be personal rather than patriotic and they are prompted by anger and hatred rather than by a sense of justice. The Mann hero does not style himself as a civilising influence. He is, compared with the Wayne hero, much more lonely and inward, his authority too elusive to embody anything akin to Wayne's granite-like ideals.

[2]

The hero as aggressive patriot must have an enemy. In the Western myth the enemy takes on certain specific aspects. He can be the personification of destructive evil. He may be a dangerous but not necessarily evil misfit who must give way to the rational forces for order and civilisation. He may be a personal rival. He may be a man whose weakness and cowardice make him a necessary casualty in the face of justice.

But more constant than any of these particular types of foe is the faceless enemy who can suggest any or all of them. Patriotism needs an enemy, not just a disruptive individual, but something that can embody a powerful threat to the community, society, the entire nation. John Wayne frequently suggests that it is an enemy on this scale that he is coping with. Who is this enemy? For decades it was the Indians. Sometimes it was marauding gangs of outlaws who could be seen to be working not just for selfish gain but directly against the interests of the nation, interfering with the stage line or the telegraph for instance. In the sixties it has most often been the Mexicans.

The prejudice against Mexico revealed itself very early on in Western fiction. The dime novels were careless in their disposal of 'greasers'. They were inferior to Indians, the dregs of a peasant race, entirely dispensable. That was one of their uses. In another light they were totally evil, gaudy, knives between their teeth, treacherous. In the early Western it was rare to find any compromise between the sloppy, gibbering peasant and the vicious, silver-studded killer. In an article on Rhodes, W. H. Hutchinson discusses this phenomenon.

The type-casting of the *hombre del pais* can be attributed to the Texas influence on the folk-ways of the free range, or it can be traced to a residual fear of the Spanish Armada and the Inquisition. In either case *Westward Ho!* presages the role the Spaniard and his New World descendants were foreordained to play in the 'Western' story.[7]

'Chili con carnage': the cavalier destruction of Mexican manhood while using the more colourful aspects of Southern life to enhance the atmosphere. If the Indians were mere savages the Mexicans could be portrayed as practitioners of a much more sophisticated kind of cruelty.

The kind of opinion that fed the popular portrayal of the Mexican was certainly much in evidence long before the Western took on any form at all. In 1857 a traveller in Texas expressed himself on the subject.

Mexico! What the hell do we want of it? It isn't worth a cuss. The people are as bigoted and ignorant as the devil's grandchildren. They haven't even the capacities of my black boy. Why, they're most as black as niggers anyway, and ten times as treacherous....[8]

When the fiction writers began to take over they had a ready made attitude waiting for them legitimised by the fact that many of America's enemies had come out of Mexico. More surprising and a great deal less palatable than the early characterisation of the Mexican is the resurrection in recent years of the Mexican enemy and by implication the Mexican threat to American civilisation. Film makers have fairly consistently used the Mexican revolutionary ferment as suitable material for Western type movies, for the most part converting real issues into slightly more exotic versions of standard action drama. In 1934 a review of *Viva Villa!* directed by Jack Conway commented, 'They have conceived the Mexican fight for independence on the lines of a Western with all the attendant plot circumstances we know so well.... The only way they could avoid the great social issues involved was to convert the revolution into cowboy fights and to concentrate on personalities.'[9] If this opinion seems to be too typically of the leftist thirties it is only fair to add that Hollywood's cheapening of Mexican history has in fact been fairly consistent, and continues.

Kazan's *Viva Zapata!* is an exception, but still the Western heroic role dominates the film. Brando's Zapata is no peasant but a man of superior mould, a natural leader. But the men who follow him appear convincingly as neither a debased nor an evil form of humanity. *Viva Zapata!* was made in 1952, a time when the Indian was beginning to emerge as a real personality with films like *Broken Arrow* and George Sherman's *Battle at Apache Pass* (1952). In fiction the nasty Mexican and the faceless Indian still appeared, but so did the noble Spaniard, owner of a vast and splendid rancho, and there were to be a whole series of novels like Logan Forster's *Proud Land* (1961) celebrating the Indian. However, the usefulness of Indians as a dispensable mass of subhumanity continues. As long as films are made about General Custer an awful lot of Indians have to die.

The romantic elements of Spanish American life were too good to miss, and have featured significantly from the Western's earliest days. The cantina, the music of the guitar, the dancing, the girls with flowers in their hair are all colourful enough to avoid the sneering attitude to 'greasers'. The spreading haciendas lend themselves to romance also. But the distinction drawn between Spanish aristocrat and native peasant is radical. The aristocrat lives his highly civilised life, his cellars stocked with fine wines, his women gracious and beautiful. His horses are thoroughbred. In spite of this he is frequently a comic figure, ridiculed amongst his splendour.

The Spanish aristocrat can also be a cruel man. Meticulously polite, courteous, gracious, serving his victims the finest brandy, he can then consign them to abominable torture. In *Day of the Evil Gun* the hero and his rival are staked out in the broiling desert sun by such a gentleman. This crude characterisation in a recent film (1968) shows how easy it still is for the Western to fall back on stereotypes. Of course there are vicious Americans too, and of course some Mexicans were bad. But in this case we are served up with a straightforward racial characterisation as recognisable as the devoted negro servant.

Where one must be most sharply critical is not so much in the use of stereotyping. The stereotype, racial or otherwise, has been an ingredient of all kinds of art for centuries. It is in the use of racial characterisation in the presentation of a faceless, dispensable, subhuman foe that the Western of the sixties reveals itself in its most unacceptable light. The Mexicans have been used in this way in a number of recent movies: *The Undefeated* (McLaglen), *100 Rifles* (Gries), *Bandolero!* (McLaglen), *The Wild Bunch* (Peckinpah), *Two Mules for Sister Sara* (Siegel). *Butch Cassidy*, where the Mexicans are Bolivians, could be added. For many Western makers the Indian is no longer a legitimate target. But there still has to be a target of some kind.

The Western writer is less open to criticism on these grounds. The writer rarely attempts to convey in words the kind of spectacle that wholesale slaughter can provide on the screen. Inevitably the writer's focus tends to be narrower. He is more likely to concentrate on individuals rather than massacre, even where it is massacre that he is writing about. The writer must generally be more committed than the camera; more depends on him making his own viewpoint clear. The camera is considerably more anonymous than the pen, and because a film must be a corporate effort, and can never be wholly the responsibility of the director in the way a book is wholly the responsibility of the author, it is generally much looser, much laxer in its point of view than a book. Western hack writers can get away with a lot of rubbish, but it is much more difficult to present triumphantly the implied racialism that Siegel and Peckinpah manage and expect it not to be noticed.

Increasing numbers of Westerns are being filmed in Mexico where it can be done cheaply and extras hired at low cost. This may be part of the explanation for Mexican slaughter—it is probably cheaper to kill Mexicans these days than to kill Indians. Mexico offers film makers a great deal of scope. The peasant can be sentimentalised while a hundred years or so of Mexican history provides a wide variety of oppressors for destruction. The guerrilla can be romanticised and the bandit vilified.

In *The Undefeated* Mexican bandits attack a ring of covered wagons and the Americans defend themselves in true frontier style. The bandits are defeated, but there are by implication good Mexicans in the movie, for the Southern relics of the Civil War are on their way to join in their fight against dictatorship. Wayne as the Yankee colonel influences them to return across the border and they all join together to contribute to the great American theme. In *Bandolero!* the bandits first appear as silent, sinister, faceless killers who slit the throats of unsuspecting Americans. Later they perpetrate an Indian style attack. In *Two Mules* there is the sketchiest characterisation of a Juarista leader, presented as a mildly comic figure, followed by casual slaughter. In *The Wild Bunch* the death toll of Mexicans is beyond calculation. In each of these films Mexicans die in anonymous heaps while the Americans, if they perish, do so with the cameras full on them and an almost reverential sense of their identity.

Thankfully a few movies contradict this trend. In *Death of a Gunfighter* John Saxon plays a Mexican who is a United States marshal. Although Saxon's cool, dry bitterness at years of prejudice is convincing, his presence in the film is self-conscious. He is there primarily to illustrate the good-heartedness of the hero rather than for his own sake. In *The Professionals* the Mexicans not only have some dimension they are in a sense triumphant. Without sentiment and without glamour their existence has a convincing aspect. It is an exceptional film in that it enters without hesitation territory which is now suspect and intelligently avoids the traps.

Mexican slaughter, and its predecessor Indian slaughter, indicates that the Western needs not only an object for its aggression, but an enemy en masse. Yet it is significant that most of those Westerns which are now considered classic build up a particular individual as enemy and do it without attendant massacre. Although there were plenty of anonymous dead in the very early days of the Western it is partly the wide screen that encourages the presentation of death on such an enormous scale. In *Red River* there are mass enemies, raiders and Indians, and they do contribute to the epic scale of the picture, but the central conflict is the rivalry between the two heroes. Violence is particularised: the shooting of a rebellious trail herd has infinitely more point than the staple Indian attack, and that is the way it is handled.

Many Westerns are conceived as epic contests between large bodies of men, and it is just these that are most difficult to control and most likely to slip altogether out of the heroic mould. Epic heroism has to be presented in individual terms in order to be effective; at the same time it is important not to lose sight of epic grandeur. Epic does not necessarily involve the large scale clash of armies, quantities of horses and extensive battlefields, for it has less to do with scale than with the stature and symbolic value of the heroes. In the most impressive Western epics size, quantity and distance are used to measure individual stature. These epic ingredients are not simply present for their own sake. *Red River* is one of the finest Western epics, but it is Ford preeminently who is able to handle detail on a large scale as an integral part of the action itself. In *Cheyenne Autumn* Ford assembles groups of people, and we see them as a community of lives, differentiated men and women acting upon each other, the Cheyennes on the one hand, the troopers on the other.

A director with epic tendencies, an imitator of Ford, who does not have the confident focus required is Andrew McLaglen. The structure of his movies is too loose, too subservient to the scale, for the result to be satisfactory. *The Undefeated* contains a jumble of clustered protagonists which fails to blend into anything approaching a convincing whole. In *The Way West* McLaglen appears to be relying desperately on the major actors, Robert Mitchum and Kirk Douglas, to take the weight of the film, while he throws in indiscriminate action in an undisciplined attempt to give them some support. Only the dignified performance of Mitchum saves the film.

The mistreatment of the mass is an insult to individuals and an insult to the history that lies behind the Western myth. When we see Mexicans dying in heaps it is not the blood or the brutality that is so offensive as the complete blotting out of identity. It is an attitude of supreme carelessness. The dead exist only as victims of American heroes. As no other artistic genre, not even the war film, is so basically concerned with aggression, this is a radical criticism. American heroism appears to be built only on anonymous dead.

The classic Westerns do contradict this and we are able to treat them with respect. The fusion of the essence of the myth and a conclusion that is morally and artistically acceptable is crucial. Even allowing for the sentiment that frames *Liberty Valance* we can see it as a powerful and legitimate example of some of the best features of the Western. If traditional heroism is to nourish a nation's image of itself it needs not only a strong myth but a strong interpretation of the myth. From the days when the frontier was still viable the Western has been filling in some of the gaps in America's cultural background and providing archetypal examples of elements that the nation as a whole has sought to emphasise. Whether this is a good thing is another question. The Western has nourished Wayne's image of himself as a good American. It is even arguable that without it the particular ruggedness of the American right wing would not be so easily identifiable. When the Western slips into mass insult at the expense of the genre itself it is therefore of some seriousness.

It makes the link between aggression and community building all the more striking. The hired gun in *Shane* is seen not just as a threat to a group of homesteaders but as a destructive force directed against the whole community. The death of Stonewall in the mud in front of the saloon is symbolic. Stonewall dies on community territory and is buried in the community graveyard. The gathering of good citizens at the graveside is meaningful. The gunman has to be eliminated because he stands in the way of the area's proper development, and that means development not under the bullying headship of one landowner but as a democratic community of individuals living and working in harmony.

It is themes of this kind that show just how important the West's solid citizenry is. They make national sense of heroic folk tales. Very often these respected individuals are victims, of a terroriser or of their own cowardice. In *No God in Saguaro* the men whose financial and professional solidity supports the town attempt to kill in order to protect themselves from the aftermath of an unjust hanging. Here, the guarding of the town's reputation is the essence of the drama. The town must survive. In Patten's book the town survives not by masking a past fault but by finding an instrument to cleanse its conscience.

Patten also wrote *Death of a Gunfighter* and his stories throw into relief the basic paradox of the West. On the one hand there is the instinct to preserve a heroic tradition that is aggressive, violent and potentially anarchic. On the other there is the deliberate building up of solid community values, the relating of the developing territories of the West to the United States as a whole and the emphasis of those warm, homely qualities that have for so long flourished side by side with the cult of the violent loner. In *Cable Hogue* nothing could be more homely than the idyllic existence shared by Cable and Hildy. Hildy in a neat cotton dress serving an ample meal is a symbol of honest American femininity. The fact that Hildy looks after Cable is an essential feature, even *the* essential feature, of the romance, and the presentation of this leans heavily on traditional ideas of the feminine role in the American community. Generally when a woman isn't around just as a piece of decoration she is there to cook for the men.

The readiest image of the Western paradox is the brothel next to the schoolhouse. While the brothel means the bawdy, rough-and-ready West of men who are never likely to settle down, the schoolhouse is the epitome of taming in action. The unison chanting of ABC by a row of fresh faced kids suggests not so much civilisation as the heavy hand of conformity. When in *Liberty Valance* the Eastern lawyer undertakes the education of the town's children he is directly challenging the heroic mode that John Wayne represents. Words rather than guns, the pen mightier than the sword. The schoolhouse and what it represents run directly contrary to the most potent aspect of the myth. It is one thing to perpetuate the process of making the frontier safe for children, and not only taming but building a suitable conformist environment. It is quite another to accept the point at which the frontier is tamed, the moment when the frontier no longer exists. At this point the Western hero is indeed obsolete. He must either fade into history or change his image. Part of the object of the Western is to keep the frontier alive at a stage before it reaches the stasis of civilisation. Recently there have been a number of Westerns set in the last years of the nineteenth century or the early years of the twentieth. They are conscious of the particular poignancy of the Western hero at this stage, his ambivalence in the face of the automobile. Some, like *Ride the High Country* demonstrate the translation into myth, in spite of and because of modern times.

What one might be looking for here is something to suggest the hero's decadence, but it isn't there. Aspects of the West's decadence can be found elsewhere; it is often integral to the plot, part of the challenge the hero has to face. There are soft livers as villains as well as toughs, and always the suggestion that the easy way of life is morally unsound. Cowardice and corruption go hand in hand with this kind of decadence. In *Bend of the River* as soon as we see Arthur Kennedy in flashy gambler's dress enjoying the amenities of booming Portland we suspect him. Kennedy's powerful projection of strength undermined by moral deficiency makes him a superb villain, never conventional.

The decadence is very much associated with towns. Money has a lot to do with it and money is centred in towns. There is often the further suggestion that decadence ultimately stems from the East. The brothels and saloons escape this, for they are an integral part of frontier life, but they can be implicated. For it is usually corruption that is at the centre, corruption amongst the powerful, and the powerful are likely to have their fingers in the profitable pies. With this the schoolhouse and brothel image becomes even more suggestive. The tarts and their customers may well be more honest than the good citizens who run the town. A saddle tramp may accept money to perform a killing but he is then entering the Western arena on its own terms. The mayor behind a front of good citizenship may well be the man who pays for the killing.

The Western offers a solution to its own paradox by harnessing violence in the cause of good. But it is a limited solution. The contrary implications are far too forceful for us to be able ultimately to accept that this is what the Western is all about. As the celebration of a period in American history we may indeed see the Western as demonstrating the progress, in dramatic and condensed form, from wilderness to civilisation. As a myth, and this is where its real potency lies, we are responding to something very different. Part of the joy is that civilisation is relatively meaningless, as Sergio Leone spectacularly acknowledges. Ideas of justice and morality are stripped down to their barest. The individual has only himself and his code.

The Western has manipulated the Westerner's independence in a variety of ways. It has geared it to community building, to the fulfilment of an American heritage, to the corporate idea. Independence has been structured, ordered into hierarchies, tamed, and castrated. But the myth has survived all this, and has provided its own reactions against it. If John Wayne harnesses his Western persona to the idea of a corporate America, spreading her wings and gloriously decimating her rivals, lonely as ever on the horizon there appears a different breed of mean and cynical action man to redeem us from the resonance of heroic patriotism.

Owners and fathers and Americans in honest business filled up the West. But the crux of it all is not that these things meant stability and continuity. As far as the Western is concerned the importance lies in that they were ready to fight for what they wanted and fight to keep what they had. In the country as a whole it was an unspoken creed. In the West it wasn't necessary to keep quiet about it. As Luke Short's honest American said, 'I don't like crooks!—I don't like bullies! They run a hell of a lot of this world, girl, too much of it. But when you see a man who has got the guts to fight them and lick them, then it's your duty to help him![10] Sentiments like these provided a licence beyond the law. The honest men went right ahead and licked their crooks—and became heroes. The less honest followed the same pattern, and ruled by graft where they couldn't rule by the gun. Mayor Daley is an inspiring reminder.

For the property owners, the husbands, the fathers and the businessmen independence became in fact less real. But they clung to the idea that it had not diminished. As the East caught on to the Western as a reminder of its frontier past and a reminder that there really was still a frontier on American soil the West preserved it as best it could to strengthen its own idea of its special qualities. Europe was already excited by the American frontier by the time the Western emerged, and has continued in a state of excitement and even reverence ever since. Now the Western hero can be said to be truly universal, not because he is America's hero and America's country is the world, but simply because he is watched and applauded in practically every country in the world. He is a constant reassurance of the delights of adventure, freedom and anarchy in a time when these words tend to mean violence, hatred, bloody oppression or the darkness of total chaos.

FOURTEEN

The Death of the West?

Suddenly we have found there is no longer any Frontier.
Frank Norris, *The Frontier is Gone*

'I've been in worse emergencies, and always emerged.'
Eugene Rhodes, *The Numismatist*

John Chisum was a New Mexico cattle king, a man who had built up his herds in traditional fashion and controlled a vast area of land. He is now probably best remembered for his part in the Lincoln County Wars, 1878, which brought Billy the Kid into prominence. Chisum himself did not carry a gun, but he was behind some shady deals and responsible for some unpalatable incidents. He engineered the murder of a large number of reservation Apaches. He was not trusted by his fellows. He was a man of ruthless independence, but above all a man who was a success.

Andrew McLaglen's film *Chisum* (1970) begins and ends with John Wayne on an immobile horse surveying his property. Wayne is Chisum. Wayne plays a patriarch, a paternalist, a man of action who has come through many hardships but who now recognises that times are changing—now is 1878. He plays a man who is good to the Indians; he considers them his brothers and a noble foe. He believes in the power of justice—'justice will prevail', intones one character solemnly. But he does not believe in leaving everything to the sheriff. He has worked hard and suffered greatly for what he has won—a vast tract of land, large quantities of men who loyally and unquestioningly fight for him, a ranch house that is solid and almost elegant, but also with just a touch of pioneer roughness, cattle—and he is lonely, unmarried and without children. The real Chisum did marry and produced a tough-looking daughter.

Wayne's paternalistic wings spread wide. He allows his lesser neighbours (Mexicans) to use his water. When a rival consortium monopolises the town's facilities and puts up the prices Chisum opens a bank and a store where the terms are reasonable. The populace flocks to them. The lesser mortals on the Chisum domain revere him and would die for him. They accept his word humbly and do what they are told.

The counterpart to Wayne's Chisum is Billy the Kid, a good looking boy of some charm, in love with his revolver and Chisum's niece. He is flanked by Pat Garrett, the man who in fact killed Billy in dubious circumstances, who is here an honest and upright fellow, even-tempered, reliable, and a much more suitable mate for Chisum's niece than the wild Billy. Billy holds his Bible in one hand while practising his lightning draw with the other. A good boy, loyal, but a killer. Twenty-five years ago, they tell the paunchy, greying Chisum, you were like that too. Billy shoots down the murderers of his mentor, the Englishman Henry Tunstall, as indeed he did in reality, and as the film ends rides off to continue his grim pursuit of justice. Chisum returns to his extensive property. A corrupt corporation has been defeated and peace reigns once again, under the benign hand of John Wayne—except that somewhere out there rides Billy and his avenging gun.

It is not so much the distortion of history that is surprising here, as the fact that those responsible for the movie found it necessary to attempt to anchor the action to real events at all. Wayne does not require the reality of Chisum to enable him to play John Wayne, especially as here he is embarrassingly flabby. The tampering with known facts is blatant. To present Pat Garrett and Billy as comrades in arms with no hint of the fact that Garrett hunted Billy to his death not long after is ludicrous. To use history to heighten legend, as Hill did in *Butch Cassidy* is one thing. To manipulate in order to celebrate the values of a man who never lived by them is a great deal more questionable.

What exactly are those values, and what kind of manipulation has been involved? *Chisum* is a corporation Western, a Western that extolls benevolent dictatorship. What gives Chisum the right to be dictator? The fact that he has fought and suffered for his gains; the fact that he has won. The Mexican peasants have not won. They are still struggling with the soil and the water. And they will never win, because they are inferior, and need the kindly protection of the big man in order to survive. It is a reflection, and the fact that we see it in the context of the Western makes it a wistful reflection, of the role many Americans would like to see their country playing in the world. There is an assumption that to win by one's own hand engenders a natural right to superiority.

The real John Chisum, symbol of the dauntless individual as he may be, did not quite win by his own hand. Certainly he won, but the men who fought his battles did it for pay. The successful men of the West owed a great deal to determination, rather less to honesty, frankness, generosity or even skill. In Wayne's Chisum all these qualities are much in evidence, along with courage and a rock-like constancy. The measurements of success in the film are of crucial import: success is the ownership of thousands of acres, thousands of cattle and thousands of dollars. Success is static. For all the film's action set pieces nothing can counteract the dominant impression of Wayne at the stage of immobility. For the first time one begins to suspect that John Wayne is getting old.

Chisum appears to be changing with the times. 'We'll try your way first', he says to Henry Tunstall, who argues for legal means. But Tunstall is killed while on his way to the State Governor and Chisum's loyal sidekick Pepper (a part that does no justice to Ben Johnson's abilities) points out laconically that the only way to settle things is through the confrontation of force. Pepper is right, and as the movie draws to a climax Chisum leads his men in a thundering charge into battle. The fight is not the elemental contest between rival claimants to the throne but the victory of good Americans over a crowd of unshaven nasties led by a man who is an unprincipled coward. There is a bounty hunter who becomes embroiled in the fight, on the wrong side of course, who bears a distinct resemblance to Clint Eastwood, of particularly vicious and sneering aspect. There is little doubt that Wayne and McLaglen between them intended a swipe at the Eastwood hero.

As the smoke and the dust are clearing Billy rides out, his charm undamaged, and the ambivalence of his character at least partially removed by the fact that the great and noble Chisum has ridden to his aid. Billy may be an anachronism, but he is not evil, nor the mindless psychopath that history suggests. He reads the Bible, and Chisum's niece, a spunky but decent girl, falls for him, a sure indication that he has a lot of good in him. The link between Billy and Chisum is obvious. Chisum does in fact resort to the methods of twenty-five years before to solve his problems. It may be that his object is justice and not revenge, the distinction that Wayne himself makes, but this makes no difference to the action. In the context that the film itself establishes—action, not words—the distinction between justice and revenge has little meaning.

Billy is Chisum's alter ego, and his riding out of the picture enables the ageing landowner to take up again his motionless stance. In this way violence is authorised while the central character makes gestures against it. In this way Chisum consolidates his holdings without losing his status as leader and respected citizen. It is exactly what Wayne's politics are all about. America has always sought to make the distinction between the corrupt and the benevolent corporation vital. On this is based an entire morality. But more often than not the distinction cannot hold. A certain kind of benevolence *is* corrupting. Any kind of organisation whose structure depends on unquestioning loyalty and obedience is potentially rotten at its centre.

So much for McLaglen's version of John Chisum. He has tampered with history to produce what is arguably an anti-Western—a Western that contradicts or ignores the most striking features in terms of the appeal and the survival of the myth. Certain moments in the movie suggest that he himself is at least partially aware of this. Why remove Chisum's wife and give him a niece instead of a daughter? Because, like all the best Western heroes, he must be a lonely man, a man who has chosen action rather than domesticity. Typically, it turns out that he was in love with his niece's mother. Typically, he affirms that it was right for her to choose his brother, safe and solid, rather than himself, wild and risky. The man of action has to deny himself the consolation of love yet he must not make it look as if he were never interested in women: as Wayne says sententiously to his niece, 'don't think there weren't women who fired my blood.' Yet what does Chisum have in the end? He has a great deal of what marriage implies: security, stasis, even domesticity. He and Pepper sit down to breakfast in the homely kitchen with glasses of milk at their elbows. Pat Garrett does the dishes!

In making Billy the Kid a relatively decent fellow, by carefully balancing his impulsive tendencies to kill, McLaglen is simultaneously trying not to lose the authentic Western hero and making him acceptable to the corporation ethic. Billy's old gang is lumpen rather than vicious, but he is always ready for a fight and once in one won't give up. Billy's loyalty is fierce, yet he is independent, by the end of the film a loner, and he doesn't get the girl. He is in fact little different from the Billy the Kid of the comics, adolescent, manly in action but shy of women, never shirking danger but basically modest. It is Garrett who is presented as the solid citizen, the younger version of the respectable side of Chisum, the man who does get the girl—yet we all know he is going to kill Billy. Garrett is the rising generation. He will be married man, property owner, responsible member of the community, *but* without losing his skill with a gun, his ability to think and act fast, in fact his status as Western hero.

This, we feel, is what the movie would like to say, but are we convinced? Are Garrett and Chisum as presented here our everlasting, universal Western heroes? Are they not as tamed, as anchored to the monolithic American structure, as unfree, as those countless heroes of American fiction who yearn for a hint of the dream on which America long ago foreclosed? If this is so, it underlines a notable aspect of the Western, that it can accommodate the conformist, the conventional and the anti-independent so readily. Wayne shows us how close the independent man of guts is to traditional strivings. Wayne is at his best and at his most admired when he is directed away from this role, as he is in *True Grit*.

Chisum is not of course unique as a corporation Western. The trend has been present almost from the beginning. It is there in Zane Grey, in Hough's *North of 36*, in *Red River*, in many of the Westerns of the fifties and in many television series. In these the hero tends to be a leader with a loyal following, the corporation boss, or he is the amanuensis of someone in this role. Sometimes the approach is matriarchal, and it is a woman at the head of the organisation. This is a favourite theme of Zane Grey (*Riders of the Purple Sage*, *Knights of the Range* and others) and is there in, for instance, *The Big Valley*, with Barbara Stanwyck drawing the rebellious into the corporation, a kind of castration by protection.

Even the most solid of corporation Westerns tries not to lose sight of the potential of the drifting loner. When this does happen, as in *Guns of Wyoming* the result is disastrously tedious. If *Chisum*, for all its unpalatable implications, is slightly less than disastrous it is because McLaglen does understand the loner's impact. But *Chisum* does come dangerously near to killing the frontier. The only alternatives after consolidation are either more consolidation (imperialism) or revolution.

Yet the Western myth does survive the onslaught that *Chisum* represents. The true Western hero, the hippie of the nineteenth century, anarchic, a-social, retains his profound appeal. He continues to attract good writers, good actors and good movie directors as well as the hacks and the third rate. He continues to survive restatements, re-examinations, questioning. About *Little Big Man* Arthur Penn says, 'It challenges the notion that the heroes of America are the ones you read about in the history books. It challenges the glorification of the gunfighter and the simple proposition that the cavalry was the good guys and the Indians the bad guys. It exposes the rotten morality of commercialism.' [1] Yet, in spite of—or perhaps because of—the unforgettable humanity of the Cheyennes, Penn has done no more than reform the myth in a slightly different image, and these reformations have been occurring in the Western continually. Penn acknowledges the myth, just as some directors of less conventional Westerns in the last ten years have acknowledged the Western paradox—Richard Brooks, Ted Post, Alan Smithee—and used it without destroying the myth. It is possible that the most serious challenger of the old assumptions is Sergio Leone but although he exposes the core of the myth he does not destroy it.

We are beginning to have anti-heroes who are anti not because they are not heroic but because they do not live up to traditional demands.

Even in a film like *The War Wagon* John Wayne and Kirk Douglas do not represent the cowboy hero in traditional form. The comedy Western is always apt to contain a challenge to authority, even the authority of the myth. It is in that that a great deal of the comedy lies. When, in *Support Your Local Sheriff*, another of Burt Kennedy's, the sheriff foils a stick-up by poking his finger down the barrel of the offending revolver, or calls a halt to a deadly earnest gunfight so that he can cross the street in safety, the comedy works because we are measuring these actions against our assumptions about the myth. In this film much of the comedy is straight-forward slapstick and all very much on the surface. In *The War Wagon*, or in *The Scalphunters*, there is an introverted satire constantly feeding on the material it must seriously use. *The Scalphunters* is on one level a comic tour with macabre overtones, on another level entirely serious about bounty hunters. On both levels it works, and Burt Lancaster is simultaneously hero and anti-hero.

Those directors who now want to show us what the Western hero was *really* like will not be doing anything new, though they may well be approaching the subject with greater seriousness and self-consciousness. We have had the vicious hero. We have had the inept hero caught in the web of a gothic situation where only instinct helps him. We have had the comic hero and we have had the Westerner who is heroic in spite of his tendencies to act unheroically. It is not possible to abolish the hero without abolishing the heroic plot, and without that there is no Western at all.

Meanwhile many of the characteristics of the traditional Western hero have been moving into the contemporary world. 'The romance of rootlessness put forward in *Easy Rider* is the essence of the American Western with its fantasy of vagabond life. This myth of rootlessness that today's youth is aching for is the same ache that their fathers sought to answer in going to John Wayne movies and their grandfathers did when they watched William S. Hart.'[2] This is director Alan Pakula. A recent batch of American movies are very much concerned with the outsider, the man who cannot accept society and whom society cannot accept. Willie Boy is not so different from Benjamin in *The Graduate*. They are both outcasts, though one is an intrinsically more dramatic situation than the other. They are both profoundly moral heroes. When Robert Redford says, 'I want to make movies about a guy who is outside society, who is flawed and a loner ... the kind of guy who appears to be a hero but isn't,'[3] he could be describing a version of the Western hero. It is a profoundly romantic preoccupation.

It is of some interest that the Western hero appears to be edging into contemporary films while the contemporary view of the Western hero is changing. It illustrates the deeply bohemian appeal of the loner. It shows, once again, that moving on, with all its anti-social implications, is at the root of much of American myth and culture. The hobo, the drifter, the saddle tramp, the hitch hiker continually re-emerge. It is possible, sometimes necessary, to challenge the dominant myths, especially where myth has become a version of history. But it is not possible, or even desirable, to dam up the streams that supply these myths. Whatever version of the West becomes current in the 1970s it is still going to contain much of what is richest in the myth so long as the Western continues to be about individuals in wide open spaces with civilisation at their backs. As long as Westerns are structured with plots and heroes or anti-heroes, in other words so long as it is acknowledged that the Western cannot imitate history, and should not, the myth will survive.

'The old heroes used to protect society from its enemies,' says Paul Newman. 'Now it's society itself that's the enemy.'[4] In the Western society has always implicitly been an enemy. In spite of many abberations this has always been one of the things the Western is about. The screen Western especially, where we cannot help drawing our own conclusions from the town on the one hand and space on the other, tends to be unequivocal about this, reminding us that one of the things the hero is up against is a monolithic, conformist, hierarchical society. Such a society may not have been much in evidence in the West at the time of its glory, but it was on its way.

The Western context allowed the Westerner to be non-conformist. It was precisely his lack of ties that made him valuable to stable communities. It was the fact that he escaped the enchainment of civilisation that made him romantic. But while the cowboy was being legitimised as a national hero other types of drifter, for all that they had something in common with the cowboy, were falling into disrepute. While the movement Westward still had something to commend it—it went on being respectable until the driving force became destitution rather than the pioneering spirit—the rambling man became an object of suspicion. The hoboes, the unemployed who hunted seasonal work in the plains states, wayfaring strangers who entered towns through their railroad yards rather than riding down main street, were not the stuff of heroes. For all their importance in American folk lore and labour history they are set firmly beyond the pale of society while the Westerner is enshrined. The contemporary outcast, the beatnik on the road or the motor cycling hippie, does share something with the Western drifter but society sees him in the less romantic and more offensive version.

The West itself has created its defensive measures against the inevitable stasis of Western society. Outdoor activities become of especial importance: hunting, camping, prospecting. It is all that can be retained of the old West where life had to be lived in the wild. The insistence on the necessity of weapons is not so much a relic from the frontier days as a deliberate emphasis on what is felt to be an aspect of independence. Western magazines exist with a wide circulation in Western states and an avid interest, expressed often in readers' letters, in minute details of the pioneer past. The history of the frontier and its heroic individuals is written over and over again for the consumption of readers who would like to believe that there is still a frontier.

[2]

It is not necessary to belong to the West to enjoy this submission to the Western heritage. It is not even necessary to be American; millions of non-Americans respond to the re-enactment of the individual facing a gigantic challenge. The sheer scope of challenge in the Western is probably unique. That and the solitariness of the hero make the confrontation both elemental and magnificent. They are two of the essential qualities of classic myth and in one form or another audiences have been responding to them for centuries. If the Western long ago evolved a formula that seemed to make the constant re-expression of these qualities redundant it is still this that provides the clue to the great Western. It is still the writers who present the confrontation in its basic terms who are the most distinguished producers of Westerns. It is those who rely on standard ingredients without bothering to restate the situation who produce the pulp.

Directors like Ford and Mann and Howard Hawks are constantly restating the situation in their different ways. It is this that makes Ford, limited as he is by a traditionalist and hierarchical view of American development and American society, a great Western director. He always starts with the basics, presents conflict in its most elemental form, handles qualities such as justice and courage as if they were profound and invariable constants, as solid as the terrain itself over which the action roams. It is to an extent Ford's solidity that limits him. He has a vision of the American family and the American community, juxtaposed with the American hero, but so firmly rooted that it almost suggests intolerance. He combines this with such fluidity of action that we are scarcely aware of it. In his pictures man has a relationship with the land itself which shapes his relationship to society. Men and women are seen in terms of a dual relationship with the landscape which involves both struggle and harmony: harmony is the reward of struggle. Ford's favourite shots of men seen through dust clouds, through water spray, against a sunset, men characterised by the elements and the country, are deeply significant. Man cannot exist in isolation from his environment. The fact that Ford himself clearly believes that it is of the highest importance that the Western environment is also American does not intrude on the Westerns he makes. His understanding of the myth is far too radical.

Anthony Mann too is profoundly concerned with man and his environment but his statement of the situation is much more individualised. The environment is a test, a threat, not just a savage land but a breeding ground for evil. The West's lack of order, its lack of rationality, is much nearer the surface than in Ford's West. While Ford's heroes are often lonely they are still sharing the experience they symbolise. They tend to be leaders rather than outcasts. In Ford's Westerns action usually exists in relation to some achievement. Mann presents action as action, life and death, cruelty and movement, clear cut and there because it has its own reality.

The Western's vitality has been maintained by directors working firmly within the myth, giving it distinction with a personal response. Directors such as Henry Hathaway, Delmer Daves, Budd Boetticher, King Vidor, though not consistent, have each created something individual out of the myth. But the great surge of Westerns in the thirties and forties, epics, B pictures, comic spoofs, were more often than not composed of material that could be carved up and served up wholesale with little interest in the function of the myth and little finesse in presentation. The mauling of history became commonplace, but this was not so damaging as the failure to explore its genuinely mythic value. The average supporting Western, and even many of the major films, were very weak versions of the rugged legends of the West.

The fifties reacted ponderously to this. With Audie Murphy Westerns providing an undistinguished mainstream there were heavy handed attempts at psychological Westerns, such as Fuller's *Run of the Arrow*, gestures towards realism that could not quite relinquish the blandishments of glossy romance which indicate a confusion arising from a wish to modernise the Western while wanting to return to the heart of the myth. Realism brought in sex and vicious killing, a new breed of baddies (some of whom survive splendidly: Lee Marvin, Jack Palance, Arthur Kennedy), a sophistication in the treatment of stereotypes, but all this seemed to bring with it a large scale blurring of issues. Yet if the fifties produced some of the most embarrassing Westerns ever, they also produced some of the best and most lasting. Many of the Westerns that we now think of as being genuinely innovational (Delmer Daves' *Broken Arrow*), genuinely classic (*Shane, High Noon*), richly epic (*The Searchers*) and the best of Anthony Mann stem from this era. The best pictures of the fifties portrayed a taut, more intense frontier, which did a great deal to feed the Westerns of the sixties, and which owed a significant debt to the pre-talkie era. The fifties saw the emergence of the 'adult' television Westerns such as *Gunsmoke, Maverick* and *Have Gun will Travel* ('a knight without armour in a savage land') which in their turn influenced screen Westerns. The television series were in fact a valuable means of channeling new blood into the Westerns of the late sixties. Burt Reynolds, James Garner, Clint Eastwood, James Coburn, to mention only a few, started their careers as television heroes. Peckinpah wrote scripts for several series. The fact that television Westerns have become largely institutionalised is clearly partly the result of so many moving on to new horizons.

At regular intervals the demise of the Western is announced. But there is a fresh vitality, sometimes modest, present not only in sophisticated Westerns that claim to portray an authentic West but also in pictures like *Sam Whiskey* or *Paint Your Wagon*—a musical and a comedy maybe, but very much within the myth—where relaxed, sympathetic and affectionate treatment produce rewarding results. It is likely that the Western myth will survive, and will survive on many different levels. It enriches a brief past for the benefit of a possibly barren present. It feeds contemporary culture, and has done so for many years, with a vision of independence which America and the world find both comforting and exciting. It can suggest anarchy, rebellion, as well as the most offensive aspects of nationalism. It can emphasise the uniqueness of a nation and the inviolability of the individual. It can provide simultaneously an escape and a challenge. All this is arguably dangerous mental pabulum for a nation that is inactive on its own ground and overactive on the territory of others, but with so much to offer the Western myth is, hopefully, invulnerable.

The Western novel is perhaps on more difficult ground, for the written word has never been able to cope with the myth as expansively as the screen. A large percentage of the Westerns to be found in bookshops and libraries are in fact reprints of standards like Max Brand, Zane Grey and Ernest Haycox. 'The start of more action than you may be able to take,' announced a recent advertisement for 'The Zane Grey Library'. 'Zane Grey's famous novels are written for tough-minded readers about some of the roughest characters who ever roamed the frontier: broken-nosed, bullet-scarred men who had to ride hard and shoot fast in order to survive.'[5] Some of these novels are sixty years old yet they still, apparently, retain their appeal, which is an interesting reflection on their basic ingredients. The Western novel has not changed significantly, and Ernest Haycox remains, deservedly, a writer to compare in skill and serious stature with anything more recent.

The committed hacks, such as Matt Chisolm, who are writing now, are probably less good than those of forty years ago. There are writers who deserve, along with Haycox, permanent status; Alan Le May, who is very variable, but whose best is haunting and impressive. And Louis L'Amour, prolific and repetitious but essentially in skilled command of his material. Lewis Patten and T. V. Olsen have produced taut, unusual Western dramas, tensely written, and are in some ways more worthwhile than a number of the serious novels about the West (novels that can be justifiably read by non-devotees) which are often ponderously conscious of their historical nature. A. B. Guthrie's novels are a little like this, a little earnest, yet containing an appropriate range of dramatic incident. Like Paul Horgan and Elliot Arnold he takes on topics of epic proportions, but of Western novels by 'serious' writers some of the more limited in scope are the more impressive. John Prebble's *Buffalo Soldiers*, though perhaps without finesse, tackles a theme beyond the usual territory of the Western with a convincing grittiness. Howard Fast, a writer whose popularity has possibly disguised his real achievements, has produced in *The Last Frontier* a book that ought to be a minor classic of the West. Slightly more tortuous, slightly less at ease technically, are Michael Straight's highly serious army novels *Carrington* and *A Very Small Remnant*. Deliberately limited and concentrated in theme these novels ignore the expansive sweep of the American continent and American rhetoric, which prove such a temptation to so many historical writers, and involve themselves probingly and provocatively in specific and detailed issues. Yet they do not lose the flavour of the West nor the impact of the myth.

What can be learnt from such novels is that it is not necessary to distort history in order to present a challenging image of the West. The mythic hero can exist happily and impressively within the bounds of authentic history. This is a part of the special character of the West itself. It can sustain characters that have a life far beyond the reach of history, yet it is history itself that breeds them. History has always been able to produce heroes of mythic stature who move with ease into an existence independent of history. In terms of America, with so much done in so short a period, the timeless quality of the legendary figure is of special significance. The days of the Western frontier were brief. For a period of thirty years to produce a figure and all his supporting detail that was going to last for more than a hundred was something like an instinctive necessity.

It was a necessity for the American imagination and American self-respect. While in the latter half of the nineteenth century the East was being exposed to all the agonies and hysteria of economic slumps, unemployment, sporadically burgeoning industry and flooding immigration the West was protected by its own rude emptiness. No safety valve, almost certainly, but a comforting thought to thousands. Whatever was happening in the clogged city out there was distance, beauty and an elemental challenge. If on the Eastern streets men were at the mercy of forces far beyond their control out West there was space for men to expand and take command. Out West gestures could be large; they could match the rhetoric of American ideals. Out West America could still make in ringing tones her magnificent promises.

Notes

I. The Frontier

1. Van Cort, *Journey of the Gun*, Berkley Medallion 1966, p. 72 (fiction).

2. Elizabeth Bacon Custer, *Boots and Saddles*, University of Oklahoma Press 1961, p. 218.

3. Quoted, G. C. Quiett, *They Built the West*, Appleton-Century Co. 1934, p. 86.

4. John Clay, *My Life on the Range*, by permission of University of Oklahoma Press 1962, p. 73.

5. Alan Le May, *The Siege at Dancing Bird*, reissued as *The Unforgiven*, 1960, p. 135 (fiction).

6. Alan Le May, *The Searchers*, Harper 1954, p. 53 (fiction).

7. Frederick Jackson Turner, *The Frontier in American History*, Holt, Rinehart and Winston 1962, p. 4.

8. Isabella Bird, *A Lady's Life in the Rocky Mountains*, John Murray 1882, p. 77.

9. Lewis Patten, *Valley of Violent Men*, Fawcett Gold Medal 1957, p. 5 (fiction).

10. Emerson Hough, 'Society in the Cow Country', *The American Frontier*, ed. C. Merton Babcock, Holt, Rinehart and Winston 1965, p. 85.

11. William Cox, *Black Silver*, Corgi 1969, p. 9.

12. Owen Wister, *The Virginian*, Harper and Row 1902, 'To the Reader', p. xviii (fiction).

13. Quoted, Larzer Ziff, *The American 1890s*, Viking Press 1966, p. 225.

II. Post Bellum

1. Quoted, James D. Horan and Paul Sann, *Pictorial History of the Wild West*, Spring Books 1962, p. 28.

2. Luke Short, *Ambush*, New English Library 1968, p. 38 (fiction).

3. John Prebble, *The Buffalo Soldiers*, Corgi 1961, p. 185 (fiction).

4. Michael Straight, *Carrington*, Corgi 1963, pp. 39-40 (fiction).

5. Henry Sell and Victor Weybright, *Buffalo Bill and the Wild West*, Signet 1959, p. 81.

6. John Hawgood, *The American West*, Eyre and Spottiswoode 1967, p. 286.

7. Howard Fast, *The Last Frontier*, by permission of Dell 1966, p. 77 (fiction).

8. William Cox, op. cit., p. 65.

9. Ibid., p. 67.

10. Ibid., p. 235.

11. Lewis Atherton, *Cattle Kings*, Indiana University Press 1962, p. 123.

12. Ibid., p. 33.

III. *Taming the Natives*

1. Fenimore Cooper, 'Civilising the Red Man', C. M. Babcock, op. cit., p. 161.

2. Peter Bogdanovich, *John Ford*, Studio Vista 1967, p. 72.

3. Fenimore Cooper, *The Pathfinder*, Signet 1961, p. 13.

4. Elliot Arnold, *Blood Brother*, Eyre and Spottiswoode 1962, p. 427 (fiction).

5. Horace Greeley, *An Overland Journey*, Macdonald 1965, p. 121.

6. John Finerty, *War-Path and Bivouac*, University of Oklahoma Press, p. 290.

7. Quoted, Sell and Weybright, op. cit., p. 86.

8. Ibid.

9. Edgar Bronson, *Reminiscences of a Ranchman*, University of Nebraska Press 1965, p. 145.

10. J. P. Dunn, *Massacres of the Mountains*, Eyre and Spottiswoode 1963, p. 382.

11. Peter Bogdanovich, op. cit., p. 94.

12. Helen Hunt Jackson, *A Century of Dishonour*, Harper 1965, p. 29.

13. Milton Lott, *The Last Hunt*, Collins 1958, p. 339.

14. Jack D. Forbes, ed., *The Indian in America's Past*, Spectrum 1964, p. 65.

15. Chief Standing Bear, 'What the Indian Means to America', C. M. Babcock, op. cit., p. 200.

IV. *Settlement*

1. Quoted, Carl F. Kraenzel, *The Great Plains in Transition*, University of Oklahoma Press 1955, pp. 140-41.

2. Henry David Thoreau, *Walden*, Time Inc. 1962, p. 9.

3. Fred A. Shannon, 'The Homestead Act and the Labour Surplus', *The Public Lands*, ed., Vernon Carstensen, University of Nebraska Press 1963, p. 298.

4. Ray Allen Billington, *America's Frontier Heritage*, Holt, Rinehart and Winston 1966, p. 73.

5. C. M. Babcock, op. cit., p. 9.

6. Walter Prescott Webb, *The Great Plains*, Ginn and Co. 1931, p. 223.

7. John Clay, op. cit., p. 24.
8. Howard Fast, op. cit., p. 77.
9. Ibid., p. 81.
10. Van Cort, op. cit., p. 30.
11. Ibid.
12. William MacLeod Raine, *Glory Hole*, Pan 1951, p. 33 (fiction).
13. Louis L'Amour, *Fallon*, Corgi 1969, pp. 2-3 (fiction).
14. William Cox, *The Duke*, New English Library 1962, pp. 5-6 (fiction).
15. Douglas Branch, *Westward*, Appleton and Co. 1930, pp. 468-69.

V. *Home on the Range*

1. J. S. Tait, *The Cattlefields of the Far West*, Blackwood 1884, p. 9.
2. E. S. Osgood, *The Day of the Cattleman*, University of Chicago Press 1929, pp. 7-9.
3. Charles Siringo, *A Texas Cowboy*, University of Nebraska Press 1966, p. 46.
4. John Leakey, as told to Nellie Snyder Yost, *The West that Was*, University of Nebraska Press 1958, p. 259.
5. Andy Adams, *Trail Drive* (abridged version of *Log of a Cowboy*), Ronald Whiting and Wheaton 1965, pp. 25-6.
6. Ibid., p. 38.
7. Douglas Branch, *The Cowboy and His Interpreters*, Appleton and Co. 1926, p. 27.
8. Ernest Haycox, *Free Grass*, Sphere 1967, p. 24 (fiction).
9. Thomas Sturgeon, *The Rare Breed*, Fawcett Gold Medal 1966, pp. 17-18.
10. Granville Stuart, *Forty Years on the Frontier*, Appleton and Co. 1925, p. 237.
11. *Rocky Mountain Husbandman*, 17-3-1887.
12. *Cheyenne Daily Leader*, 12-7-1892.
13. John Clay, op. cit., pp. 276-7.
14. Quoted, A. S. Mercer, *The Banditti of the Plains*, University of Oklahoma Press 1961.
15. Frank Canton, *Frontier Trails*, Houghton Mifflin 1930, p. 106.
16. David Lavender, *The Penguin Book of the American West*, Penguin 1969, p. 438.
17. Ernest Haycox, *Riders West*, Sphere 1967, p. 111 (fiction).
18. John Clay, op. cit., p. 221.
19. Wayne Gard, *Frontier Justice*, University of Oklahoma Press 1949, p. 107.
20. Ibid., p. 118.
21. John Clay, op. cit., pp. 291-92.
22. Jack Schaefer, 'Miley Bennet', *The Big Range*, Heinemann 1967, pp. 53-4 (fiction).

VI. *Pas de Cheval, Pas de Cowboy*

1. Quoted, Frank Dobie, *A Vacquero of the Brush Country*, Hammond 1949, p. 11.
2. Ibid.
3. Elizabeth Bacon Custer, op. cit., pp. 85-6.
4. Bret Harte, 'A passage in the Life of Mr. Oakhurst', *The Outcasts of Poker Flat and other Tales*, Signet 1961, p. 238 (fiction).
5. Clarence Mulford, *Hopalong Cassidy*, Hodder 1953, p. 52 (fiction).
6. Jack Schaefer, *Shane*, Heinemann 1967, p. 140 (fiction).
7. Ibid., p. 141.
8. Arthur Miller, *The Misfits*, Penguin 1961, pp. 135-36 (fiction).
9. Leo Tolstoy, *War and Peace*, Penguin 1967, p. 215.
10. Ibid.
11. Frank Dobie, *The Mustangs*, Hammond 1954, p. 43.
12. Charles Siringo, op. cit., p. 93.

VII. *The Law of the Gun*

1. Stephen Crane, 'The Bride Comes to Yellow Sky', *The Red Badge of Courage* and other stories, Oxford University Press 1969, p. 303.
2. John Clay, op. cit., p. 83.
3. Jack Schaefer, *First Blood*, Penguin 1958, p. 124 (fiction).
4. Frank Dobie, op. cit., p. 85.
5. Walter Prescott Webb, *The Texas Rangers*, Houghton Mifflin 1935.
6. Louis L'Amour, *Heller With a Gun*, Hodder Fawcett 1967, p. 106 (fiction).
7. Ibid., p. 43.
8. Mark Twain, *Roughing It*, Chatto and Windus 1901, p. 5.
9. Jack Schaefer, op. cit., p. 61.
10. Zane Grey, *Riders of the Purple Sage*, Grosset and Dunlap 1912, p. 272 (fiction).
11. Ibid., p. 157.
12. Van Cort, op. cit., p. 44.
13. *Young Wild West's Whirlwind Riders*, New International Library, n.d., p. 7 (fiction).
14. Ibid.
15. Owen Wister, op. cit., p. 316.
16. Ibid., p. 311.
17. Ernest Haycox, op. cit., p. 190.
18. J. T. Edson, *The Ysabel Kid*, Corgi 1968, p. 111.

VIII. *Vigilance and Violence*

1. Walter Van Tilburg Clark, *The Oxbow Incident*, Four Square 1964, p. 189 (fiction).

2. Ibid., p. 190.

3. 'Afterward', Ibid., pp. 223-24.

4. Wister, op. cit., pp. 250-51.

5. David Lavender, op. cit., p. 365.

6. Wayne Gard, op. cit., p. 176.

7. Th. Roosevelt *Ranch Life and the Hunting Trail*, T. Fisher Unwin 1888, p. 14.

8. Glenn Shirley, *Law West of Fort Smith*, Collier 1961, p. 137.

9. Philip Oakes, 'The Violent Eye', *Sunday Times*, 17-5-70.

10. Ernest Haycox, *Bugles in the Afternoon*, Corgi 1961, back cover.

11. Van Cort, op. cit., back cover.

12. Clair Huffaker, *The War Wagon*, Fawcett Gold Medal 1957, p. 104.

13. Hugh Davis Graham and Ted Robert Gurr, *A History of Violence in America*, Bantam 1969, Introduction to Part ii, p. 106.

14. Joe B. Frantz, 'The Frontier Tradition: an Invitation to Violence', ibid., p. 128.

15. Quoted, ibid., p. 137.

16. Richard Mazwell Brown, 'The American Vigilante Tradition', ibid., p. 201.

17. Philip Oakes, op. cit.

18. Max Caulfield, 'Clint Eastwood Tells Why I'm a Loner', *Woman*, 12-4-1969.

19. Philip Oakes, op. cit.

20. Raymond Chandler, *The Big Sleep*, Penguin 1948, p. 194 (fiction).

21. Chester Himes, *The Real Cool Killers*, Panther 1969, p. 127.

IX. *Gold and Locomotives*

1. Eugene Smalley, 'Coeur D'Alene Stampede', *Century Magazine*, October 1884.

2. Luke Short, *Western Freight*, Fontana 1961, p. 15 (fiction).

3. Quoted, Ray Allen Billington, op. cit., p. 78.

4. Quoted, Muriel Sibell Wolfe, *The Bonanza Trail*, Indiana University Press 1955, pp. 48-9.

5. Ray Allan Billington, op. cit., p. 215.

6. Quoted, Muriel Sibell Wolfe, op. cit., p. 244.

7. Quoted, ibid, p. 348.

8. Quoted, ibid., p. 48.

9. T. V. Olsen, *Savage Sierra*, Fawcett Gold Medal 1962, p. 156 (fiction).

10. Luke Short, op. cit., p. 5.

11. From 'The California Stage Company', *Cowboy Songs and other Frontier Ballads*, collected by John A. Lomax and Alan Lomax, Macmillan 1966, p. 394.

12. Quoted, G. C. Quiett, op. cit., p. 86.

13. Ernest Haycox, op. cit., p. 14.

X. *Women in the West*

1. Isabella Bird, op. cit., p. 53.
2. Frederick Woods, 'Hot Guns and Cold Women', *Films and Filming*, March 1959.
3. Andrew Sinclair, *The Better Half*, Jonathan Cape 1966, p. 205.
4. Walter Prescott Webb, op. cit., p. 505.
5. Alan Le May, op. cit., p. 53.
6. Horan and Sann, op. cit., p. 236.
7. Isabella Bird, op. cit., Introduction, p. vii.
8. Hamlin Garland, *The Mocassin Ranch*, Harper 1909, p. 32 (fiction).
9. J. J. Lynx, ed., *The Film Fan's Bedside Book*, 1948.
10. Zane Grey, *To the Last Man*, Hodder and Stoughton 1921, p. 299 (fiction).
11. John Coleman, 'Why Go to the Movies?', *New Statesman*, 9-10-70.
12. William Cox, *The Duke*, New English Library 1968, p. 6 (fiction).
13. Andy Adams, op. cit., p. 274.
14. Muriel Sibell Wolfe, op. cit., p. 424.
15. Robert Riegel, op. cit., p. 320.
16. Elliot Paul, *A Ghost Town on the Yellowstone*, Cresset Press 1949, p. 37.
17. Peter Dawson, *High Lonesome*, Collins, n.d., p. 188 (fiction).
18. Louis L'Amour, *Last Stand at Papago Wells*, Hodder Fawcett 1967, p. 34 (fiction).
19. Louis L'Amour, *Hondo*, Hodder Fawcett 1966, p. 159 (fiction).
20. Eugene Cunningham, *The Trail from the River*, Collins 1939, p. 123 (fiction).

XI. *Saddle Tramp*

1. Kenneth Allsop, *Hard Travellin'*, Hodder and Stoughton 1967, p. 73.
2. Eugene Rhodes, 'The Bird in the Bush', *The Rhodes Reader*, University of Oklahoma Press 1957, p. 185.
3. Ibid., p. 187.
4. Louis L'Amour, op. cit., p. 41.
5. Kenneth Allsop, op. cit., p. 72.
6. Richard Jessup, *Chuka*, Fawcett 1961, p. 6.
7. Ibid.
8. Ibid., p. 13.
9. Ibid., p. 14.
10. John Clay, op. cit., p. 120.
11. Eugene Rhodes, 'The Fool's Heart', op. cit., p. 132.
12. Alan Le May, op. cit., p. 9.

XII. *Who Are These Guys?*

1. Dennis John Hall, 'Tall in the Saddle', *Films and Filming*, October 1969.
2. F. Maurice Speed, ed., *Western Film Annual*, 1955, pp. 25-6.
3. Quoted, Jim Kitses, *Horizons West*, by permission of Secker & Warburg 1969, pp. 98-9.
4. *Young Wild West's Green Corn Dance*, p. 56.
5. Richard Schickel, *Movies*, MacGibbon and Kee 1965, pp. 70-71.
6. Peter Bogdanovich, op. cit., p. 86.
7. Ibid.
8. Fenimore Cooper, op. cit., p. 69.

XIII. *There* Must *Be a Lone Ranger*

1. Tom Horn, *Life of Tom Horn*, University of Oklahoma Press 1964, pp. 137-38.
2. 'John Wayne as the Last Hero', *Time*, 8-8-1969.
3. Ibid.
4. Ibid.
5. Ibid.
6. Ibid.
7. Eugene Rhodes, op. cit. Introduction by W. H. Hutchinson, p. xi.
8. Frederick Law Olmsted, 'A Journey Through Texas', Forbes, op. cit., p. 17.
9. D. F. Taylor, review of *Viva Villa*, *Cinema Quarterly*, summer 1939.
10. Luke Short, *Hurricane Range*, Panther 1968, p. 45 (fiction).

XIV. *The Death of the West?*

1. 'The New Movies', *Newsweek*, 7-12-1970.
2. Ibid.
3. Ibid.
4. Ibid.
5. *Golden West*, November 1970, back cover.

Films

The following is a chronological list of films mentioned in the text with
their directors.

The Great Train Robbery, 1903, Edwin S. Porter.
The Battle of the Red Men, 1912, Thomas Ince.
Indian Massacre, 1912, Thomas Ince.
Blazing the Trail, 1912, Thomas Ince.
The Spoilers, 1914, Rex Beach.
The Gunfighter, 1917, W. S. Hart.
The Covered Wagon, 1923, James Cruze.
To the Last Man, 1923, Victor Fleming.
North of 36, 1924, Irvin Willat.
The Iron Horse, 1924, John Ford.
The Pony Express, 1925, James Cruze.
Cimarron, 1931, Wesley Ruggles.
To the Last Man, 1933, Henry Hathaway.
Viva Villa!, 1934, Jack Conway.
The Plainsman, 1937, Cecil B. de Mille.
Union Pacific, 1937, Cecil B. de Mille.
Stagecoach, 1939, John Ford.
The Return of Frank James, 1940, Fritz Lang.
Gone With the Wind, 1940, Victor Fleming.
When the Daltons Rode, 1940, George Marshall.
Western Union, 1941, Fritz Lang.
The Oxbow Incident, 1941, William Wellman.
My Darling Clementine, 1946, John Ford.
Red River, 1948, Howard Hawks.
The Left-Handed Gun, 1948, Arthur Penn.
Paleface, 1948, Norman Z. McLeod.
Fort Apache, 1948, John Ford.
Winchester '73, 1950, Anthony Mann.
Broken Arrow, 1950, Delmer Daves.
Copper Canyon, 1950, John Farrow.
Bend of the River, 1952, Anthony Mann.
Viva Zapata!, 1952, Elia Kazan.
Battle at Apache Pass, 1952, George Sherman.
High Noon, 1952, Fred Zinneman.
Denver and Rio Grande, 1952, Byron Haskin.
Rancho Notorious, 1952, Fritz Lang.
Calamity Jane, 1953, David Butler and Jack Donahue.

Powder River, 1953, Louis King.

Shane, 1953, George Stevens.

Johnny Guitar, 1954, Nicholas Ray.

Hondo, 1954, John Farrow.

The Far Country, 1954, Anthony Mann.

Bad Day at Black Rock, 1954, John Sturges.

Apache, 1954, Robert Aldrich.

The Man From Laramie, 1955, Anthony Mann.

Friendly Persuasion, 1956, William Wyler.

The Searchers, 1956, John Ford.

Run of the Arrow, 1957, Samuel Fuller.

War and Peace, 1958, King Vidor.

The Law and Jake Wade, 1958, John Sturges.

The Horse Soldiers, 1959, John Ford.

The Hanging Tree, 1959, Delmer Daves.

Rio Bravo, 1959, Howard Hawks.

Cimarron, 1960, Anthony Mann.

The Alamo, 1960, John Wayne.

The Unforgiven, 1960, John Huston.

Sergeant Rutledge, 1960, John Ford.

North to Alaska, 1960, Henry Hathaway.

The Man Who Shot Liberty Valance, 1961, John Ford.

El Cid, 1961, Anthony Mann.

One Eyed Jacks, 1961, Marlon Brando.

The Last Sunset, 1961, Robert Aldrich.

The Magnificent Seven, 1961, John Sturges.

Lonely Are the Brave, 1962, David Miller.

Ride the High Country (Guns in the Afternoon), 1962, Sam Peckinpah.

Guns of Wyoming (Cattle King), 1963, Tay Garnett.

Four for Texas, 1963, Robert Aldrich.

How the West Was Won, 1963, John Ford.

Invitation to a Gunfighter, 1964, Richard Wilson.

Hud, 1963, Martin Ritt.

Cheyenne Autumn, 1964, John Ford.

Major Dundee, 1965, Sam Peckinpah.

The Professionals, 1966, Richard Brookes.

The Rare Breed, 1966, Andrew McLaglen.

South West to Sonora (The Appaloosa), 1966, Sidney J. Furie.

The Scalphunters, 1967, Sidney Pollack.

Chuka, 1967, Gordon Douglas.

Hondo, 1967, Lee H. Katzin.

The War Wagon, 1967, Burt Kennedy.

The Good, the Bad and the Ugly, 1967, Sergio Leone.

Hour of the Guns, 1967, John Sturges.

Killer on a Horse, 1967, Burt Kennedy.

Rough Night in Jericho, 1967, Arnold Laven.

Custer of the West, 1967, Robert Siodmark.

El Dorado, 1967, Howard Hawks.

Firecreek, 1967, Vincent McEveety

Bandolero!, 1967, Andrew McLaglen.
Will Penny, 1967, Tom Gries.
Hombre, 1967, Martin Ritt.
The Undefeated, 1968, Andrew McLaglen.
Day of the Evil Gun, 1968, Jerry Thorpe.
Duel at Diablo, 1968, Ralph Nelson.
100 Rifles, 1968, Tom Gries.
Bonnie and Clyde, 1968, Arthur Penn.
The Stalking Moon, 1968, Robert Mulligan.
Support Your Local Sheriff, 1968, Burt Kennedy.
Coogan's Bluff, 1969, Don Siegel.
The Wild Bunch, 1969, Sam Peckinpah.
Tell Them Willie Boy Is Here, 1969, Abraham Polonsky.
Death of a Gunfighter, 1969, Alan Smithee.
Hang 'Em High, 1969, Ted Post.
Paint Your Wagon, 1969, Joshua Logan.
Sam Whiskey, 1969, Robert Aldrich.
The Graduate, 1969, Mike Nichols.
Easy Rider, 1969, Dennis Hopper.
Young Billy Young, 1970, Burt Kennedy.
Little Big Man, 1970, Arthur Penn.
Once Upon a Time in the West, 1970, Sergio Leone.
Chisum, 1970, Andrew McLaglen.
True Grit, 1970, Henry Hathaway.
Two Mules for Sister Sara, 1970, Don Siegel.
The Culpepper Cattle Co., 1972, Dick Richards.

Bibliography

CONTEMPORARY ACCOUNTS

A great deal of the most interesting material on the West is to be found in contemporary accounts and memories. Some are dull and repetitive, but all those mentioned here have a special appeal. A number have been reprinted in the last ten or a dozen years and are still available. Accounts of their experiences by well-known figures include Horace Greeley's *An Overland Journey* (1882), Theodore Roosevelt's *Ranch Life and the Hunting Trail* (1888), Mark Twain's *Roughing It* (1872) and the products of the two Custers, George Armstrong's *My Life on the Plains* (1874) and Elizabeth Bacon's *Boots and Saddles* (reprinted by the University of Oklahoma Press, 1962). For impassioned and committed statements on particular issues J. P. Dunn's *Massacres of the Mountains* (Eyre and Spottiswoode, 1963) and Helen Hunt Jackson's *A Century of Dishonour* (Harper, 1963) present different views of the Indian question, while A. S. Mercer's *Banditti of the Plains* (University of Oklahoma Press, 1961) is an anti-invader account of the Johnson County War, supported in Mari Sandoz's history *The Cattlemen*. John Clay's *My Life on the Range* (University of Oklahoma Press, 1962) is one of the most revealing of autobiographies, Charles Siringo's *A Texas Cowboy* one of the most exuberant and John Leakey's *The West that Was* (University of Nebraska Press 1958) is honest and attractive. It is worth reading Frank Canton's *Frontier Trails* (University of Oklahoma Press) as a partner to John Clay. Edgar Bronson's *Reminiscences of a Ranchman* (University of Nebraska Press, 1965) has an unpretentious interest and Andy Adams' *Log of a Cowboy* (Signet, 1962), just one of many accounts based on his own experiences, perhaps the best known of all Western memoirs. Two of the most enjoyable accounts are Isabella Bird's *A Lady's Life in the Rocky Mountains* (1882) and Elliot Paul's *A Ghost Town on the Yellowstone* (1949). The curious ambiguity of Tom Horn makes his own *Life of Tom Horn* (University of Oklahoma Press) worth looking at, along with Lauran Paine's biography *Tom Horn: Man of the West*. A volume of memoirs with no special vitality but full of information is E. White's *Experiences of a Special Indian Agent* (University of Oklahoma Press, 1965).

NON FICTION

Histories of the West and particular aspects of the West are legion. Two recent general histories which are good reads in themselves are

John Hawgood's *The American West* (Eyre and Spottiswoode, 1967) and David Lavender's *The Penguin Book of the American West* (Penguin, 1969). Other standard authorities are Walter Prescott Webb, whose two books *The Great Plains* (1931) and the *Texas Rangers* (1935) are voluminous classics of scholarship on the West and E. S. Osgood whose more modest *The Day of the Cattlemen* (1929), an account of the cattle industry in Wyoming, is a key work. Frederick Jackson Turner's essay *The Frontier in American History* (Holt, Rinehart and Winston, 1962) is always cropping up in discussions of the West's history and ripples from the debate he provoked are still discernible. Henry Nash Smith's *Virgin Land* and Robert Riegel's *America Moves West* are important histories, crucial aids to an understanding of the West, and *The American Frontier*, a useful collection of essays edited by C. Merton Babcock is also helpful. For a jollier read see James D. Horan and Paul Sann's *A Pictorial History of the Wild West* (Spring Books, 1962)—it's full of facts—and Henry Sell and Victor Weybright's *Buffalo Bill and the Wild West* (Signet, 1959). On particular areas of the West's history Lewis Atherton's *Cattle Kings* (Indiana University Press, 1962) is a standard work on the cattle empires and Wayne Gard's *Frontier Justice* (University of Oklahoma Press, 1968) is an immensely informative book on the subject the title suggests. Wayne Gard is a consistent historian of the West who has also written books on *Sam Bass* (1936) and *The Chisolm Trail* (1954). Glenn Shirley's *Law West of Fort Smith* (Collier, 1961) is a description of the activities of Judge Parker and his marshals in what became Oklahoma. Frank Dobie is a vastly prolific writer who has written on practically every imaginable aspect of the West. It is not possible to list all his titles but worth remarking that his books are really for devotees. Of books on Indians the classic is John Collier's *The Indians of the Americas* (1947) and William Brandon's *The American Heritage Book of Indians* (1961) is first-rate. *The Indian in America's Past* is a useful little collection of essays edited by Jack D. Forbes (Spectrum, 1964). Mari Sandoz has written with committed sympathy about the Cheyennes and the Sioux in *Cheyenne Autumn* (Eyre and Spottiswoode, 1966) and *Crazy Horse*. Dee Brown's *Bury My Heart at Wounded Knee* (1971) describes the tragic finale of the Sioux's nineteenth century history. Books on the cowboy are countless, but Frank and Choate's *The American Cowboy* (1955) and Douglas Branch's *The Cowboy and His Interpreters* are worthwhile. Finally, it is of some relevance to look at Hugh Davis Graham and Ted Robert Gurr's *A History of Violence in America*, a meaty and illuminating volume (Bantam, 1969).

The above list is drastically selective. Books on the West have been pouring out steadily for approaching one hundred years. The list that follows, of fiction, is of necessity even more drastic in its exclusions. I have tried to pick out the better and more entertaining writers.

FICTION

It is probably scarcely necessary to mention Zane Grey: suffice it to say that for the addict Zane Grey is a must. Titles such as *Riders of the Purple Sage* and *Knights of the Range* are characteristic and many of his novels are still in print. A writer of similar status is Max Brand, who will be long remembered if only for the many almost unrecognisable film versions of *Destry Rides Again*. Roughly contemporaneous with Grey are Eugene Cunningham and Emerson Hough, but their popularity has not lasted. A writer of great sympathy and humour is Eugene Rhodes, but he is not as available as he should be. For some of his stories see *The Rhodes Reader* (University of Oklahoma Press, 1957). He is much more worthwhile than Owen Wister, now remembered for *The Virginian*, but author of many other Western novels and stories, such as *Red Men and White* (1896) and *When West was West* (1928). Clarence Mulford, creator of Hopalong Cassidy borrows somewhat from Eugene Rhodes, as most Western writers in a comic vein are almost bound to do. Ernest Haycox is a solid and distinctive Western writer who is way above average in his characterisation. Two of his best are *Bugles in the Afternoon* (Corgi, 1961) and *Free Grass* (Sphere, 1967). He is still in print after forty years. Readable mainstream writers of solid Westerns are Luke Short and William MacLeod Raine. A more distinctive writer, particularly good at tense, claustrophobic situations, is Lewis Patten. *No God in Saguaro* is one of his best. Always readable, but with that tendency endemic amongst Western writers to be repetitive, is Louis L'Amour. *Last Stand at Papago Wells* (Fawcett, 1967) and *Heller With a Gun* (Fawcett, 1967) are brisk examples of his wares. Alan Le May's *The Searchers* (Harper, 1954) is something of a classic. He is an uneven writer, but *By Dim and Flaring Lamps*, perhaps not strictly a Western, and *The Siege at Dancing Bird* are as good. A writer who has been more or less embraced by the establishment—his books are now being issued as school text books—is Jack Schaefer. As the creator of *Shane* he will never be forgotten but he has written many first-rate Western stories and is rarely lured by a romantic version of his material. Most of his best stories have been reissued by Heinemann —see, for instance, *The Big Range* (1967). Two writers now producing are T. V. Olsen and W. C. Tuttle. The latter has quarried a vein of dry humour which is highly pleasurable. There are a number of writers of Westerns, or writers who have used Western material, who have some claim to being considered 'serious' writers. Walter Van Tilburg Clark's *The Oxbow Incident* (Four Square, 1964) is undoubtedly a classic. A. B. Guthrie's *The Big Sky* (1947), Elliot Arnold's *Blood Brother* (Eyre and Spottiswoode, 1962) and Milton Lott's *The Last Hunt* (1955) are all large scale narratives and have been highly regarded. Michael Straight's two novels *Carrington* (Corgi, 1963) and *A Very Small Remnant* are less expansive and probably better. Howard Fast's *The Last Frontier* is an acute, committed narrative and again perhaps preferable to more ambitious enterprises. John Prebble's *The Buffalo Soldiers* (Corgi, 1961) is worth reading but not quite of the same standard. Dorothy Johnson's stories, in *Indian Country* and *The Hanging Tree* are memorable, muted sketches of Western life with hints of tragedy. Will Henry's *From Where the Sun Now Stands* is one of the few good novels about Indians. Finally, a few titles which are not unequivocal Westerns, but should be mentioned: Arthur Miller's *The Misfits* (Penguin, 1961), an almost essential coda to the Western myth, Thomas Berger's *Little Big Man* (Penguin, 1968), an anarchic and unexpected treatment of familiar material, and Charles Portis's *True Grit* (Penguin, 1969), a novel which can rank with the best of American fiction of the last ten years.

Index